THE CREST JEWEL OF WISDOM

(Viveka-Cūḍāmaṇi)

THE CREST JEWEL OF WISDOM

(Viveka-Cūḍāmaṇi)

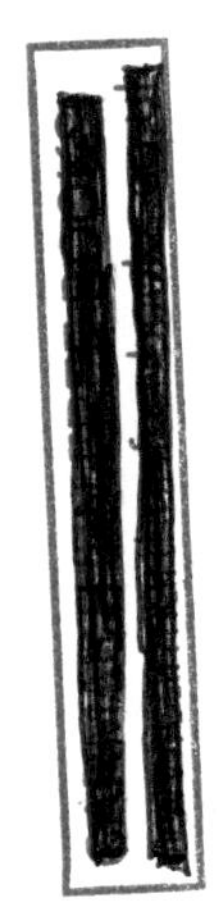

attributed to
Shri Shankaracharya

translated by A J Alston

commentary by Hari Prasad Shastri

SHANTI SADAN
LONDON

First published in 1997 by Shanti Sadan

29 Chepstow Villas
London W11 3DR

ISBN 0-85424-047-0

Printed and bound by
J W Arrowsmith Ltd, Bristol BS3 2NT

CONTENTS

About the commentator

Hari Prasad Shastri (1882-1956) was an accomplished scholar in the direct line of one of the oldest teaching schools of the classical Yoga. Through his own teacher, Shri Dada of Aligarh, Dr Shastri achieved mastery of the methods of Yoga. He came to London in 1929 at the wish of his teacher, in order to introduce Adhyatma Yoga (the Yoga of Self-Knowledge) to the West. He founded a Centre called Shanti Sadan in Notting Hill Gate, London, in 1933, where instruction in the traditional Yoga is still given, according to his guidelines.

In addition to his commentary on the *Viveka-Chudamani*, Dr Shastri translated several important Advaita Vedanta classics from the Sanskrit, and wrote many original works. His translations include *Panchadashi*, the *Avadhut Gita*, the *Ashtavakra Gita*, and sections from the *Yoga Vasishtha* (published as *The World Within the Mind*), as well as a complete translation of the epic poem, *The Ramayana of Valmiki*. Several of Dr Shastri's translations are accompanied by illuminating commentaries, based on his experience as a master of Yoga.

PREFACE

'SHANKARA'S teaching (simultaneously theoretical and practical, as is that of all true exponents of the Perennial Philosophy) is conveniently summed up in his versifed treatise, *Viveka-Chudamani* (The Crest Jewel of Wisdom).' Aldous Huxley published this testimonial followed by two pages of quotations in his book *The Perennial Philosophy* in 1946.

Four years earlier, in the winter of 1941-42, our Teacher, the late Hari Prasad Shastri, had already given a series of public lectures in Shanti Sadan to make this celebrated classic and its themes more widely known in the West. His comments included in the present volume have been selected and transcribed from notes of those lectures and from his many other writings on its themes.

If the authorship of *Viveka-Chudamani* is today disputed, what remains undisputed is its authority as one of the best popular introductions to the traditional doctrine of Advaita Vedanta which Shri Shankara himself taught and practised. Hari Prasad Shastri also belonged to Shri Shankara's tradition and so was fully qualified to expound its meaning.

Dr A.J.Alston has translated the complete work, supplying a transliterated text based mainly on the edition prepared by Muni Lāl for the Gita Press, Gorakhpur. Some readings have been taken from those of Swami Mādhavānanda (Mayavati, 1921, often reprinted) and H.R. Bhāgavat (*Minor Works of Shri Shankaracharya*, Poona, 1925). Diacritical marks have been preserved in the translation and footnotes, but not elsewhere. For more elaborate notation, consult Swami Mādhavānanda's excellent version.

We are pleased to have the opportunity of making more widely available in published form our Teacher's illuminating exposition of a justly famous and authentic practical guide on how to fulfil the spiritual purpose of human life. This publication is reverently dedicated to him.

INTRODUCTION

by

Hari Prasad Shastri

OUR desires are like the arrows in the quiver of our personality, and the divine will is the bow. Each desire has to be directed like an arrow from the bow of our will. No archer wastes his arrows. We too must be most careful in conceiving and directing our desires to a definite purpose. The desires find fulfilment according to the intensity and the concentration applied to their execution. We always have one great desire and many minor desires subordinate to that one. Let us have one great desire in life—you cannot have two—but we may have many minor desires helping the execution of that one great desire. I feel thirsty: this is one desire. I desire a rope and a bucket and look for a well, and I desire the cleanness of my glass, and so forth. Such ought to be our life.

What should be that one great desire? Experience teaches us that our one great desire should be the accomplishment of something higher than anything else which exists, and that is infinite bliss, universal sovereignty, infinite fame and infinite power. It is summed up in one word: Godhead. This is what we ought to desire. In the *Bhagavad Gita*, the oft-repeated expression is: 'He who steadfastly, with a pure heart and devotion, desires Me, he becomes Myself'.

As a tiny river, desiring union with the ocean, becomes the ocean, so the human mind, desirous of universal happiness, infinite sovereignty, infinite fame and infinite power, undoubtedly becomes that. This is the one ambition which a man ought to possess. All others must be subsidiary to it. If anything else is desired, the result will be disappointment, despair, heartache and failure all round.

This is a new education, a new ideal, a new orientation of the deep-seated volcanic urge in the human heart called love. What we desire we accomplish, but beware what you desire. The object of our desire must influence our whole being. We must dream of it, we must live it, we must sleep it, we must walk it. It is then that the desire is fulfilled. The way to the fulfilment of this supreme desire, Godhead, is called Yoga.

To sum up: What should we desire? Godhead. Not to be slaves of a God—not to occupy a secondary position to God—but to be God Himself. Unless a lover has become the object of his love, he does not know the meaning of love.

Love is a process of eliminating the distance between lover and beloved. 'He is my friend, who shows me the way to the house of Vasudeva, the Son of Nanda', says the poet Sur Dasa. The word 'Vasudeva' means: 'He in whom the universe dwells and who dwells in the universe'. This ring dwells in gold and gold dwells in this ring. Infinite bliss, infinite sovereignty, infinite fame, infinite power and infinite capacity to love—these five things together are called Vasudeva, the Lord of the universe.

That on which a man concentrates he eventually becomes. If you concentrate on God, you become God; if on your pet dog, you become that dog. The love of his ideal by Columbus needs no repetition; the love of the navigator Magellan for his ambition needs no mention; the love of Alexander of Macedon for the conquest of the world is well-known. Alas, Columbus died in chains and his chains were buried with him; Magellan succumbed to physical exhaustion without any friends and in disappointment; Alexander was poisoned by his marshals and generals, and died in utter despair.

My friends, let your desire be Godhead, Vasudeva. As we take His name in love, we create Him in our personality. Godhead lies buried in the human personality. Through self-control, benevolence, devotion, enquiry and meditation, we discover Him within us, and then we become Vasudeva Himself. Let us therefore offer salutations to Him before we start our study of this classic by one of the greatest teachers of all time.

ANALYTICAL TABLE OF CONTENTS

TRANSLITERATED SANSKRIT WORDS

The following table gives the most elementary indications of the value of the vowels that are variable in English (but regular in Sanskrit) and of the unfamiliar symbols and groupings of letters found in transliterated Sanskrit words. It is not intended as an accurate guide to correct pronunciation, for which see M. Coulson, Sanskrit (Teach Yourself Books), pp.4-21.

a = u in but (elided a = ')

ā = a in father (elided ā = '')

ai = ê in French crême

au = au in audit

c = ch in chant

ch = ch aspirated (said with extra breath

ḍ = d in drake

e = ay in hay (better, French é elongated)

h immediately after a consonant aspirates it without altering the value (bh, ph)

ḥ = strong h

i = i in hit

ī = ea in eat

jñ = ja or gya (as in big yard)

ṃ = m before b, p, v, y and at the end of a word; elsewhere = n

ṅ = n in king

ṇ = n in tendril

ñ = n (except in jñ, q.v.)

o = o in note

ṛ = ri in rich

s = s in such

ś = sh in shut

ṣ = sh in shut

ṭ = t in try

u = u in put

ū = oo in boot

THE CREST JEWEL OF WISDOM
(VIVEKA-CŪḌĀMAṆI)

'Viveka' means 'spiritual discrimination'; 'cūḍāmaṇi' means 'crest jewel'. Those who have discrimination are real human beings.

1. Invocation

sarva-vedānta-siddhānta-gocaram tam-agocaram
govindaṃ paramānandaṃ sadguruṃ praṇato'smy aham

[1] I bow to my true Guru Shri Govinda who is of the nature of supreme Bliss. Though his true nature transcends mind and speech, it is approachable indirectly as the final teaching of the Upanishads considered in their entirety.

The tradition is that the disciple ascribes to his teacher all that he is or what he wants to become. The negation of individuality is the secret of supreme, as well as minor, success in life. (Note: Shankara's Guru is traditionally held to have been Govindapada Acharya). We can learn from this verse the right way of doing things.

We can say we know the teacher, but do we? Can any scientist in the world say that he knows what a plate really is? 'Plate' is its name; 'circular' is its form. How can we know what it really is? By the study of ontology. Ontology tells us what a thing is, independently of what we see. It is wrong to say that we know a thing by seeing and touching it. Sensual knowledge is most imperfect. Real knowledge is that which reveals supreme bliss. What is dearest to us? Satisfaction. A thing may be very great, but if it does not satisfy our spirit, the greatest is of little meaning to us.

In India, everybody has three kinds of teacher: one who teaches us secular knowledge, one who is the family priest, and one who gives knowledge of truth. The holy Acharya in this one verse tells us how to have knowledge through discrimination by bowing down to the teacher and seeing all in him.

2. Importance of realization of the Absolute

jantūnāṃ nara-janma durlabham ataḥ
  puṃstvaṃ tato vipratā
tasmād vaidika-dharma-mārga-paratā
  vidvattvam asmāt param
ātmānātma-vivecanaṃ svanubhavo
  brahmātmanā saṃsthitir
muktir no śata-koṭi-janmasu kṛtaiḥ
  puṇyair vinā labhyate

[2] It is hard for living creatures to attain human birth, harder still to become a man, harder still to become a Brahmin, harder still to be one devoted to the spiritual path of the Veda, harder still to acquire learning in that domain. But to effect a complete discrimination of the Self from the not-self and to have direct experience of one's true nature and liberation in the form of establishment in the Self as the Absolute—that is not attained without the good deeds of many millions of lives.

In this second verse is shown how valuable is human birth. There are millions of species, vertebrates, primates, etc., but human birth is a rare achievement. Why? Because man can become God. If a cat could express its ambition what would it say? 'A room filled with fresh delectable mice, cushions to lounge upon, numbers of kittens frisking around'. Can a cat think, or want to become a Newton?

How fortunate we are to be human beings. That superior force, called God, who has made us human beings, ought never to be forgotten.

Among men, those who walk the path of righteousness and wisdom are more fortunate, but those who are spiritually learned are still more fortunate. In olden times, Christians and Jews showed infinite reverence for learning. Why? Because it is the key to the opening of the mysteries of creation.

Still more fortunate is that man who can discriminate between the Self and the not-self. In the whole world there are two kinds of objects, sentient and insentient, Self and not-self. According to Aristotle, no insentient object can move without receiving an impetus from outside. Those who confound these two together are called ignorant men.

Wisdom is discrimination. It means to understand: 'That which is Self is Self; that which is not-self is not-self. There is only one Self pervading all the objects of the world'. 'O Arjuna, know Me to be the Knower of the Field' (*Gita* 13.2). Hence the acme of wisdom is discrimination between what is Self and what is not-self: 'The not-self is the abode of suffering; Self is happiness. Self is Vasudeva (God); not-self is inert matter'.

The highest human beings are those who have realized the identity of the individual self with the cosmic Self. Imagine you are standing on the shore at Brighton. Before you waves are dashing high and low, here and there. The small wave looks at the big wave and says 'How unfortunate I am!' Bubbles are still less satisfied; they organize a revolution. All is misery. But misery goes when each wave knows 'I am water, we are one, there is no difference between us!'

The acme of the consummation of life is realization of God in all. To those who have identified their individual ego with the cosmic ego, there is no bondage, no suffering. They are absolutely free. This state is called liberation-in-life (jivan-mukti).

How is this state acquired? By the merit of many incarnations. Everyone is destined to be one with God. Nothing worthwhile is easy. This state is acquired when the merits warrant it. Merits are good kind deeds, prayer, devotion, study, compassion and leading others on the right path. This conduct continued for a long time leads to God-realization.

durlabhaṃ trayam evaitad devānugraha-hetukam
manuṣyatvaṃ mumukṣutvaṃ mahā-puruṣa-saṃśrayaḥ

[3] Three things are hard to obtain and are only obtained through the grace of God—human birth, desire for liberation and access to the society of spiritually perfect souls.

What is the grace of God? That mighty, conscious, compassionate force which has constructed the universe.

Spiritual truth cannot be learnt by studying books only, nor by prayers alone, nor by self-taught methods. You need one who himself has experimented on spiritual methods and is competent to pass this experience on. He should be loving, because otherwise the teaching does not fully fructify. Alexander of Macedon had two teachers, one was Aristotle, the other Homer, and he was brought up on the *Iliad* and *Odyssey* of the latter. As a result he shaped his life to the pattern of Homeric ideals and, just as Homer's heroes are in reality scoundrels, so Alexander proved no exception, doing little that was worthwhile, while Aristotle contributed to his education the few great essentials of knowledge. There ought therefore to be a bond between teacher and pupil.

labdhvā kathaṃcin nara-janma durlabhaṃ
tatrāpi puṃstvaṃ śruti-pāra-darśanam
yaḥ svātma-muktau na yateta mūḍha-dhīḥ
sa hy ātma-hā svaṃ vinihanty asad-grahāt

[4] He who, having attained human birth as a man and intellectual mastery of the Veda, is so foolish as to fail to strive for liberation, commits spiritual suicide in pursuit of the unreal.

Physical suicide is bad, mental suicide is worse, but worse still is spiritual suicide, for the mind endures millions of years and the Spirit is immortal. Why should one know the nature of one's Self? Because without it, life is just a series of afflictions and miseries, since the intellect or reasoning faculty, which looks for order and sequence in phenomena, also expects to know the reason for life. Hence the supreme necessity of knowing the answer to the questions: 'What am I?' 'What is my nature?' 'What am I here for?' These are problems that man must study with great care.

itaḥ ko nvasti mūḍhātmā yas tu svārthe pramādyati
durlabhaṃ mānuṣaṃ dehaṃ prāpya tatrāpi pauruṣam

[5] Who indeed would be so foolish as to neglect his true interest when he had obtained human birth and a masculine body as well?

We know that just drinking and enjoying name and fame and mere domination over others is not the end of life. Therefore the really ignorant man is he who, having been given all the opportunities to light the flame of wisdom in his heart, fails to do so. Why wisdom? Because wisdom alone gives us real freedom and happiness, making us more compassionate, charitable, kind and loving.

vadantu śāstrāṇi yajantu devān
kurvantu karmāṇi bhajantu devatāḥ
ātmaikya-bodhena vinā vimuktir
na sidhyati brahma-śatāntare 'pi

[6] One may repeat the Vedas, offer sacrifices to the gods, perform good works and worship deities—but without direct realization that all is one as the Self, one would not get liberation even after a hundred world-periods.

How is this freedom obtained? To me, political freedom means very little; it is merely a slogan exploited by cunning people for their own ends. Real freedom means that state in which we are masters of our minds, masters of immortality, having overcome death. It is not obtained through charity, nor through duty, but by knowledge alone. By prayer you can obtain the grace of God, but the real means to freedom is the knowledge which terminates ignorance forever.

It has been said that the most important thing in life is knowledge of truth. What man wishes for more than anything else is always immortality. Lao Tzu says that knowledge is the means of obtaining that freedom for which the human soul hungers.

amṛtatvasya nāśāsti vittenety eva hi śrutiḥ
bravīti karmaṇo mukter ahetutvaṃ sphuṭaṃ yataḥ

[7] The Veda says, 'There is no hope of immortality through wealth'. Hence it is clear that liberation cannot come through action.

3. The means to metaphysical knowledge

ato vimuktyai prayateta vidvān
saṃnyasta-bāhyārtha-sukha-spṛhaḥ san
santaṃ mahāntaṃ samupetya deśikaṃ
tenopadiṣṭārtha-samāhitātmā

[8] And so the man of learning should strive for liberation, giving up desire for joy from external objects. He should take refuge with some great and holy man as his teacher and concentrate his whole soul on the teaching he is given.

If he desires freedom, immortality, bliss, he has first to make himself master of his taste, sound, touch and sight. Aristotle has said that man would have been a much nobler creature if he had not fallen a slave to his sense of touch. Health and keenness of intellect can only be enjoyed when a man has mastery over the external pleasures of our existence. How wise are the words of Christ who says that 'Man does not live by bread alone'—he means 'by the senses alone'. What of the joys of forgiveness, of philosophy, of the acquisition of learning? These in truth are the real joys in life. In the *Katha Upanishad* it is said that the soul is the chariot-driver, the mind the reins, and the senses the horses. Must not the charioteer control the horses to prevent his chariot being hurled into the ditch? First, then, we must hold our five senses in rein.

Secondly, we must have a loving preceptor. What we learn in books is easily forgotten. It is the Spirit that communicates with the Spirit, and it is love that induces the flow of wisdom from teacher to pupil, as from a cow to its calf.

uddhared ātmanā ''tmānaṃ magnaṃ saṃsāra-vāridhau
yogārūḍhatvam-āsādya samyag-darśana-niṣṭhayā

[9] Drowned as he is in the ocean of repeated births and deaths, he should raise himself out by his own efforts, attaining perfection in yoga through constant concentration on vision of the real.

saṃnyasya sarva-karmāṇi bhava-bandha-vimuktaye
yatyatāṃ paṇḍitair dhīrair ātmābhyāsa upasthitaiḥ

[10] Wise and courageous souls should give up all resort to self-interested action in the interests of release from rebirth. They should apply themselves to sustained concentration on the Self.

As long as a man has to die, what is the use of fame, wealth and learning? Therefore the Acharya says we should have an iron determination to acquire wisdom. When we want to make a change in our lives, it is essential that we should change our companions and works. The result of knowledge is the realization that finite works are limited, and nothing that is limited ever satisfies the human soul. Therefore the candidate for wisdom must be one-pointed, resolute and changed from the life of limited pleasure to that of infinite freedom.

It may be asked: 'If all works are useless, how does knowledge arise out of the mind?'

cittasya śuddhaye karma na tu vastūpalabdhaye
vastu-siddhir vicāreṇa na kiṃcit karma-koṭibhiḥ

> [11] One may engage in disinterested action to purify the mind, but it will not bring knowledge of reality. It is through introspective reflection that one comes to know the real: in this domain, nothing whatever is gained by a million good deeds.

Our mind is like a sea in constant motion, some of the waves being anger, some attachment, some ambition and so forth, but there is also a deeper wave there. The book of the mind is hard to read, but in it can be found knowledge. Knowledge dwells in the deeper layers of the mind and when the upper layers are controlled and pacified, wisdom will appear.

But first the mind must be made calm and pure. Not merely by asceticism, for purity of the mind means having fewer and fewer desires. Knowledge requires that desires should be few and wise. To allow oneself to be assaulted by an army of desires is to face a pack of mad hounds. When the mind is made calm and unagitated, pure wisdom arises in it. How is it made pure? By the practice of wisdom, devotion and desirelessness. If the mind is agitated, life is a great burden. The practice of compassion, desirelessness and friendliness to all is necessary for creating those conditions in the mind which are conducive to the germination of the plant of wisdom. Remember that the sighs of the oppressed are stronger than all the cannons, guns and torpedoes in the world, for they rise directly to the throne of God.

samyag-vicārataḥ siddhā rajju-tattvāvadhāraṇā
bhrāntyodita-mahā-sarpa-bhaya-duḥkha-vināśinī

[12] It is through right reflection that one comes to know the true nature of the rope. And it is that knowledge alone which can remove the great fear arising from the erroneous notion of a snake.

If one day you see in your house a rope, but you imagine it to be a snake, how will you get rid of this illusory snake? Will you pray, or give charity, or fast? These means will be fruitless. Bring in a light—that is, a knowledge of the rope, and this will dispel the snake. Bondage of all kinds is illusory, like the snake. Try to know what you are and banish these illusions.

In order to cook a curry you need many things; but the one essential is fire, for without it all the condiments will not make the curry. What is the essential in life? It is to know your own nature; and when you do, all bondage and restrictions will disappear. In order to appreciate the real blessing of birth as a man, it is necessary to know our mind, to approach a teacher who is practised in truth, to give up self-interested works and to devote ourselves to acquiring knowledge of Self by studying such books as *The Crest Jewel of Wisdom.*

'God' and 'Self' are synonymous terms, as one is interchangeable with the other. Therefore we should devote ourselves to such means as conduce to the acquisition of knowledge of God and bring it to others. Where a wise man lives who knows God and controls himself, he, like the sandal tree, sheds fragrance on all who contact him. 'He acquires My state' says the Lord in the *Gita* (18.55). This is the ideal of humanity and it should be adopted and followed.

arthasya niścayo dṛṣṭo vicāreṇa hitoktitaḥ
na snānena na dānena prāṇāyāma-śatena vā

[13] It is through reflection over the words of a truly benevolent soul that one comes to a knowledge of reality, and not through bathing at sacred places, charity or hundreds of breathing practices.

A deep conviction of the holy truth is necessary. What is it? It is that God alone exists and all else is His shadow, and that He abides in the heart of each and every being. The eternal question is 'What is truth?' Truth is a statement about a fact which is not contradicted by time—this is a working definition of truth. This fact, that God is, is not contradicted by time. That all else is His shadow and that He abides in the heart of each and every being, is the only truth, and nothing other than this can be called truth.

William James has founded what is called the pragmatic test: 'How does knowledge affect our experience?' He is not wholly right but there is some truth in it. Pragmatism means to accept nothing which does not affect our experience favourably. How does this fact that God alone exists and abides in the hearts of all affect our life and our experience? It makes one a philanthropist, a lover of all beings, a saint of God and a freed man independent of all limitations and conditions. William James turned the tables on atheists, hedonists and agnostics, such as Spencer and Hegel, by reason of this test, and proclaimed the doctrine of the existence of God and personal immortality.

We do not begin to live well until we hold this conviction. We must not hold opinions, because opinions change and they are of no use; but conviction is that for which we will willingly sacrifice our life. Many saints of God have sacrificed their lives, not for opinions but for this conviction.

How does this conviction come? Through reflection. But you must hear the truth from a saint of God and then reason it. John Stuart Mill applied the closest logical test to the existence of God and then proclaimed 'There is no God!' Hear the truth from the lips of a living student of God-knowledge. Do not accept blindly. 'A living soul can be lit only by a living soul'. Books do not teach that. Come into touch with the living soul in love and devotion and hear from those lips the truth.

Many people say that by controlling the breath you can know God, but nothing physical can lift the soul to the spiritual. Bathing in a sacred river, or giving in charity, is useful, but it is not the direct means to knowledge of God as one's Self.

4. The qualifications for study

adhikāriṇam āśāste phala-siddhir viśeṣataḥ
upāyā deśa-kālādyāḥ santy asmin saha-kāriṇaḥ

[14] Success here demands above all a properly qualified student. Considerations of what has to be done, when and where, are secondary by comparison.

This means that a man who wants to know God must first have a conviction of the spiritual truth which will not change. First he hears the truth from a loving teacher, and then he leads the life of a disciplined disciple.

Then comes time. The best time for prayer and meditation is from a little before to a little after dawn. The rays of the sun have a special effect at dawn. At that time the holy ones in their retreats commune with the Maker of heaven and earth in themselves and pour blessings on all. Your moods, thoughts and life in general during the whole day are very much influenced by your thoughts and life during these half-hours. In Sanskrit it is called 'divine time'. The night and day of the full moon is also a very useful time.

Places free from gross materialistic associations, such as the solitary bank of a river, a valley, a hill, are the fittest places for devotion to God. The Chinese have built a temple to Buddha wherever the voice is echoed in mountains. The banks of the holy Ganges are a place consecrated by the presence of holy saints of God. Always retire for devotion to a spot unsullied by the thoughts and subtle forms of the matter-worshipping people.

ato vicāraḥ kartavyo jijñāsor-ātma-vastunaḥ
samāsādya dayā-sindhuṃ guruṃ brahmavid-uttamam

> [15] Therefore the serious enquirer must reflect over the nature of the Self as the real after resorting to some great teacher who has himself realized the Absolute and who is an ocean of compassion.

A few worshippers of the Lord sit down together and, taking the existence of God as a hypothesis, seek to establish it by reasoning. The atheists and agnostics do not know how to reason. They frame arguments and then argue about it.

The teacher must be an ocean of compassion and he must have known God. The more compassion we show, the nearer we are to the holy throne of the Maker of heaven and earth. To love is difficult; to have compassion is easier.

In the nuns' convent founded by St Ignatius Loyola, when discipline was not being fully observed, a few young men used to find their way to its inmates. The saint took the requisite steps and restored discipline. The young men, finding themselves deprived of their joy, one night caught hold of the saint and nearly killed him. He knew them all, but when he recovered and was asked to identify those who had attacked him, he only said, 'Some misguided fools' and did not betray the name of a single person—an example of mercy and compassion. In the Jewish scriptures it is said: 'Jehovah is the hardest to displease and the easiest to reconcile'. So are the saints of God. Shri Dada was never known to be angry—the anger of a saint is momentary, like a flash of lightning.

Who is qualified to know God?

medhāvī puruṣo vidvān ūhāpoha-vicakṣaṇaḥ
adhikāryātma-vidyāyām ukta-lakṣaṇa-lakṣitaḥ

> [16] The student qualified for knowledge of the Self must be an intelligent and learned man, skilled in understanding proof and disproof, and possessed of the virtues to be enumerated below.

He ought to be intelligent, but for those who are not intelligent there is faith. If you cannot dig your own well for water, use the well dug by another.

Abelard spoke of authority as having a waxen nose because it could be twisted this way or that through reason. How to apply reason? Whoever wants to know God should reason in favour of the scriptural texts in order to establish them. Do not reason to demolish the doctrines of the immortality of the soul and the existence of God; reason to establish them, refuting arguments against them. Shri Shankara Acharya, in his brilliant commentaries, has anticipated all arguments against the holy philosophy and has demolished them.

Some people find fault with the Bible because some of the statements are not corroborated by physical science. It is as if they were to say that because their father is not able to do a sum of calculus, whatever he says is wrong. The Bible is a book of spirituality and not a book of science. When did holy Christ say: 'I give you a book of science'? You cannot understand the Bible, the *Gita*, or the Quran unless you approach it with great reverence and with the feeling 'this book is much greater than I am'. He who has this characteristic can receive the knowledge of God.

Be intelligent, be learned and be skilled in arguing in favour of God. It is said in the *Katha Upanishad*, 'This Self is not to be known by arguments' (1.2.23). As Descartes says, you can neither prove nor disprove the existence of God by argument, but counter-arguments can be met by reasoning.

What are the qualifications?

vivekino viraktasya śamādi-guṇa-śālinaḥ
mumukṣor eva hi brahma-jijñāsā-yogyatā matā

[17] Only he is held to be fit for enquiry into the Absolute who is possessed of discrimination, detachment, the six-fold qualities of inner control and the rest, along with deep desire for liberation.

These qualifications are called the ground for knowledge of God. Discrimination (viveka) means discrimination between the real and the unreal—nothing else is meant by discrimination. The greatest qualification is the desire for liberation and knowledge of God (mumukshuta). All this is summed up by the holy teacher in the next two verses.

5. The four-fold discipline

sādhanāny atra catvāri kathitāni manīṣibhiḥ
yeṣu satsveva san-niṣṭhā yad abhāve na sidhyati

[18] The wise speak of four items of discipline. Only if these are present can a person become permanently established in reality, otherwise not.

Note it very carefully. Mere church-going, praying, gift-giving, will not give the light of direct knowledge of God. They ought to be accompanied by these four great qualifications, also a teacher and the appropriate time and place.

ādau nityānitya-vastu-vivekaḥ parigaṇyate
ihāmutra-phala-bhoga-virāgas tad anantaram
śamādi ṣaṭkasampattir mumukṣutvam iti sphuṭam

[19] The first qualification is discrimination of the permanent from the impermanent, then an attitude of detachment towards

the enjoyment of all rewards in this life or in lives to come, then the six-fold spiritual wealth consisting of inner control and the rest, and finally deep desire for liberation.

brahma satyaṃ jagan mithyety evaṃ-rūpo viniścayaḥ
so 'yaṃ nityānitya-vastu-vivekaḥ samudāhṛtaḥ

[20] Discrimination of the permanent from the impermanent is said to be the conviction 'The Absolute is real and the world illusory'.

The first mental equipment that a disciple has to have and to cultivate is discrimination (viveka). To discriminate in daily life between what is fugitive and what is real, to evaluate the unreal and the real, and to give only as much attention to the unreal as will enable us to pursue the real—this is discrimination.

There are two kinds of things in this world, passing and permanent. Everything which is compound has a transitory existence. In the *Gita* (2.28) the Lord says that is called unreal which does not exist in the beginning and the end, but only has existence in the middle. Why is a dream unreal? Because it only has a temporary intervening existence. When a messenger from Rome brought news from Augustus to Mark Antony in Egypt, who was under the spell of 'the Serpent of the Nile', Antony said: 'Let Rome in Tiber melt...Kingdoms are clay' *(Antony and Cleopatra*, I.1). The death in obscurity of Kaiser Wilhelm II proved that 'kingdoms are clay'.

What is 'real'? The religious man calls reality God, a yogi calls it Self, the scientist calls it truth. Reality is the substratum of all so-called facts. The pyramids exist, Rome existed, Carthage existed; what is common to all? Existence. Will existence ever be destroyed? No! If you imagine that there is nothing before you and you say that nothing exists, still you who make that statement exist. When you know existence, then you know God. Dr McTaggart comes to the same conclusion, that the cognizer, or perceiver, is real. When children chase after a rainbow, we laugh, but are not our little ambitions as impermanent as a rainbow? Do not our dreams end suddenly? To understand this is discrimination.

If we devote our life from morning to evening to perishable things, we are called ignorant; for their knowledge brings no satisfaction. We cannot know God unless we cultivate discrimination (viveka). The holy Lord said: 'Leave all and follow Me'. Turn your back on the perishable and follow reality, the Light of the world. Every faculty grows when exercised, and deteriorates when not used. Let us exercise this faculty of discrimination (viveka). You will say: 'How can we pursue that which is real?' Yoga is the answer. By prayer, inner silence, renunciation and universal love we pursue what is eternal.

tad vairāgyaṃ jugupsā yā darśana-śravaṇādibhiḥ
dehādi-brahma-paryante hy anitye bhoga-vastuni

[21] Detachment implies disgust for the whole realm of impermanent enjoyments perceived through the senses, stretching from the body to the world of Brahmā.

The second qualification is detachment (vairagya). 'Raga' means hankering, thirst or attachment; 'vi' is a prefix meaning 'from which they are gone'. When my hand is full like the hand of the monkey thrust into the jar of nuts, I cannot grasp any other thing. Vairagya does not mean to be careless and indifferent, but to live as Christ lived, as Ashoka, as Shri Dada, as Krishna lived. What rich full lives they lived. To be so absorbed in the contemplation and love of God that nothing else has a binding force upon us, that is detachment (vairagya). It is not a doctrine of escape, nor an irrational attitude, nor a makeshift; but a one-pointed, fuller and freer life.

There was once a Buddhist monk who used to live in retirement far from the world, proud of the fact that he had renounced the world and was a disciple. Once he visited a fellow disciple who was in charge of a school with a large number of monks, a library and a dispensary. They lived together for a few days and the renunciate used secretly to scorn the other monk. One day, when both disciples were walking about five miles from the institution, the renunciate said: 'I am sorry for your delusion. Why have you collected all this around you? Why not be a renunciate like me and leave the world?' The other thought for a moment and then replied: 'Brother, you are right. Let us go now!' The renunciate answered: 'Yes, but I have left my blanket and staff behind. I will get them and then we will go'. Where was his renunciation?

Acharya Shankara says: 'The attached ones accumulate pain-giving relationship even in the woods and forests'. In Yoga, renunciation is an inner subjective quality. The teacher of the *Gita* was the greatest yogi, yet no life has been fuller than his. It is the mind that is tied and the mind that is free. Marcus Aurelius, sleeping in marble palaces, lived a more saintly life than many who lived apart from the world. Yoga does not mean running away from the world; it means creating a mood of the mind that does not admit of any attachment to name, form, wife, child and so forth.

Detachment (vairagya) means the assignment to desire of its proper value. Desires are like people flocking to a show of jewellery. Some only come to look, some to touch, others to help themselves on communistic grounds such as 'He has jewels and I have not!' The jeweller chooses real customers. The yogi chooses those desires which lead his soul higher and higher to God.

virajya viṣaya-vrātād doṣa-dṛṣṭyā muhur-muhuḥ
sva-lakṣye niyatāvasthā manasaḥ śama ucyate

[22] Inner control means that constant fixing of the mind on the spiritual goal every moment that can be obtained after acquiring detachment through seeing the defects in all sense-objects.

I assure you, my friends, nervousness can be easily cured. You need not go to a psycho-analyst, only come to God. The meditations we practise take away all neurosis and soothe the soul. Unless you are tranquil, all you have is valueless. The bud receives in silence the kiss of the morning sun and opens into a blossom. A little irritant passing into the shell of an oyster sets in motion a fluid, and a pearl is created in the silent depths of the ocean.

Mind reacts to suggestion. When it is restless, try to analyse the object by centring the mind on that which disturbs it. Yoga says 'be wise', that is, be thoughtful. When a man who has never smoked opium experiences the first few puffs of the pipe he feels great nervous relaxation and says, 'Now I have got all I want in life'. If the man at that time were to see all the effects of opium, he would abhor it for what it brings in its train. This should be applied to life, and it will add to tranquillity.

Another aspect of inner control (shama) is constant remembrance of the holy name of God, whether in the form of Christ, Buddha, Krishna, Rama or OM. It is a psychological fact that the mind cannot apply itself to more than one object at a time. If the mind is filled with remembrance of God, His wisdom, His Yoga, His incarnations and His saints, it cannot stray or become agitated. The mind transforms itself into the pattern of an ideal after long and constant thought on that ideal.

viṣayebhyaḥ parāvartya sthāpanaṃ sva-sva-golake
ubhayeṣām-indriyāṇāṃ sa damaḥ parikīrtitaḥ

[23] Outer control is described as the withdrawal of the sense-organs and organs of action from objects and confining them to their place in the body.

The senses are five—taste, smell, sight, touch and hearing. If the ears become fond of hearing ill of others, which they can easily do, at once stop and withdraw hearing to the ear. Roman gladiator shows, as described by St Jerome, prove to what degradation our eyes can lead us. We must see what is beautiful, we must taste what is conducive to health. See that the tongue never gets out of control, that it speaks only what is good not for yourself alone, but for others.

Outer control (dama) is very important. The classical way to self-control is to train the ear to hear, whenever you have time, stories of holy Christ, of his display of mercy to Mary Magdalene, of his exposition of Truth on the Mount of Olives. Or hear of Rama blessing his enemies, those who had come to assault him; he gave high station in heaven to them when slain. With your hands serve your spiritual community, the poor, the miserable, and always serve with humility—such is outer control.

bāhyānālambanaṃ vṛtter eṣoparatir-uttamā

[24] The finest form of withdrawal (uparati) is refusing to allow the mind to dwell on external objects.

Withdrawal (uparati) is an excellent discipline. We should be able to withdraw our mind instantaneously from any object. If anyone spoke ill of anyone else in the presence of my teacher, Shri Dada, he rang a bell and said: 'The temple bell is ringing!' Unless we are able to control anger and inordinate affection, our life is not ours but belongs to those thieves, the passions.

sahanaṃ sarva-duḥkhānām apratīkāra-pūrvakam
cintā-vilāpa-rahitaṃ sā titikṣā nigadyate

[25] Endurance (titikṣā) is said to be the acceptance of all pain without taking measures to alleviate it and without anxiety or lamentation.

Endurance can be full of a vituperative vocabulary, but here patient endurance is indicated. To bear afflictions without seeking to remove them, meanwhile keeping the mind free from anxiety, is titiksha. Bearing afflictions but going about grumbling is not the right way. Can we bear contradiction, heat and cold, opposition to our views and ideas? The life of the early disciples of Christ is a limpid stream of crystal-clear water in which flourish the pearl oysters of peace and beauty. To be a perfect yogi, one must put the mind in touch with the fountain of bliss which never diminishes. There is really no point when the weather is bad in remarking 'beastly weather!' The Japanese would say; 'Very cold, I sympathize with you!' and that ends the matter. Suffer, have forbearance without anxiety. Then the mind has strength to devote itself to peace and higher light.

Once Shri Dada urgently needed money. He took a few gold ornaments from the holy mother and said to the money-lender: 'Can you advance me some money?' 'No, I have none', was the reply. 'But you are reputed to be a rich man', said Shri Dada. 'Yes, but my money is all invested', said the money-lender. If all our life is invested in likes and dislikes, passions and pleasures, where have we the resources to invest in the inner beauty of the love and wisdom of the Lord?

śāstrasya guru-vākyasya satya-buddhy-avadhāraṇam
sā śraddhā kathitā sadbhir yayā vastūpalabhyate

[26] The wise say that faith is the conviction of the truth of the teaching of the Veda and the words of the Guru. It is the means to knowledge of the real.

Without this faith, God-realization is impossible. Many a frail boat of spiritual life has been wrecked because of lack of faith. What did the man say when told to sell all and follow Christ? There must be acceptance by an unwavering mind of the judgement of the teacher and the holy scriptures in matters relating to Yoga. This is a most important part of the discipline—the most important. That much maligned, but nevertheless great philosopher, Pythagoras, used to take a pledge of faith from those whom he initiated. Not one of the modern philosophers, John Stuart Mill, Hobbes, Freud or Hume, knew the true spiritual meaning of freedom—which is, freedom to surrender the mind to God.

Spiritual science needs no innovation; it is not subject to the law of evolution. Astronomy, psychology and other sciences have evolved, but spiritual science remains as it was given at the beginning of the world-period (kalpa). It is complete in the Bible, complete in the *Gita*, complete in the Buddhist scriptures, complete in the Quran, where it is said: 'I give you this book, which is the book of life'. If you want truth, refer to the *Gita* or the Fourth Gospel. You will find it complete with nothing new to add. If a teacher says he can give you something new, he is no teacher but an imposter.

The first task undertaken by Aristotle was to attend to the destruction of the philosophy of Plato. Hegel asserted that the last word in philosophy had been said, but see what William James, McTaggart, Bergson and Moore say. The philosophy of all of these is based on the intellect and therefore will have to be rubbed out every few years, but spiritual philosophy will endure forever. Hence we see the necessity for faith (shraddha).

The Guru is your best friend. How true are the words: 'Many Gurus there are, who are skilful in removing the wealth of their disciples, but I know of only one who removes the sufferings of the pupil, he who belongs to Shri Shankara and his line'. The teacher shares the physical suffering. He takes upon himself much of the affliction that would otherwise fall upon the pupil.

sarvadā sthāpanaṃ buddheḥ śuddhe brahmaṇi sarvathā
tat-samādhānam ity uktam na tu cittasya lālanam

[27] Concentration (samādhāna) is the continual fixing of the mind on the Absolute in its pure form, and not allowing the mind to dwell on whatever it likes.

Then alone can one meditate on God. Let us not quarrel with any religion, denomination or creed. I bow down to those who worship Mary, I bow down to those who worship the Cross or the Crescent, I bow down to those who worship the eternal Absolute. He only is a lover who does not forget the beloved even for a moment.

ahaṃkārādi-dehāntān bandhān ajñāna-kalpitān
sva-svarūpāvabodhena moktum-icchā mumukṣutā

[28] Deep desire for liberation (mumukṣutā) is the desire to free oneself through knowledge of one's own true nature from all the bonds imagined through ignorance, beginning with the ego-sense and ending with the body.

Every human being has a desire to know God but misreads his desires and imagines he can be freed by indulging in objects of the senses, in acquiring power over others, in being vain and in accumulating possessions, both material and academic. The main desire must be to know Him alone.

A man suffering from tuberculosis expresses the disease in about a hundred symptoms, but to treat him successfully you do not treat the symptoms; you treat the bacteria and then the symptoms will disappear. Similarly, hunger, thirst, lunacy, restlessness, want of peace, being out of focus with our companions and so on are all indications of one grand error—that is, want of understanding of the real nature of the individual as the universal Self, or God. The spiritual diagnosis of the millions of diseases that the human mind is subject to—physical, mental, social, national, international—is called ignorance; and this medicine is given by the holy saints of God to cure the malady.

A most important factor in the growth of the soul is called mumukshuta, or conscious desire to be free from all limitations, but unless the desire is strong, we shall not apply the proper remedy. We may postpone the treatment, or we may not recognize the disease, but the bacteria of ignorance are at work all the time and death leads to another birth and yet another birth.

When a diagnosis of all these ills is made, there is found to be only one disease and one cure. The disease is ignorance of the nature of the Self, and the cure is knowledge of its true nature.

manda-madhyama-rūpāpi vairāgyeṇa śamādinā
prasādena guroḥ seyaṃ pravṛddhā sūyate phalam

[29] Even though desire for liberation may initially be weak or mediocre, it grows and eventually bears fruit through detachment, through the six-fold spiritual wealth and through the grace of the Guru.

The Acharya says that mumukshuta, a strong yearning for freedom, is created, by the grace of the Guru, through non-attachment (vairagya) and tranquillity of the mind (shama). These two things are indispensable. Neurotics, fanatics and power-mad ones will die the death of Richard III on the battlefield of life.

Non-attachment (vairagya) means not minding inordinately whether possessions and worldly matters are according to our desire or not. The one supreme formula is: 'Let Thy will be done'. The holy Veda says: 'All-knowing Father, take away from us all that is an impediment to our spiritual unfoldment, whether it be sons, wife, husband, or anyone. I submit to Thy desire'.

The other indispensable thing is shama, inner tranquillity, to be equiminded—that is, not to be elated when success comes and boast of it, for this leads to greater and greater suffering. We educate the mind in an inner calmness. This inner calmness will not fall like a ripe plum from the tree; we have to cultivate it, and meditation is the chief means. Life without meditation is a walk on a road of absolute insecurity.

Holy meditation comes by the grace of the Guru. The human mind is affected by the human mind. If Homer had not given the world his *Iliad*, there would have been no Napoleon, no Alexander, no Caesar. It was the influence of Homer's *Iliad*, imbibed in childhood, that turned the minds of these men into so-called conquerors. Real education begins with the mother. How beautiful it is to see a mother rocking her babe and singing: 'O my child, thou art ever awakened, ever free from the taints of Maya (illusion)'.

What does the Guru do? He pours out his soul in a continuous stream on the visible plane to lift up the soul of his disciple.

vairāgyaṃ ca mumukṣutvaṃ tīvraṃ yasya tu vidyate
tasminn evārthavantaḥ syuḥ phalavantaḥ śamādayaḥ

[30] And the six-fold spiritual wealth is meaningful and fruitful only for him whose detachment and desire for liberation are keen.

For the man who has strong passionlessness (vairagya) and yearning to be free from all suffering (mumukshuta) all the other items of discipline follow. These two are most important. The patient has followed the instructions of the physician, but he must have the desire to be cured.

etayor mandatā yatra viraktatva-mumukṣayoḥ
marau salilavat tatra śamāder bhāsamātratā

[31] Where detachment and desire for liberation are weak, there is only an appearance of the six-fold wealth, like the water of a mirage.

mokṣa-kāraṇa-sāmagryāṃ bhaktir eva garīyasī
sva-svarūpānusandhānaṃ bhaktir ity abhidhīyate
svātma-tattvānusandhānaṃ bhaktir ity apare jaguḥ

[32] But of all the means to liberation, the greatest is devotion (bhakti). Devotion is defined as the investigation of one's true nature—or, according to others, investigation of the true nature of the Self.

6. The approach to the Guru

ukta-sādhana-sampannas tattva-jijñāsur ātmanaḥ
upasīded gurum prājñam yasmād bandha-vimokṣaṇam

[33] One who is endowed with the spiritual equipment mentioned above and who wishes to know the true nature of the Self should approach a wise Guru from whom he may receive liberation from bondage.

śrotriyo 'vṛjino 'kāma-hato yo brahma-vittamaḥ
brahmaṇy uparataḥ śānto nirindhana ivānalaḥ

ahaituka-dayā-sindhur bandhur-ānamatām satām
tam ārādhya gurum bhaktyā prahva-praśraya-sevanaiḥ
prasannam tam anuprāpya pṛcchej jñātavyam ātmanaḥ

[34-36] The Guru should be learned in the texts, sinless, desireless, a knower of the Absolute in the highest sense, withdrawn from all except the Absolute, at peace like a fire that has consumed its fuel, an ocean of disinterested compassion, a true friend to all good souls who bow before him. The spiritual enquirer should first honour the Guru devotedly with service and marks of respect, and then, when the latter is pleased, should approach him and ask what has to be known about the Self.

If you follow the tradition, it is the kings and emperors who go to the sage. If you are thirsty you go to the well, the well does not come to you. Worship means service by word, deed or thought and with devotion. There can be service without devotion; the gaol warder gives service to the prisoner, but not devotion. Service purifies the body and devotion purifies the heart and mind. These are the two instruments with which the pupil crosses the ocean of being and becoming: 'Know Him, O Arjuna, through service and devotion, and then the knowers of wisdom will speak to you of the divine secret, That which transcends all' (*Gita* 4.34). Let man go to the Guru with passionlessness, the best gift, and take fuel and offer service to him (cp. *Mundaka Upanishad* 1.2.12), then ask the question.

How to ask the question:

svāmin namaste nata-loka-bandho
kāruṇya-sindho patitaṃ bhavābdhau
mām uddharātmīya-kaṭākṣa-dṛṣṭyā
ṛjvyātikāruṇya-sudhābhivṛṣṭyā

[37] He should say: 'O Master, O friend of those who bow before you, O ocean of compassion, I offer my reverence. Rescue me from the ocean of rebirth with a single glance of your eye which is utterly sincere and overflowing with the nectar of compassion.

He is not a teacher unless he is a friend of the universe. A Vedic prayer says: 'Grant, O Lord, that everyone may look upon me as a friend and that I may look upon all as friends'. The holy Lord of Galilee taught the same.

The recognition of one's state of suffering has a mystic significance. Unless a vessel is empty it cannot be filled; similarly, unless the pupil realizes his present state to be one of suffering, he cannot be freed. If a man thinks: 'I have a motor car, a charming wife, many secretaries, a good position, am I not a happy man, an efficient man?'—Oh this efficiency! The Englishman is spiritual for one reason, that he is not an efficient man, neither is the Hindu!

The pupil says: 'Lift me up by one kindly glance'. Note it well: by glance, not by word. Our eyes express our most sacred emotions. Love cannot be expressed by word of mouth, it is then befouled. The real teachings are expressed only by the glance of the eye of the Guru.

durvāra-saṃsāra-davāgni-taptaṃ
dodhūyamānaṃ dur-adṛṣṭa-vātaiḥ
bhītaṃ prapannaṃ paripāhi mṛtyoḥ
śaraṇyam anyaṃ yad ahaṃ na jāne

[38] 'Save me from death, who stand before you scorched by the forest-fire of rebirth so hard to quench, battered by the winds of evil karma and thoroughly frightened. I know of no other refuge but yourself.

A little consideration will show that this world is a bed of sufferings. Every joy experienced in this world is necessarily pursued by sufferings. According to the Dialogue of Plato called *Phaedo*, on the morning of Socrates' death, when the gaoler cut the chains from his hands and feet, Socrates stretched his legs and said: 'Crito, I do feel a little relieved. Pleasure and pain are like two birds, one tied to each end of a piece of string—where one goes the other necessarily follows'.

The human soul wants unalloyed joy. It is said that even Indra in heaven is always suffering from headache! So the pupil says: 'Lift me up from samsara (the realm of transmigration), O Guru! Death is staring at me and I am afraid! Protect me, protect me! For I do not know of any other man with whom to seek shelter'. He is not a pupil who regards two Gurus at the same time. Philosophy is a most jealous wife. One cannot be a deep student of philosophy if there is any other intent in life; and with divine knowledge, much more so. Let us not make it a luxury. The used key is ever bright. Detachment and complete relaxation of the mind—these two qualities are expressed here in the attitude of the disciple.

śāntā mahānto nivasanti santo
vasantaval-loka-hitaṃ carantaḥ
tīrṇāḥ svayaṃ bhīma-bhavārṇavaṃ janān
ahetunā 'nyān api tārayantaḥ

[39] 'Great and holy souls live in the world at peace, doing good to the people like the coming of spring. Having themselves crossed the terrible ocean of rebirth, they help others to cross over without any interested motive.

ayaṃ svabhāvaḥ svata eva yat para-
śramāpanoda-pravaṇaṃ mahātmanām
sudhāṃśur eṣa svayam arka-karkaṣa-
prabhā-'bhitaptām avati kṣitiṃ kila

[40] 'The great ones are by nature inclined towards the removal of the sufferings of others. Does not the moon come to the aid of the earth of its own accord when the latter has been scorched by the cruel rays of the sun?

You do not know what a moon can mean. In the Gobi desert every grain of sand is like a bullet in the day; but when the moon comes, then soft breezes blow.

brahmānanda-rasānubhūti-kalitaiḥ pūtaiḥ suśītaiḥ sitaiḥ
yuṣmād-vāk-kalaśojjhitaiḥ śruti-sukhair vākyāmṛtaiḥ secaya
saṃtaptaṃ bhava-tāpa-dāva-dahana-jvālābhir enaṃ prabho
dhanyās te bhavad-īkṣaṇa-kṣana-gateḥ pātrīkrtāḥ svīkṛtāḥ

[41] 'O my Master, I am burning in the flames of the forest-fire of reincarnation. Pour on me the pure, cool and holy nectar in the form of words that fall from the pitcher of your lips, flavoured with your experience of the bliss of the Absolute and pleasing to the ear. Fortunate are those who are rendered acceptable by a momentary visit of your glance—and are accepted.

This is how the approach is to be made:

kathaṃ tareyaṃ bhava-sindhum etaṃ
kā vā gatir me katamo 'sty upāyaḥ

jāne na kiṃcit kṛpayā 'va māṃ prabho
samsāra-duḥkha-kṣatim ātanuṣva

[42] 'How is this ocean of rebirth to be crossed? What path should I take? Which means should I choose? I know nothing. Show me your compassion. Help me to put an end to the sufferings of rebirth.'

The pupil asks: 'O Lord, tell me how I can cross this ocean of phenomenal existence (samsara), this world of relativity in which there is no security and no lasting joy?' What a delusion is this word 'joy'! There is a bitter concoction which is given to a child when born, but after it tastes the sweetness of the milk of its mother, it shows aversion to it. These 'joys' are a state of delirium in which we are unaware of the presence of the Lord about us. We do not know the real bliss at all. So the pupil says: 'Give me this bliss'. 'What means shall I adopt—at present I know nothing?' Those who think they know are miserable souls. The disciple says: 'There is no joy anywhere, so I come to thee, O Master of mercy, to learn that science which relieves the soul forever'.

7. The method of instruction

tathā vadantaṃ śaraṇāgataṃ svaṃ
saṃsāra-dāvānala-tāpa-taptaṃ
nirīkṣya kāruṇya-rasārdra-dṛṣṭyā
dadyād abhītim sahasā mahātmā

[43] The great soul (mahātmā) should look upon his pupil, who had been scorched by the forest-fire of rebirth and had come to him speaking these words and seeking refuge, with a glance softened with compassion and should at once offer him his protection.

We know that a compassionate man realizes that the world is

full of suffering which he tries to alleviate at the expense of his own life. So the Master looked at the pupil with a glance of compassion and delight. The eyes are more eloquent than the tongue. He said to him: 'Give up all fear!' The whole of philosophy and religion is concerned with the presence and absence of fear. We study religion to get rid of fear. That which causes fear is weakness and is wrong.

Compassion is considered to be of two kinds—karuna and daya. Karuna (the word used in this verse) is where there are no reasons for forgiveness; daya is where there are reasons for forgiveness. Hari (the Lord) is He who forgives His devotees before they have even asked for forgiveness.

vidvān sa tasmā upasattim īyuṣe
   mumukṣave sādhu-yathokta-kāriṇe
praśānta-cittāya śamānvitāya
   tattvopadeśaṃ kṛpayaiva kuryāt

[44] To him who approached him thus, dutiful and with a deep desire for liberation, peaceful at heart and possessed of inner control, the sage should give metaphysical teaching out of pure compassion.

Three qualifications are essential for one who seeks protection under the master and is most eager for liberation: (i) Obedience to the injunctions of the scriptures and the teacher; (ii) conquest of the mind and senses; (iii) possession of tranquillity. To such a one the teacher gives the holy Yoga as a matter of sheer grace.

mā bhaiṣṭa vidvaṃs tava nāsty apāyaḥ
   saṃsāra-sindhos taraṇe 'sty upāyaḥ
yenaiva yātā yatayo 'sya pāraṃ
   tam eva mārgaṃ tava nirdiśāmi

[45] 'Have no fear, O learned one', he should say, 'You

> are not in danger. There exists a way to cross over the ocean of rebirth. I will teach you that path by which it was crossed by ascetics in days of yore.

'O learned one'. Note that the teacher speaks to the disciple in the highest terms. This has psychologically a great effect; for what you call a person you infuse into him. In the East it is customary for the husband to address his wife as 'Princess'.

asty upāyo mahān kaścit saṃsāra-bhaya-nāśanaḥ
tena tīrtvā bhavāmbhodhiṃ paramānandam āpsyasi

> [46] 'There is one great means by which you may overcome the danger of rebirth, and if you make use of it to cross over the ocean of worldly life, you will attain to perfect felicity.

The means which will reveal it to you is knowledge. Knowledge means cognition of the supreme Principle, knowledge of the nature of one's own Self. This is neither a biological nor a physiological truth. Science has done more harm by its dogmatic attitude than by anything else. To say that life originates in protoplasm is entirely stupid. That kind of knowledge is not wanted here.

True knowledge is acquired by meditation on the teachings of the holy philosophy. Through this a new cognition will arise. The subject matter of this philosophy is: 'What is God?' 'What am I?' 'What is the purpose of life?' If you think of it with a restrained mind, a purified heart and faith in the teacher, you will have a new cognition, a new light. What a man knows with his mind is 1% correct and 99% illusion. What do you know of the stars? They appear to be as small as a pinhead, yet they are a million times as large as the earth. The sky appears over the earth as a dome. These are illusions.

Thus the Guru says:

vedāntārtha-vicāreṇa jāyate jñānam uttamam
tenātyantika-saṃsāra-duḥkha-nāśo bhavaty anu

[47] 'It is by reflecting over the teachings of the Upanishads that one gains the highest knowledge. From this there follows the total cessation of worldly suffering.

With a prepared mind, following the injunctions of the scriptures and the teacher, meditating on the subject matter, a new knowledge will arise and through it will come annihilation of all sufferings of the world. This knowledge is not a palliative; it is a sovereign remedy and, once cured, you will be mad with desire to relieve the sufferings of others.

There is a painting by a Chinese artist of Shakyamuni (Buddha). It is a painting of a desert and a barren tree. Under the tree sits an emaciated, thin, starved figure dressed in rags. Underneath, it says: 'After illumination, going to preach to the world'. And here is another picture: blind and crippled, a little figure is seen being led by a disciple from village to village. He can neither see nor speak, but the hands are lifted in blessing to all. This is the figure of St Francis of Assisi. Once this knowledge has arisen in you, you will be possessed with the desire to work for the relief of the suffering of others.

A commentator on this verse remarks that it makes one point clear which is never to be forgotten—suffering will end only by a vital and direct knowledge of the unity of the local self with the universal Self. In the opening chapter of the *Imitation of Christ*, the saintly author says: 'The teachings of Christ are greater than that of any holy man. They are the gateway'. The mind must be made colourless. All affection for this or that, attachment, desire and resentment of the world ought to be washed clear.

The mind, which today has many colours—the red of anger, green of jealousy, orange of ambition, blue of infinity—has to be washed clear by meditation, group devotion and equanimity. Then dip the mind into the colourless dye of the contemplation of the

Attributeless. When it is dyed in that colour it is called colourless, because the colours of the rainbow are inadequate to describe it. They fade, but that dye is permanent.

In the *Shrimad Bhagavata*, a gopi (cowherd maiden) goes to the dyer to have her sari dyed. He asks her: 'Lady, what colour do you want it dyed?' The reply is: 'That colour which will make me dearer to the King of Vraj, to Shyama (the Lord Krishna)'. This is the real life. All before this is life in the kindergarten.

śraddhā-bhakti-dhyāna-yogān mumukṣor
mukter hetūn vakti sākṣāc chruter gīḥ
yo vā eteṣv eva tiṣṭhaty amuṣya
mokṣo 'vidyā-kalpitād deha-bandhāt

[48] 'The voice of the Veda says that faith, devotion, meditation and yoga are the methods whereby he who has a deep desire for liberation attains it. Whoever remains firmly established in these acquires liberation from bondage to the body, imagined through ignorance.

Remember that faith means faith coupled with devotion. It implies one thing, the unfailing power of the grace of God to redeem our life. There must be faith in the authority of the holy scriptures and in the teacher, and devotion to the practice of Yoga and meditation. Faith, devotion and practice lead the soul to liberation. Bondage is conjured up by ignorance and is removed by these three means and by no other.

ajñāna-yogāt paramātmanas tava
hy anātma-bandhas tata eva saṃsṛtiḥ
tayor vivekodita-bodha-vahnir
ajñāna-kāryaṃ pradahet sa-mūlam

[49] 'It is through association with ignorance of your own Self in its true (lit. supreme) form that you are in bondage

to the not-self and are on that account undergoing rebirth. But the fire of enlightenment arising from the discrimination of Self and not-self will burn up the effects of ignorance together with their cause (ignorance itself).'

It is through ignorance that the great Spirit in man dreams of bondage. It does not become bound, but dreams of bondage—of birth, death, parenthood, dictatorship, sin and sorrow, hell and heaven. These are all dreams due to ignorance of the presence of the Lord in the soul. The fire of knowledge, born of discrimination, burns up this ignorance and destroys the root of suffering. This is a claim which no poet, scientist, doctor, or politician ever makes, or has ever made; it is only made by the holy saints of God.

8. The pupil's questions

śiṣya uvāca

kṛpayā śrūyatāṃ svāmin praśno 'yaṃ kriyate mayā
yad uttaram ahaṃ śrutvā kṛtārthaḥ syāṃ bhavan-mukhāt

[50] The pupil said: 'O my Master, please listen to my question. My ends will be realized if I can hear the answer from your lips.

How politely and gently he speaks. Even Shakespeare's clowns speak more politely than we do in these days! Then he asks the fundamental questions of life:

ko nāma bandhaḥ katham eṣa āgataḥ
katham pratiṣṭhā 'sya katham vimokṣaḥ
ko 'sāv anātmā paramaḥ ka ātmā
tayor vivekaḥ katham etad ucyatām

[51] 'What is bondage? How does it arise? What keeps it

> in being? How may one escape from it? What is the not-self? What is the supreme Self? How can one discriminate between the two? Please tell me that'.

What is the cause of all this suffering, death, birth, loss and gain (for gain often brings suffering)? How has it victimized the Self? If there is bondage and it does not touch us, we do not worry. What makes it continue? How can we be freed from it? What is this not-self? Here the pupil understands two categories in the world, Self and not-self—all that which is objective is not-self. What is the supreme Self? I am conscious of being the local self. How can one discriminate one from the other?

In daily life we are identified with the not-self. What we call 'love', in the worldly sense, is identification with the not-self.

Swami Rama Tirtha, through his spiritual sense, two years before his final release gave the following law: 'We invite suffering on ourself and on any object if we give the place of God to it. If a wife gives to her husband the place of God, she invites suffering'. This is the final experience of one of the greatest spiritual exponents of our time.

What is a poet? He is one who conveys a divine truth through emotional and rhythmic language. Our poet Shakespeare at every step tells this story. What was the end of Lear's love for his daughters, or the love of Othello for Desdemona? Each is a tragedy. It does not mean that we should not love others, but we must love them for God's sake. It is He who makes them worthy of love. Aristotle's difficulty as to the origin of forms was solved by his postulate of God. He says that God is the being who confers form on matter. Forms are attractive in husband, wife and so forth because they are the effect of the presence and thought of the Lord. Those who love things, forgetting God, make things their possessors.

It is said: 'What is the not-self? What is the supreme Self?' Every pupil and reasonable person should think of these questions.

śrī gurur uvāca

dhanyo 'si kṛta-kṛtyo 'si pāvitaṃ te kulaṃ tvayā
yad avidyā-bandha-muktyā brahmībhavitum icchasi

[52] The Guru said: 'Blessed are you! You have attained your ends! Your whole family is purified through you since you wish to realize the Absolute through liberation from the bondage of metaphysical ignorance.

Those are indeed blessed who desire to know God. A Persian poet says: 'What comparison is there between a king and a God-loving beggar! O Humay (a legendary bird), kings come to kiss the feet of that beggar'. There is something wrong, too, with the individual who is not ready to take the dust of the feet of holy saints of God and adorn his forehead with it.

9. The importance of personal effort

ṛṇa-mocana-kartāraḥ pituḥ santi sutādayaḥ
bandha-mocana-kartā tu svasmād anyo na kaścana

[53] 'Sons and others can release a father from his debts. But there is no one but oneself who can effect one's release from bondage.

The son has a supreme duty to pay the debts of his parents. The Sanskrit for 'son' is 'putra', or 'one who saves his parents from descending into hell'. That civilization cannot last where parents are not treated with respect. The debt to be paid does not mean only a material one. If our mother is not a goddess to us, can we approach the heavenly goddess? But one's own debt can only be paid by oneself, and so also, one's own ignorance can only be removed by oneself.

mastaka-nyasta-bhārāder duḥkham anyair nivāryate
kṣudhādi-kṛta-duḥkhaṃ tu vinā svena na kenacit

[54] 'A load that one is carrying on one's head can be removed by others, but no one but oneself can relieve oneself of the pain caused by hunger and similar personal complaints.

pathyam auṣadha-sevā ca kriyate yena rogiṇā
ārogya-siddhir dṛṣṭā 'sya nānyānuṣṭhita-karmaṇā

[55] 'It is those diets and herbs that the patient himself takes that cure him of illness. He is not cured of it by the actions of others.

vastu svarūpaṃ sphuṭa-bodha-cakṣuṣā
svenaiva vedyaṃ na tu paṇḍitena
candra-svarūpaṃ nija-cakṣuṣaiva
jñātavyam anyair avagamyate kim

[56] 'The reality has to be known through the eye of one's own clear knowledge, you cannot hire a scholar to do it for you. One can only know the form of the moon through one's own eye. Of what help will be the knowledge of others?

avidyā-kāma-karmādi-pāśa-bandhaṃ vimocitum
kaḥ śaknuyād vinātmānaṃ kalpa-koṭi-śatair api

[57] 'Who but oneself could relieve oneself of the bonds of metaphysical ignorance, desire and action in a million world-periods?

The holy truth and sovereign remedy must be practised by the disciple himself and by no other person.

10. The importance of Self-knowledge

na yogena na sāṃkhyena karmaṇā no na vidyayā
brahmātmaikatva-bodhena mokṣaḥ sidhyati nānyathā

[58] 'One cannot obtain liberation through yoga, through the Sāṃkhya philosophy, through rituals or through the prescribed meditations on the ritual. It can be obtained only through awakening to one's identity with the Absolute.

The only way out of grief and the magic show of delusion called sansara is the inner realization of the identity of the individual soul with Brahman (the Absolute). Devotion, practice of charity and benevolence, learning and heroic actions can be used as means to this realization but they are not the end of life, which is liberation (moksha). The embodied soul in all walks of life experiences sorrow. The king on his throne, the youth who imagines that life is all a bed of roses, the dictator fanned by the winds of power, the poor man in his hut, are all subject to grief, desire and aversion. Is even the man who is in love with his family, or the man given to chivalrous deeds, happy? No. As thirst is quenched only by cool pure water, so the soul of man is only truly happy when freed from the delusion which makes the mirage of the world, sansara, appear real and makes its support and substance, Brahman, appear unreal.

vīṇāyā rūpa-saundaryaṃ tantrī-vādana-sauṣṭhavam
prajā-rañjana-mātraṃ tan na sāmrājyāya kalpate

[59] 'The beauty of one's lute and one's skill at playing the instrument will only please the ears of the people—it will not establish an empire.

vāg-vaikharī śabda-jharī śāstra-vyākhyāna-kauśalam
vaiduṣyaṃ viduṣāṃ tad-vad bhuktaye na tu muktaye

[60] 'Similarly, copious eloquence, a torrent of words, skill in expounding the texts and scholarship generally, are for the delight of a few other scholars but not for liberation.

Learning and cleverness, unless attended by spiritual discrimination and devotion, are dangerous. Let us beware of the false pride of learning which makes one think: 'I am learned, others are fools'. This is a dangerous state of mind. One must be led by the light of the scriptures and one's own tranquil and educated mind.

avijñāte pare tattve śāstrādhītis tu niṣphalā
vijñāte 'pi pare tattve śāstrādhitis tu niṣphalā

[61] 'One's study of the texts is useless if one does not come to have a knowledge of the supreme reality. And when one has gained a knowledge of the supreme reality, one's study of the texts is also useless.

śabda-jālaṃ mahāraṇyaṃ citta-bhramaṇa-kāraṇam
ataḥ prayatnāj jñātavyaṃ tattva-jñāt tattvam ātmanaḥ

[62] 'A network of words is like a great forest in which the mind wanders about lost. One should bend all one's efforts to know that true nature of the Self that has to be known from one who actually knows it.

People who think that by intellectual argument or mere study they can know the nature of the Self, will always be disappointed. Arguments are meant to settle worldly truth and not spiritual truth, because the Self of man is not subject to proof. It is a great mistake to think that each and everything can be proved. The *Katha Upanishad* says: 'Not by argument is the truth to be known, but it is easy to see it when it is proclaimed by a teacher who sees no differences'.

The really earnest seekers who keep the discipline and reduce their egoism by service of Guru and God will find the Self revealed in their own intellect in the absolute silence of the mind. The individual soul (jiva) can make efforts to know the Self but can never know it unless the Self reveals itself.

ajñāna-sarpa-daṣṭasya brahma-jñānauṣadhaṃ vinā
kimu vedaiś ca śāstraiś ca kimu mantraiḥ kim auṣadhaiḥ

[63] 'He who has been bitten by the snake of metaphysical ignorance can only be cured by the herb of realization of the Absolute. Of what use to him are the Vedas, the traditional sciences, mantras and medicines?

na gacchati vinā pānaṃ vyādhir auṣadha-śabdataḥ
vinā 'parokṣānubhavaṃ brahma-śabdair na mucyate

[64] 'An illness will not go away at the mere mention of the name of the potion that cures it; you actually have to drink it. Similarly there can be no liberation through talk about the Absolute, but only through immediate experience of it.

akṛtvā dṛśya-vilayam ajñātvā tattvam ātmanaḥ
bāhya-śabdaiḥ kuto muktir ukti-mātra-phalair nṛṇām

[65] 'How can there be liberation (mukti) through external objects like words when the true nature of the Self has not been known and the realm of objects dissolved? Words will not then bring liberation (mukti) but only bring the labour of human speech (ukti).

akṛtvā śatru-saṃhāram agatvā 'khila-bhū-śriyam
rājā 'ham iti śabdān no rājā bhavitum arhati

[66] 'No one becomes a king merely by saying, "I am king" and without conquering the enemy and establishing his power over the whole land.

āptoktiṃ khananaṃ tathopari-śilādy-utkarṣaṇaṃ svīkṛtim
nikṣepaḥ samapekṣate na hi bahiḥ śabdais tu nirgacchati
tad-vad brahmavidopadeśa-manana-dhyānādibhir labhyate
māyā-kārya-tirohitaṃ svam amalaṃ tattvaṃ na duryuktibhiḥ

[67] 'For acquisition of a buried treasure one needs the instructions of one who knows about it, digging, removal of the boulders and so on lying on the top and taking it up at the end. It will not just jump out at the sound of words spoken from without. Similarly, one's own stainless true nature that has been hidden by the effects of Māyā can only be attained through such disciplines as reflecting over and meditating on the teachings of one who himself knows the Absolute—and not through weak reasoning.

Theory is one thing and practice another. Vedanta can be learned only by practice. Theories are innumerable but the practice is only one. Who will deny the world of limitations which covers the light of the Self? As all the limitations are illumined or revealed by the light of the Self, they are mere adjuncts to it. To keep the mind in a liquid state, to prevent it from being crystallized into attachment to worldly objects, we must devote ourselves to the study of the scriptures.

Although the Upanishads hold a position of the utmost importance in the practice of the Vedantic ideal, it is not easy to understand their appeal. Their essential meaning is not in the words but in the great experience of the sages which they describe. We cannot know this real meaning and its secret without the help of one who has himself experienced the substance of it. In his commentary on the *Kena Upanishad* (1.3) Shri Shankara says: 'Brahman is cognized by repeated instruction of the Acharya'. It is the living contact with a teacher which enlightens our heart with the secret of an art. What is true in the case of aesthetics is equally true in the spiritual realm. A lamp is lit only from a lighted lamp and not by mere words and books.

tasmāt sarva-prayatnena bhava-bandha-vimuktaye
svaireva yatnaḥ kartavyo rogādāv iva paṇḍitaiḥ

[68] 'Therefore the wise should bend all their efforts to attain liberation from bondage. They have to make independent efforts on their own, as in the case of illness and the like.

It is by practice that we know the real truth of Vedanta. What practice shall we follow? Withdrawal of our attachment from the outer objects, conversion of the mind into the light of the Spirit by self-control, selfless devotion and benevolence and, finally, evaporation of the mind into the light of the stream of knowledge through meditation.

11. The means to liberation

yas tvayā 'dya kṛtaḥ praśno varīyāñ chāstravin-mataḥ
sūtra-prāyo nigūḍhārtho jñātavyaś ca mumukṣubhiḥ

[69] 'The questions you have raised today are held by those who know the texts to be the best. They are succinct but full of hidden meaning. They are just what those who truly long for liberation need to know.

śṛṇuṣvāvahito vidvan yan mayā samudīryate
tad etac chravaṇāt sadyo bhava-bandhād vimokṣyase

[70] 'Listen carefully, O learned one, to what I have to say in answer to them. Through listening to this you can acquire liberation from bondage in this very life.

mokṣasya hetuḥ prathamo nigadyate
vairāgyam atyantam anitya-vastuṣu
tataḥ śamaś cāpi damas titikṣā
nyāsaḥ prasaktākhila-karmaṇāṃ bhṛśam

tataḥ śrutis tan-mananaṃ sa-tattva-
dhyānaṃ ciraṃ nitya-nirantaraṃ muneḥ
tato 'vikalpaṃ parametya vidvān
ihaiva nirvāṇa-sukhaṃ samṛcchati

[71-72] 'The first means to liberation is said to be total detachment in regard to impermanent things. Then follow inner and outer control, endurance, and the total renunciation of all self-interested action. Next comes listening to the metaphysical texts of the Veda, then pondering over them, accompanied by long, regular and unbroken meditation on their content by the sage. Then the enlightened one passes beyond the vagaries of the mind here in this very life and attains the joy of nirvāṇa.

Purification of the mind is an essential antecedent to release. This purification is not the result of actionlessness. In this preliminary stage ethical actions performed selflessly by way of adoration to God and benevolence to man are most helpful.

The real meaning of renunciation in the Vedanta philosophy of Shri Shankara is renunciation in action; that is, to practise selfless service, devotion and observance of the high ethics of Vedanta with a view to set an example to others, and not to practise the renunciation of such actions.

The essential teaching is that the individual point of view, which gives precedence to physical and worldly matters over the pursuit of the ideal of Vedanta, has to be modified and reformed. It is the reversal of our valuation of worldly matters which really counts. In Vedanta, renunciation (samnyasa) is a part of the spiritual discipline; it is not the metaphysical end of life. In some quarters, the sages of Vedanta have assigned the highest position to samnyasa, but the Upanishads do not support this point of view unconditionally or absolutely. The seers (rishis) of the Upanishads were not all monks.

Let us understand from Shri Shankara Acharya himself the system of the cognition of the Self. First the truth is known from the scriptures and the Acharya. This is known as shravana, listening. Then follows reasoning and logical corroboration (manana); and in the end it is spiritual contemplation (nididhyasana) which leads to the direct experience. The possibility of direct cognition of the Self depends on manana, the chief purpose of which is to understand by mental processes the meaning of the Upanishads, which implies the identity of the individual soul (jiva) and Brahman (the Absolute). The scriptures can only throw light on the truth; they cannot give us the inner eyes to see the truth. The Guru only shows the path to spiritual cognition, but to walk it well and speedily is in the power of the yogi himself. It is clear that both the scriptures and the Acharya are necessary; but spiritual contemplation (nididhyasana) is equally if not more important. The spiritual experience of the cognition of Self is possible only through nididhyasana. This is the complete course of the Yoga.

yad boddhavyaṃ tavedānīm ātmānātma-vivecanam
tad ucyate mayā samyak śrutvā ''tmany avadhāraya

[73] 'I will now give you a correct description of the discrimination of the Self and the not-self, about which you have to know. Having heard it, keep it steadily in mind.

12. The physical body

majjāsthi-medaḥ-pala-rakta-carma-
tvag-āhvayair dhātubhir ebhir anvitam
pādoru-vakṣo-bhuja-pṛṣṭha-mastakair
aṅgair upāṅgair upayuktam etat
ahaṃ mameti prathitaṃ śarīraṃ
mohāspadaṃ sthūlam itīryate budhaiḥ

[74] 'That body that is the source of delusion and is known as "me" and "mine" and has feet, thighs, chest, arms, back, head and other members and subordinate members and is composed

of matter called marrow, bones, fat, flesh, blood and skin, is termed "the physical body" by the wise.

nabho-nabhasvad-dahanāmbu-bhūmayaḥ
sūkṣmāṇi bhūtāni bhavanti tāni

[75] 'There exist subtle elements of ether, wind (air), fire, water and earth.

parasparāṃśair militāni bhūtvā
sthūlāni ca sthūla-śarīra-hetavaḥ
mātrās tadīyā viṣayā bhavanti
śabdādayaḥ pañca sukhāya bhoktuḥ

[76] 'When parts of them are intermingled together, they form the gross elements of which the physical body is composed. Their subtle forms make up the sense-objects such as sound and the rest (touch, sight, taste and odour in the classical Hindu physics) for the pleasure of the experiencer.

ya eṣu mūḍhā viṣayeṣu baddhā
rāgoru-pāśena su-dur-damena
āyānti niryānty adha ūrdhvam uccaiḥ
sva-karma-dūtena javena nītāḥ

[77] 'Those deluded ones, who are bound to those objects by the wide-spread noose of attachment, so hard to master, come and go relentlessly, upwards and downwards (to different wombs), led by the fleet messenger of their merit and demerit.

13. The danger of sense-objects

śabdādibhiḥ pañcabhir eva pañca
pañcatvam āpuḥ sva-guṇena baddhāḥ
kuraṅga-mātaṅga-pataṅga-mīna-
bhṛṅgā naraḥ pañcabhir añcitaḥ kim

[78] 'The deer, the elephant, the moth, the fish and the bee—these five (pañca) creatures go to their death (pañcatva) through bondage to one of the five senses each (hearing, touch, sight, taste and odour respectively). How will it be with man, who is inclined towards all five? (The deer is caught by the horn of the hunter, the elephant betrays his position to the hunter by scratching himself against trees, the moth falls for the flame and the fish for the bait, while the bee, attracted by the odour of the flower, may perish if its petals close in upon it at nightfall.)

doṣeṇa tīvro viṣayaḥ kṛṣṇa-sarpa-viṣād api
viṣaṃ nihanti bhoktāraṃ draṣṭāraṃ cakṣuṣāpy ayam

[79] 'A sense-object is a worse evil than the poison of a black snake. Poison only kills one who partakes of it, while a sense-object may lead one who merely sees it to destruction.

viṣayāśā-mahāpāśād yo vimuktaḥ su-dustyajāt
sa eva kalpate muktyai nānyaḥ ṣaṭ-śāstra-vedy api

[80] 'He who escapes from the great noose of hope for happiness from the sense-objects—so hard to escape from—only he is fit for liberation and not another, be he learned in all the six systems of philosophy.

āpāta-vairāgyavato mumukṣūn
bhavābdhi-pāraṃ pratiyātum udyatān
āśā-graho majjayate 'ntarāle

nigṛhya kaṇṭhe vinivartya vegāt

[81] 'The shark of hope seizes by the throat the seekers of liberation who have but temporary detachment from the sense-objects, and swiftly turns them back as they seek to cross the ocean of rebirth and drowns them in the middle.

viṣayākhya-graho yena su-virakty-asinā hataḥ
sa gacchati bhavāmbodheḥ pāraṃ pratyūha-varjitaḥ

[82] 'Only he who slays the shark of sense-objects with the sword of well-sustained detachment reaches the further shore of the ocean of rebirth without impediment.

viṣama-viṣaya-mārgair gacchato 'naccha-buddheḥ
pratipadam abhiyāto mṛtyur apy eṣa viddhi
hita-sujana-gurūktyā gacchataḥ svasya yuktyā
prabhavati phala-siddhiḥ satyam ity eva viddhi

[83] 'Know that death in this form attends every step of him of clouded mind who walks by the rocky paths of the sense-objects. And know, too, that he succeeds in his ends who walks by the light of his own clear reason, guided by the truly helpful words of the kindly Guru.

mokṣasya kāṅkṣā yadi vai tavāsti
tyajāti-dūrād viṣayān viṣaṃ yathā
pīyūṣavat toṣa-dayā-kṣamārjava-
praśānti-dāntīr bhaja nityam ādarāt

[84] 'If you want liberation, then shun sense-objects from afar, like poison, and taste fervently and continuously the ambrosial joy of contentment, compassion, honesty, peace and self-control.

14. The danger of attachment to the body

anukṣaṇaṃ yat parihṛtya kṛtyam
anādy-avidyākṛta-bandha-mokṣaṇam
dehaḥ parārtho 'yam amuṣya poṣaṇe
yaḥ sajjate sa svam anena hanti

[85] 'He who, abandoning his true duty of liberating himself every moment from the bondage created by beginningless metaphysical ignorance, becomes attached to the nourishment of the body, which exists merely as an instrument for the sake of another, kills himself by this very fact.

Ignorance is without a beginning. Why? Because time is itself a product of ignorance. So how could ignorance be in time and have a beginning? The city you see in a dream is beginningless.

Despite the great attempts we make, our body will become the food of others, for if it is thrown into a field, vultures or jackals feed on it, and if it is buried, vermin feed on it. Verily this is the fate of the body, and of the man who devotes all his attention to keeping it comfortable and well-nourished and ignores the necessity of breaking the fetters of ignorance. Unless checked, the tendency to worship the body by providing it with comfort and luxury leads to the depth of degradation; nor can proficiency in any art be acquired unless the body is recognized for what it is, and no more. The body is not God. The mind is more important and the Spirit infinitely more important. The beginning of wisdom is to devote to the body just as much attention as it needs.

The mind lasts longer than the body, because it migrates after the body has become a conglomeration of dead matter. Mind is energy, and energy escapes from the matter holding it after death; hence it is important to take care of the mind. What does this mean? To keep it pure in love, compassion, equanimity, fellowship, devotion to God and a knowledge of the nature of the ultimate reality. This is the right way of feeding the mind and taking care of it. A mind which is debased to the worship of a fetish, a nation, religion or creed, is a great burden.

It is not the person who forces me to labour who is the real oppressor but the man who influences my mind by making it narrow, fanatical, ultra-patriotic, inflated with false exaggerated idealism. That man is my real enemy. It is a pity that the human race is yet so weak that the idealism of a silly doctrine like that of Hitler's *Mein Kampf* can prevail over the doctrine of Lord Christ or Plato. The Acharya says, 'Such a man is a suicide'. In fact he is worse, for he prepares for himself gloomy dungeons to be inhabited in the next incarnation.

śarīra-poṣaṇārthī san ya ātmānaṃ didṛkṣati
grāhaṃ dāru-dhiyā dhṛtvā nadīṃ tartuṃ sa gacchati

[86] 'Desiring to nourish the body, he loses the desire to see the Self. It is as if he were to try to cross a river by grasping a crocodile under the impression that it was a log of wood.

These two things will not go together. The holy prophets of Israel used to live in mountains and dressed most coarsely, disregarding all physical comforts; yet they could say: 'Thus saith the Lord'. The more attention is bestowed on the body, the more it will claim. On the peak called Nanda Devi, in the state of Bilaspur, I met a mahatma in the holy temple who honoured me with his attention and affection. Though it was the month of June, it was as cold as it is in winter here, yet he was nude. I offered him a blanket. He asked why? I said: 'Perhaps Your Holiness will catch a cold'. He said: 'Do those who live in palaces not catch cold?' I understood how ignorant I was. Body-consciousness includes sex and age consciousness. Holy Christ was always poorly clad, so were Buddha, Swami Mangalnath and Swami Rama Tirtha.

moha eva mahā-mṛtyur mumukṣor vapur-ādiṣu
moho vinirjito yena sa mukti-padam arhati

[87] 'Over-affection for the body and so on is the fatal disease

> that afflicts the (half-hearted) seeker of liberation. He who overcomes this undue affection is fit for liberation.

After body-consciousness, attachment is the greatest enemy of man. Attachment to class, caste, nation, youth, false idealism—all these attachments are fatal, says the Acharya. This piece of advice entitles the holy Acharya to our greatest gratitude. What more can be said? How true it is when the yogis say that only two people sleep in peace, a God-realized Avadhut and the son of a king! (The son of a king enjoys wealth and power without the anxieties of his father).

mohaṃ jahi mahā-mṛtyuṃ deha-dāra-sutādiṣu
yaṃ jitvā munayo yānti tad viṣṇoḥ paramaṃ padam

> [88] 'Give up this fatal disease of over-affection for the body, wife, children and so on, through conquest of which the sages attain the highest state of Vishnu.

In this single verse is laid down the law of a real and great life. To admire a picture, a book, a friend and a husband is all right, but to be enslaved by any of them and to base all our liberty, progress and peace on them and them alone, is the height of ignorance. He is called a madman who cannot control his thoughts. Infatuation for an object gives us an erroneous vision of that object and always leads to suffering. The infatuation of King Lear for his daughters and of Romeo for Juliet led to innumerable sufferings for all parties. Even infatuation for power—one's own greatness and extraordinariness—is equally harmful. A freed man loves his friends, relatives and objects without becoming spiritually a slave to them. Infatuation means tenacity of the mind to the desire for the maintenance of physical connection under any circumstances. There are some people who are called affectionate people, but if they fall in love with any object or person they become slaves and suffer immensely. A great requisite of spiritual freedom is absence of infatuation or attachment to any object in the world. 'Oh, I cannot live without you!' This expression is the effusion of an unenlightened mind. Love is possible only in mutual freedom, and there is no other way to its maintenance.

The first thing to which we should not become a slave is our body. To give it our sole consideration, to let others suffer for its sake, or to devote time and energy to its maintenance and its beautification, is a very great spiritual error. The body will not go with you when you die. Make use of it, but do not think of it as eternal and do not devote time and attention to it only. The same applies to the wife and child. Children ought to be loved, wife or husband ought to be loved, but they must not become enslavers. We must not feel we exist only for them and for no higher purpose. Are these expressions heartless? No, they are expressions of wisdom.

Mere detachment is of no value. It is a means to a higher end, not the end in itself. If detachment were an end in itself, then the sheep and lambs of Wensleydale, absorbed as they are in munching the green grass of the fields, should be considered great philosophers, which they are not.

It is said in the *Vishnu Purana* that the whole universe (jagat) is divided into many sections, of which the earth is one, and that billions of miles above the earth there is a region of inexpressible light where there is no death, no hunger, no illness, no sins or limitations. There, in the company of the holy Incarnations and saints, truth is showered day and night. That glorious region is called the abode of Vishnu (vishnu-loka), and there Vishnu is manifest in His divine form. Love is in the atmosphere, a perpetual spring of celestial nature prevails, and the Lord is accessible in His spiritual form to His holy saints in that region of light.

Higher than this objective Vishnu-loka is the region of pure Consciousness, the light which is the mother of all beauty and truth, of colours that have never been seen here. And that region is also called the abode of Vishnu (vishnu-loka). It is in the heart of man. The holy saints have the privilege, whenever they like, of reaching it in an instant—where Christ, Shankara and others are—and if you can create the same vibration, you can do so too. I assure you that Christ, St

Teresa and others can be seen today; but the worshippers of fetishes of the three dimensions will never see them. The height of awareness is to be aware yet undesirous of all worldly objects. In this, aim to be a stranger to any other aims.

15. Body, senses, mind, vital energy

tvaṅ-māṃsa-rudhira-snāyu-medo-majjāsthi-saṃkulam
pūrṇaṃ mūtra-purīṣābhyāṃ sthūlaṃ nindyam idaṃ vapuḥ

[89] 'This physical body is a despicable object, a compound of skin, flesh, blood, muscle, fat, marrow and bones, filled with urine and ordure.

This is said in order to demonstrate the unimportance of the body and to detach our minds from it. Kabir has said: 'Why dost thou look at thy face in the mirror? If thou hast compassion and righteousness in thy heart, why lookest thou?' That civilization is sick which judges man by the condition of his body. If Christ were to appear today, He would be thrown into prison as a vagrant in no time. Let us therefore rise above body-consciousness.

paṇcīkṛtebhyo bhūtebhyaḥ sthūlebhyaḥ pūrva-karmaṇā
samutpannam idaṃ sthūlaṃ bhogāyatanam ātmanaḥ
avasthā jāgaras tasya sthūlārthānubhavo yataḥ

[90] 'This gross physical body arises through previous karma, from the elements five-folded into their gross manifest form, as a seat of experience for the soul. Its characteristic state is waking, as it is in this body that there is experience of the gross objects (of the world of waking).

How is it that I have an ugly, sickly, unattractive body, whereas others have handsome, healthy and charming bodies? The kind of body I have now is the result of evil deeds I have done in the past. Others have Venus-like bodies because they have done good deeds. If in this life they do not do good, kind, compassionate, humane, philanthropic and altruistic deeds, they may receive the body of a Caliban in the coming incarnation. The body is the result of our karma. It is composed of the gross elements, but there are also subtle, more refined elements in its make-up.

bāhyendriyaiḥ sthūla-padārtha-sevāṃ
srak-candana-stry-ādi-vicitra-rūpām
karoti jīvaḥ svayam etad-ātmanā
tasmāt praśastir vapuṣo 'sya jāgare

[91] 'Identifying himself with this, the soul enjoys a variety of external sense-objects like garlands, sandalpaste, women and so on. Hence this body is pre-eminent in the waking state.

What is the body for? To be paraded in the streets as was the Madonna of Cimabue? No, the body is the medium of experience for the soul. The soul uses the eyes and sees through them, uses the ears and hears through them, uses the nose and smells through it. You know that the body does not function in dream, nor in dreamless sleep. It is used by the soul in the waking state to gain experience of gross objects.

sarvo 'pi bāhya-saṃsāraḥ puruṣasya yad āśrayaḥ
viddhi deham idaṃ sthūlaṃ gṛha-vad gṛha-medhinaḥ

[92] 'Know that this physical body is the seat of all the external dealings of the soul, like the house of the householder.

The house must be well-kept; but mind, feelings, discrimination and faith are much more important. The body is a mere house; the condition of the dweller in it is much more important. Oh, to forget the soul and care only for the house, what ignorance it is!

It is said 'The earth is the Lord's and the fullness thereof'. Therefore the house belongs to the Lord and I am only the tenant.

What are the characteristics of the body?

sthūlasya sambhava-jarā-maraṇāni dharmāḥ
sthaulyādayo bahuvidhāḥ śiśutādy-avasthāḥ
varṇāśramādi-niyamā bahudhā 'mayāḥ syuḥ
pūjā-'vamāna-bahumāna-mukhā viśeṣāḥ

> [93] 'The attributes of the physical body are birth, old age (decrepitude) and death, along with many different states, such as childhood, becoming stout and so on. The rules of caste and station of life[1] pertain to it. It is the special object of marks of reverence, respect, contempt and so on.

The soul does not die, but after a certain age the body decays and dies. The upper limit of the age of the body is 120 years, but who lives up to that age? Let us not be deluded by those money-grabbers who offer talismans by means of which they allege you can perpetuate your youth. The emperors of the Tang dynasty spent years and fortunes in trying to obtain the elixir of life. A short life devoted to love of man and God is much better than a long life devoted to pleasure and the destruction of others, 'We live in deeds not in years'. The body is gross, stout, thin, corpulent and so forth; these are its different conditions. It has different restrictions, such as, 'He is a student, a monk, a householder'. The body meets with high honours and worship, insults and kicks and so forth. These are the concomitants of the body. They will go with it.

buddhīndriyāṇi śravaṇaṃ tvag akṣi
ghrāṇaṃ ca jihvā viṣayāvabodhanāt
vāk-pāṇi-pādā gudam apy upasthaḥ
karmendriyāṇi pravaṇena karmasu

1. For example, when born in the womb of a Brahmin or on attaining the age specified in the Law Books for retirement from the world.

[94] The sense-organs are those of hearing, touch, sight, smell and tastė, since these are what illumine objects. The organs of action are those of speech, carrying, walking about, excretion and procreation, being concerned with action.

The body is the result of the actions (karma) of past incarnations. One must not get attached to it. When Queen Elizabeth I was on her death-bed, she cried: 'A million pounds to anyone who can keep me alive for five more minutes!' However beautiful a woman is, she will not be so charming in her old age. The body should be kept in proper order, but should not be made an idol. It has an object—that is, to enable the soul to progress towards perfection.

So far we have spoken of the physical body. There is another body within the physical body, and within this is a little flame of Self.

nigadyate 'ntaḥkaraṇaṃ mano dhīr
ahaṃkṛtiś cittam iti sva-vṛttibhiḥ
manas tu saṃkalpa-vikalpanādibhir
buddhiḥ padārthādyavasāya-dharmataḥ

[95] 'The inner organ, on account of its various modifications, is known sometimes as the lower mind, sometimes as the higher mind, sometimes as the ego and sometimes as the faculty of feeling and memory. The lower mind is so called because it functions by way of tentative propositions and rejections. The higher mind is so called because it has the attribute of determining exactly the nature of objects.

The lower mind (manas) is that which thinks, i.e., which performs any motion of the mind such as purpose, disposition, rejection or acceptance. In short, manas is the faculty which 'considers the pros and cons of a thing'. The higher mind (buddhi) is the determining faculty (in will and cognition) which determines the truth about objects.

atrābhimānād aham ity ahaṃkṛtiḥ
svārthānusandhāna-guṇena cittam

> [96] 'The inner organ is called "the ego" insofar as it identifies itself and its own modifications with the feeling "I am"; that same inner organ is called the faculty of feeling and memory (citta) insofar as it enquires into the way to realize personal ends.

The ego (ahamkara) is the function of the personal sense which identifies the body as the self. The body is only a vehicle, the sheath in which the soul 'rides'. The faculty which causes this error of identification with it is called the ego. Patriotism is a form of ego; if misapplied, it is a curse. To think that a nation or country is God, superior to any other, is as ignorant as to think that a piece of stone, taken by itself, is God. The faculty of feeling and memory (chitta) is the mental function which seeks for pleasurable objects, and it includes imagination.

prāṇāpāna-vyānodāna-samānā bhavaty asau prāṇaḥ
svayam eva vṛtti-bhedād vikṛti-bhedāt suvarṇa-salilādivat

> [97] 'The vital energy modifies of its own accord into the forward-moving vital energy (the outgoing breath), the down-going vital energy, the vital energy of vigorous action, the upward-moving vital energy and the distributive vital energy.[1] These active modifications constitute the various forms that it adopts like (molten) gold or water.

16. The subtle body and vital energy

vāg-ādi-pañca śravaṇādi-pañca
prāṇādi-pañcā 'bhra-mukhāni pañca
buddhyādy avidyāpi ca kāma-karmaṇī
puryaṣṭakaṃ sūkṣma-śarīram āhuḥ

1 On the various sub-divisions of the vital energy cp. Shankara's commentary on *Bṛhadāraṇyaka Upanishad* 1.5.3 trans. Mādhavānanda, p.149 and on *Brahma Sūtra* 2.4.12 trans. Gambhīrānanda, p.540.

> [98] 'The subtle body called the "eightfold abode" (puryaṣṭaka) consists of (1) the five organs of action beginning with speech, (2) the five sense-organs beginning with hearing, (3) the five modifications of the vital energy beginning with the out-going breath, (4) the (subtle form of) the five elements beginning with ether, (5) the higher mind and other forms of the inner sense, (6) metaphysical ignorance, (7) desire and (8) action.

The Lord says in the *Gita*: 'O Arjuna, this is My eightfold Nature (prakriti)' (7.4). Of what is this subtle body made?

> idaṃ śarīraṃ śṛṇu sūkṣma-saṃjñitaṃ
> liṅgaṃ tv apañcīkṛta-bhūta-sambhavam
> sa-vāsanaṃ karma-phalānubhāvakaṃ
> svājñānato 'nādir upādhir ātmanaḥ

> [99] 'Listen. This "liṅga-śarīra" known as "the subtle body" is composed of the non-five-folded (subtle) elements. Associated with impressions ripe for manifestation (vāsanā)[1] it renders possible the experience of the results of one's previous deeds. It is a beginningless, apparent conditioning adjunct of the soul arising from ignorance of the Self.

It is produced out of the elements (earth, air, fire, water and space) before they subdivide and combine with each other. In physical matter, mutations take place and the equilibrium is lost. This is that of which the subtle body is made.

What are its characteristics? It is the field of desires. Desire is the principle of differentiation. It is the disturbing element. It is under the influence of desire that human beings make decisions. Control and elimination of desire give the revelation of the Lord

1 Cp. Shankara's commentary on *Brahma Sūtra* 2.2.30 trans. Gambhīrānanda, p.425.

seated within. The mind or inner sense (antahkarana) is a beginningless superimposition on the Self. It is beginningless because time is a creation of the mind and so we cannot say that the mind has its origin in time. 'Beginning' presupposes time; in the Self there is no time. The mind is a beginningless superimposition on the Self, or Spirit, caused by ignorance of Its true nature. When the divine fragment does not know Itself, it superimposes the mind on Itself.

svapno bhavaty asya vibhakty-avasthā
svamātra-śeṣeṇa vibhāti yatra
svapne tu buddhiḥ svayam eva jāgrat-
kālīna-nānāvidha-vāsanābhiḥ
kartrādi-bhāvaṃ pratipadya rājate
yatra svayaṃ-jyotir ayaṃ parātmā

[100] 'Dream is that special state of the soul where it shines on its own (i.e., illumined by a reflection of pure Consciousness, but without the help of external luminaries like the sun). In dream the mind on its own assumes the form of actor, act and object with various impressions derived from the time of waking, there where this supreme Self is the self-luminous light.

The divine ray, as identified with the mind, has three functions—that is, it undergoes three states—the waking state, the dreaming state and the dreamless sleep state. The dream state is distinct from the waking state. In dream the higher mind (buddhi) takes on the role of agent owing to the various desires of the waking state. The desires of the waking state influence the higher mind (buddhi) and from these it weaves its dream pictures. Freud says: 'Dreams are unfulfilled desires'. This statement of his is nothing new. The Self shines in glory in the dream state: the divine ray in the buddhi becomes creative, creating suns, stars and so forth. The buddhi even of the poorest man becomes creative—potentially each soul is divine: 'O Arjuna, My fragment becomes the soul (jiva), or embodied Self' (*Gita* 15.7).

This Self or Consciousness (chit) is self-luminous. Nothing in the objective world is self-luminous—this brass bowl (on the table) is not self-luminous; it needs light, space and also someone to see it. There is no object of knowledge which does not need something else to illumine it; but in order to know 'I am', you do not need the assistance of a sun, or moon, or dictionary or anything else.

dhī-mātrakopādhir aśeṣa-sākṣī
na lipyate tat-kṛta-karma-leśaiḥ
yasmād asaṅgas tata eva karmabhir
na lipyate kiñcid upādhinā kṛtaiḥ

> [101] 'When the Witness of all thus has the mind alone for its apparent conditioning adjunct, it is not stained by the little "acts" performed by the mind in that state. Hence the Witness is relationless and is not affected in any way by anything done by any apparent conditioning adjunct.

The Self in the dream is not touched by what is happening, it is merely the Witness (Freud does not tell us who co-ordinates the experiences of the dream). The Self (atman) is not attached to the objects of the dream. Alas, that he becomes attached to the objects in the waking state!

sarva-vyāpṛti-karaṇaṃ liṅgam idaṃ syāc cidātmanaḥ puṃsaḥ
vāsyādikam iva takṣṇas tenaivātmā bhavaty asaṅgo 'yam

> [102] 'This subtle body is the instrument of the Spirit as pure Consciousness for all its (apparent) actions, as the chisel and the rule are the instruments of the carpenter. Therefore (since the carpenter is independent of his chisel and may lay it down at will) this Self is actionless.

The subtle body is the instrument of all activities. The mind moves the hand; the mind tastes, not the tongue. As it is at the root of all activities, it must be purified, and this is done by meditation and devotion. When the mind is purified, actions become purified. Actions divorced from mind have no significance at all.

The gross and subtle bodies are the vehicles through which the Self functions. Their destruction or transformation comes to pass through the light of the Self, yet this does not affect the great universal Self. The divine ray in us is not affected by our actions; it is the mind that is so affected.

andhatva-mandatva-paṭutva-dharmāḥ
saugunya-vaigunya-vaśāddhi cakṣuṣaḥ
bādhirya-mūkatva-mukhās tathaiva
śrotrādi-dharmā na tu vettur ātmanaḥ

[103] 'Blindness, weak vision and sharp vision are due to the defects or virtues of the eye, and deafness and dumbness and so on are due to characteristics of the ear and larynx and other organs, not to characteristics of the Self, which merely beholds them as a Witness.

Blindness, weakness and strength are conditions indicative of the fitness of our sense organs. The knower of defects is not touched or affected by the defects. The knower is distinct from that which it knows and hence is not affected.

ucchvāsa-niḥśvāsa-vijṛmbhaṇa-kṣut-
praspandanādy-utkramaṇādikāḥ kriyāḥ
prāṇādi-karmāṇi vadanti taj-jñāḥ
prāṇasya dharmāv aśanā-pipāse

[104] 'Those who understand about the vital energy say that the functions of its various modifications are out-breathing, in-breathing, yawning, sneezing, secretion and rising up out of the physical body at death. Hunger and thirst, too, are attributes of the vital energy.

17. The ego

antaḥkaraṇam eteṣu cakṣurādiṣu varṣmaṇi
aham ity abhimānena tiṣṭhaty ābhāsa-tejasā

[105] 'The inner sense (antaḥkaraṇa) stands in the sense organs such as the eye within the body, illumined by a reflection of the light of pure Consciousness and identifying itself with them as "that am I".

ahaṃkāraḥ sa vijñeyaḥ kartā bhoktā 'bhimāny ayam
sattvādi-guṇa-yogena cāvasthā-trayam aśnute

[106] 'In this form it is known as "the ego-sense", also as the actor and experiencer and the one who says "this am I". According to the constituents sattva, rajas and tamas [see below, p.68], it attains three different states.

The doer or enjoyer is the ego sense (ahamkara). It is the principle of identification with the emotions. All experiences come through the ego sense. It has to be spiritualized.

viṣayāṇām ānukūlye sukhī duḥkhī viparyaye
sukhaṃ duḥkhaṃ ca tad-dharmaḥ sad-ānandasya nātmanaḥ

[107] 'It is happy when it feels that the sense-objects are favourable to it, unhappy when it feels that they are unfavourable. Happiness and unhappiness are its attributes; they are not attributes of the Self, which is eternal and constant bliss.

What is the source of joy and pleasure? Very much of our life depends on an understanding of this subject. There are some who hold that the locus of pleasure is the object. They say that flowers, birds, music, rivers and so forth are the loci and that our mind is like a bumble bee that goes to them and sucks out the nectar. Another theory is that pleasure is created by the contact of the senses with the objects of the senses—that is, it is not located in either but is created when the contact between them is made. A third theory is that pleasure is located in the mind and the object serves to stimulate the pleasure there. What is the yogic theory about it?

If the pleasure that we seek is in the objects, how is it that sometimes we get it and frequently we do not? If the Parisian drink absinthe is competent to create pleasure in the mind, how is it that after a certain stage, even increased doses fail to bring it? We find pleasure in drinking cold water on a hot afternoon, but if we have ague, we shun it even on the same hot afternoon. How is it? (It is a logical rule that contradiction is falsity of principle.) Having been born in a very poor family, I used to think that kite-flying would be the height of pleasure. When I became a teacher, I had money but there was no desire to buy a kite. It is evident that pleasure is not in the object. If a friend is very dear today, but after some time we cross swords with him, how can we say that pleasure is in the object?

Is pleasure located in the mind? In dreamless sleep the mind is temporarily absorbed in its cause, yet there is great pleasure in dreamless sleep. But if the mind is the source of pleasure, how can this be? And if the mind is the source of pleasure, why is it not able to extract always the same intensity of joy from the same objects?

From these arguments we conclude that the locus of pleasure is not in the objects, nor in the senses, nor in the mind, but somewhere else. If we only learn this one lesson, our life can change very much for the better.

Some may say that there is real joy in the achievement of an ambition or ideal in life. But was Hitler satisfied with his achievement in driving out the Jews? No, when it was done he spoke in the same maniacal way as before. The difficulty with ambition is that it is like a will-o'-the-wisp inviting us into darker and darker woods.

Let me illustrate this. There was a man who needed money very badly. He dreamt, thought and imagined money. One day, whilst grazing his cows, he came into a deep wood and found the ruins of an old castle. He entered, and forcing his way through a heavy door, found heaps and heaps of copper coins. He was glad. Looking round, he saw another door and, after opening it with difficulty, found piles of thousands of silver coins. Then he saw another door which he forced open and discovered gold. He said: 'It is yet not enough!' Opening another door he found heaps of pearls, rubies and other precious jewels. After a while he was still not satisfied. He saw a small door, heavily barred. This, too, he forced open and came face to face with a huge monkey which caught him and held him prisoner. So it is with ambition. We become its prisoner and its tool. If the achievement of ambitious ideals brought happiness and pleasure, then we should be satisfied, but it is not so. Kabir says: 'Some get joy in palaces, some in conquest. O Sadhu, Kabir gets much greater joy in singing songs in praise of Him'. When the sense-objects are according to one's desires, one is happy; when they are not so, the mind feels miserable. Therefore the empirical happiness and misery are not characteristics of objects but of egoism (ahamkara).

The Self (atman) is ever blissful. The ego-sense (ahamkara) is like a collection of iron filings which, when stimulated into activity by the presence of a magnetic bar—the bar being the Self (atman)—is happy, but when not stimulated is unhappy. If an orange is full of juice, you want to put your nose into it; but if it is sour, you do not like it. Therefore the real locus of the pleasures that come and go, the joys that turn into their opposite, is the ego. Eternal bliss is the very nature of the Self; transitory joy is a passing, occasional characteristic of egoism.

18. All love is for the Self

ātmārthatvena hi preyān viṣayo na svataḥ priyaḥ
svata eva hi sarveṣām ātmā priyatamo yataḥ
tata ātmā sad-ānando nāsya duḥkhaṃ kadācana

[108] 'Objects are not dear in their own right, but for the sake of the Self. For the Self is dearest above all in its own right. Hence the Self is eternal and constant bliss and never experiences pain.

Sense-objects are dear and desirable on account of the Self and not for themselves. This is a truth which has to be carefully understood. 'Not for the sake of the husband is the husband dear; but for the sake of the Self the husband is dear...' (*Brihadaranyaka Upanishad* 2.4.5 and 4.5.6). To every man, the object of his greatest love is his Self. As long as the husband promotes the interest of the fancied self, he is dear. As long as Cardinal Wolsey promoted the welfare of Henry VIII, he was virtually ruler. So we conclude that the Self is the home of bliss and never suffers misery.

There were two young friends in a village; one was the son of the village barber and the other the son of the village carpenter. They decided, secretly, to run away and seek their fortune abroad. When they had travelled for three or four days, the son of the barber fell sick and died. The carpenter's son mourned him. He saw a man from the village who was returning home and asked him to tell the barber that his son was dead, but the man was confused and went to the carpenter and told him that *his* son was dead. The carpenter grieved for his son who was alive, whilst the barber was happy thinking his son was still alive. If misery really depended on the death of the son, then it was the barber who should have been mourning and the carpenter who should have been happy. This shows that the mind or ego is the real cause of misery.

There are two kinds of joy; one is followed by suffering and the other is the bliss which is permanent. The ego is like the moon which borrows its light from the sun—the sun is the Self (atman). God pervades the human soul (jiva) and also matter, and it is He who is the real Self (atman) and is bliss—not the mind and not the sense-objects.

yat suṣuptau nirviṣaya ātmānando 'nubhūyate
śrutiḥ pratyakṣam aitihyam anumānaṃ ca jāgrati

[109] 'That is why the bliss of the Self is experienced in dreamless sleep when no objects are present. The Veda, perception, tradition and inference are the evidence in the waking state (that the Self is bliss).

19. Maya, rajas, sattva, tamas

avyakta-nāmnī parameśa-śaktir
anādy-avidyā triguṇātmikā parā
kāryānumeyā sudhiyaiva māyā
yayā jagat sarvam idaṃ prasūyate

[110] 'There is a supreme power of the highest Lord, beginningless ignorance composed of the three constituents and known as "the Unmanifest". It is that "Māyā" which can be inferred by an intelligent person from its effects, and that whereby this whole world comes into being.

The question is this: Why do we see creation, maintenance and dissolution? Is there any answer to this question?

The reply of the holy philosophy is in the word Maya. No philosopher has ever given a satisfactory reply, for the mind cannot understand it. Only by the inner light can it be understood. During my days of greater ignorance I met a great saint. I was proud of my learning and plied him with this question. He said: 'My son, you seem to be fairly intelligent. My advice to you is, put aside this question for the time being and try to cultivate the spiritual light within'. I understood.

Maya means the aggregate of limitations and conditions which the Absolute has applied on Itself. This theme is most important but difficult for the untrained and uninitiated mind to grasp. Sometimes we ask questions, but are not entitled to the answers on account of our undeveloped reason and lack of intellectual capacity. A child of five asks why the sun sinking below the horizon appears much bigger than it was at the meridian. Can anyone explain this to a child? You have to know the laws of physics and other factors involved in it. Why do certain objects when placed in water submerge entirely, some only half and some not at all? Will the child understand the laws of physics, such as weight, which are responsible? No, he will not understand. We are very fond of asking questions, but not very fond of developing our understanding so that we can understand the answers. A question which has been continually asked way back to the time of Zarathushtra is: 'Why is there death and destruction and why are dictators allowed to come to power, and so forth?' These are variations of the same theme: 'Why has God created the world? Why has the Infinite limited Himself?' When the speaker was a student of fifteen, a materialistic philosopher—a friend of my father—said: 'Did God become mad when He evolved the world?' The speaker could not answer him.

The mistake of the human mind is its insistence on intellectual satisfaction previous to any discipline or understanding. In geometry the problem attributed to Pythagoras is well-known, but unless you have done all the forty-six propositions going before it, you will not understand the forty-seventh.

These questions are easy to ask, but to have a satisfactory answer you have to open those hitherto dormant capacities of your intellect which will enable you to understand it. When I first saw in the Peking Museum the paintings of the great painter Li Lung Nyang, I paid no attention to them, but when I understood their technique I loved to stand for hours before them and drink of the beauty of the eleventh century. This book we are studying gives an explanation of these questions. People never ask: 'Why is there pleasure and why are there good things in this world?' They blame the Creator for evil, but they do not understand that anything that is limited and finite is evil and the womb of suffering. It is the Infinite alone which is bliss.

The question rightly formulated is: 'Why has the Absolute become conditioned?' This question includes 'why', 'how', 'when' and 'where'. These are the four most important adverbs in our vocabulary. What is at the root of them? They are called ontological questions: 'What is the nature of the Absolute, or God?' 'Why has He assumed a conditioned form?'

The reply given in the holy philosophy is that the Absolute, or God, alone exists and there is no variation, no plurality, no sin and no vice in Him; but that there is a principle which is responsible for the phenomenal limitations and conditions, and that principle is called Maya. Everyone in the East knows this word, a most important word in philosophy.

What is the philosophical definition of Maya? 'This world is a product of a principle which is phenomenal by nature—that is, not real—and that principle is termed "Maya"'. Some call it illusion, some call it a dream, but it is not totally unreal.

This Maya, which makes God appear as the world, is also called 'the unmanifest'. In its original form, it is one homogeneous mass. Another name for it is 'nescience'—not want of knowledge but want of correct knowledge, that is, erroneous knowledge. Maya is like a cloud, and a cloud cannot be formed without the rays of the sun.

Maya is the power of the Lord. Power in what sense? Something which is the nature of the Lord, just as compassion, grace and the saving of abject ignorant ones are powers of the Lord. This Maya is beginningless, a point to be remembered. Maya is not co-eternal with the Lord, it is only beginningless like the snake in the rope, and can be inferred from its effects. It is prior to its effects. How? This wooden plate is an effect. What is its cause? Wood. The whole world is the effect of this beginningless divine power of Maya which exists before all.

What does Maya consist of, what is its analysis? Its three constituent attributes (gunas) are equilibrium (sattva), motion (rajas) and rest (tamas); it is made up of these three. The whole world and every object in the world can be resolved into these three gunas. Equilibrium (sattva) corresponds to light; motion (rajas) corresponds to ambitions, desires and so forth; inertia or rest (tamas) means sloth, laziness and so forth.

This Maya can be inferred from its effects. The first category of proof is direct perception, the second category is called inference. I see smoke and then infer that there is a fire—this is called inference in logic. But Maya cannot be perceived and it can only be inferred by a clear intellect. A clear intellect is one that wants to understand. Understanding comes through humility and true enquiry. The whole world is the product of Maya.

san nāpy asan nāpy ubhayātmikā no
bhinnāpy abhinnāpy ubhayātmikā no
sāṅgāpy anaṅgāpy ubhayāymikā no
mahādbhutā 'nirvacanīya-rūpā

[111] 'It is neither existent nor non-existent nor both existent and non-existent. It neither accepts differentiation nor rejects it, and it does not both accept and reject it. It neither possesses nor lacks subordinate parts, neither does it both possess and lack them. It is a great wonder and its nature is inexplicable.

Neither can you call it existent, nor can you say it is non-existent. F.H. Bradley has spoken of a theory in which the opposites are reconciled. He did not know the Jaina philosophy. How erroneous are our logical perceptions! Is it possible for opposites to meet in the same principle? But Maya does not conform to logic.

Most wonderful is Maya. Not wonderful in the ordinary sense of the word, but in the Platonic sense that 'wonder is the beginning of philosophy', or as we look at the starry heavens and wonder. Whatever we say, Maya is beyond understanding and there are no words by which to explain it. But this Maya is responsible for the whole universe. This is the explanation given by one of our greatest intellects, Shri Shankara Acharya. If one can understand this principle then the whole philosophy becomes clear. All that can be grasped by the senses or mind is in this Maya. Our minds are made up of this Maya and they can only function in Maya.

It is the established theory of yoga that the mind cannot know God. The mind is like a cloud in which there is a ray of Consciousness. When, by the grace of God, the mind becomes no mind, like a cloud dissolving, then the ray of Consciousness knows its own nature, knows that it is a ray of the Lord and that it has never been in illusion. Speech and mind are the effects of Maya and therefore cannot understand this principle, for the effect cannot fully know its cause. This principle Maya is responsible for the grand phenomenon of the universe. Time and space are factors of Maya, and so also is the law of cause and effect. Where is space? Where is time? These are the children of Maya.

śuddhādvaya-brahma-vibodha-nāśyā
sarpa-bhramo rajju-vivekato yathā
rajas tamaḥ sattvam iti prasiddhā
guṇās tadīyāḥ prathitaiḥ sva-kāryaiḥ

[112] 'It is subject to abolition through an awakening to the pure non-dual Absolute, as the snake for which a rope has been mistaken is abolished when the rope is known. The constituents (gunas) of which it is composed are rajas, tamas and sattva, so-called through their known effects.

Maya can be destroyed for a given individual by a knowledge of the Absolute, God. God is one-without-a-second—or rather, is not two, non-dual (if you say that He is one, you limit Him). Today we are bound by time, space and the law of cause and effect (karma). Without knowing God, there is no freedom for man. St Augustine says: 'O Lord, I wish I had known Thee in my youth, but I was too proud of my intellect'.

How is Maya destroyed? As the illusory snake in the rope is destroyed—by correct knowledge. How will all the sufferings of the world end? How will all pairs of opposites and all petty considerations of our prestige and name and fame end? When the knowledge of God comes. It is the only way. Renunciation is one of the means of destroying Maya.

The word 'guna' does not only mean 'constituent attribute', it also means 'a thing that binds'. The three gunas are the three instruments that bind the deluded soul (jiva). In its conceptual form, Maya, the principle of which the world and the human mind are composed, consists of these three sub-principles: sattva (harmony, or light), manifesting as benevolence, charity, love of truth and so forth; rajas (activity), expressing itself in love of power, fame, wealth and domination over others; and tamas (inertia), characterized by sloth, sleep and laziness.

vikṣepa-śaktī rajasaḥ kriyātmikā
yataḥ pravṛttiḥ prasṛtā purāṇī
rāgādayo 'syāḥ prabhavanti nityaṃ
duḥkhādayo ye manaso vikārāḥ

[113] 'The power of rajas is a power of projection, of the nature of action. Action has flowed from it from primordial time. From rajas there constantly flow attachment and suffering and other such modifications of the mind.

First is explained the second sub-aspect of Maya, rajas. Its chief effect on the human mind is activity. All the primordial activity of matter is due to it. From it come the mental modifications of grief, joy, conceit, egoism and attachment. The Acharya speaks of its effects on the mind alone and they are those just enumerated.

kāmaḥ krodho lobha-dambhādy asūyā
'haṃkārerṣyā-matsarādyās tu ghorāḥ
dharmā ete rājasāḥ puṃ-pravṛttir
yasmād esā tad rajo bandha-hetuḥ

> [114] 'Its dire characteristics are lust, anger, greed, hypocrisy, intolerance, egoism, jealousy, envy and the like. Because our familiar self-interested activity arises from it, rajas is a source of bondage.

What are the further effects of rajas on the mind? (1) Inordinate desire for pleasure. If one is engrossed in sense-pleasures—food, jazz music, soft flattering words—that person is on the way to ruin. When nations or individuals begin to decay, pleasure-sense takes possession of them. Pompey the Great, in order to please the Roman citizens, gave a gladiatorial show in which a thousand human beings were devoured by lions and tigers, and when they could eat no more the remaining slaves were bidden to kill each other. In order to avoid killing their fellow-men they killed themselves. Let us be warned against this demon sense-pleasure. (2) Anger: a great enemy of man. People sometimes say 'I am not angry, but indignant'. It is the same thing! Anything that agitates the mind and interferes with calm and quiet reasoning is condemnable. (3) Avarice: a leprosy that grows with years and knows no end. (4) Arrogance and spite. (5) Egoism: of which selfishness is the first expression. Dante was a good Roman Catholic and when he spoke of the seven mortal sins, the seventh, egoism, is so heinous that he did not name it! (6) Envy or jealousy: a most unreasonable, blinding, narrow and intellect-clouding quality. These are all due to the attribute of rajas.

Everything in the world has rajas in it, but these are the ways in which the mind expresses it. What is the chief cause of bondage? Rajas. In the *Gita*, Arjuna asks why man performs actions he knows will be disastrous—what forces him to this course? And the Lord replies: 'O Arjuna, know pleasure-sense and anger born of rajas to be the enemies' (3.37). This poison permeates every human mind. Education is real and friends are true only when they help us to overcome these enemies in the mind. Let us avoid all associations which encourage them. He is not our friend who assists us in promoting them. When will the world understand the Advent of Lord Christ? He called it 'victory over sin'. Let us be careful. Our life is short. We are on a par with the lower animals if we live in the senses and allow anger to overcome us. If we sell our liberty to these brutes, we sink lower and lower. I shall forfeit the right to take into my hand the hand of any human being unless by doing so I exalt his mind and soul. People ask where is the enemy? It is rajas in our mind.

eṣā ''vṛtir nāma tamo-guṇasya
śaktir yayā vastv avabhāsate 'nyathā
saiṣā nidānaṃ puruṣasya saṃsṛter
vikṣepa-śakteḥ prasarasya hetuḥ

[115] 'Concealment is the power of the constituent tamas, whereby the real appears as other than it is. This is the ultimate cause of man's reincarnation and the source of the power of projection.

There is the light of God in each human heart in the form of Consciousness. This is veiled by inertia (tamas). Things appear to be what they are not: it makes the enemy appear as friend and *vice versa*.

prajñāvān api paṇḍito 'pi caturo 'py atyanta-sūkṣmārtha-dṛg
vyālīḍhas tamasā na vetti bahudhā saṃbodhito 'pi sphuṭam
bhrānty-āropitam eva sādhu kalayaty ālambate tad-guṇān
hantāsau prabalā duranta-tamasaḥ śaktir mahaty āvṛtiḥ

[116] 'Even a wise and intelligent man, a scholar capable of

understanding extremely subtle points, may fail to understand if he is deceived by tamas, even though the thing be clearly explained to him over and over again in different ways. He supposes that what has merely been superimposed through error is excellent, and relies on its properties. Great and forceful indeed is the concealing power of tamas, hard to bring to an end.

The attitude of the man who encourages me to act lightly and degrade the Self and my friends and says: 'Oh, it is all right!' is due to tamas. Our duty is not to talk and argue and reason, but to enlighten our mind. When Goethe lay dying he cried for more light for humanity. What is light? 'I am the light of the world', says Christ. Swami Nirbhayanandaji says in one of his songs: 'Krishna is the light of all. He lifts a mountain of suffering on one finger. Give Him quarter in your heart'.

The Thugs were people who believed in killing. They once captured a child who later said that when he was fifteen he was told by them that he must learn the art of killing. He was horrified. They said to him: 'My boy, do you not believe it is better to know a thing than not to know it?' This seemed reasonable and he had no reply to make. As a result of this little mistake in reasoning, a life was ruined. Thus tamas veils. It is darkness and covers our minds, making the good appear to be bad and *vice versa*. So, friends, beware of your reason. Let the mind be enlightened. The enlightened man when he reasons utters wise words. 'O Lord, propeller of our reason, let Thy Will be done'.

abhāvanā vā viparīta-bhāvanā
'saṃbhāvanā vipratipattir asyāḥ
saṃsarga-yuktaṃ na vimuñcati dhruvaṃ
vikṣepa-śaktiḥ kṣapayaty ajasram

[117] 'As long as a person is associated with this power of concealment in tamas, he is constantly dogged by failure to

form any conception, formation of conceptions that are the opposite of the truth, inability to comprehend even the possibility of what is in fact the case, and disagreement with others. And then he is ceaselessly tormented by the power of projection in rajas.

How is it that to many people the Self is not evident? Many remain bound to the mind and do not see that there is something common to all. The Self is unknown to many because of tamas covering and veiling it. Many consider the body to be the Self, and others the mind. If you harm some people bodily they do not mind, but if you insult them they are up-in-arms, for they are identified with their mind.

ajñānam ālasya-jaḍatva-nidrā-
pramāda-mūḍhatva-mukhās tamo-guṇāḥ
etaiḥ prayukto na hi vetti kiṃcin
nidrāluvat stambhavad eva tiṣṭhati

[118] 'The typical attributes of tamas are ignorance, laziness, inertia, sleep, neglect of duty and mental confusion. One afflicted by these deficiencies knows nothing. He just stands still like a post, or like one dazed by sleep.

These are manifestations of the gross veil called tamas. It is the duty of man to overcome them. In the realm of purely secular knowledge, a man will only become more ignorant. Plato, Aristotle, Spencer, Huxley and Darwin were highly ignorant about many things. In this realm, the only thing worthwhile to know is that we do not know. No one can know everything about an atom of carbon, or about this little leaf. But there is one thing a man can know for certain: what he is, what God is, 'That by knowing which one knows all' (*Prashna Upanishad* 4.11). When we know a nugget of gold, we know all the gold in the world. When the Self is known, all becomes known.

Once when passing through the Gobi desert I saw a city. Towers which seemed to touch the heavens, beautiful domes and pleasure gardens could be seen at a distance. 'What a beautiful city!' I exclaimed. My guide replied: 'There is no city. What you see is only a mirage'. Is it necessary to know each tower and to measure and study the details of such a city? Shankara says: 'What is this world? What is its nature? How was it born? What is its cause? Do not waste time on these considerations. Let the wise know it is all an illusion, but let them know the Lord of the illusion'.

sattvaṃ viśuddhaṃ jalavat tathāpi
tābhyāṃ militvā saraṇāya kalpate
yatrātma-bimbaḥ pratibimbitaḥ san
prakāśayaty arka ivākhilaṃ jaḍam

[119] 'Although the constituent sattva is by nature pure like water, yet it makes for reincarnation when mingled with rajas and tamas. When the Self is reflected in sattva, it illumines the whole realm of the non-conscious like the sun.

Life is a pilgrimage of which each incarnation is a stage. It is man's duty to go straight to God, that is, to realize Godhead as his true nature. This is to be undertaken by every means in one's power and with steps that do not falter. All are striving towards this goal unconsciously. Those who do so consciously become subjective pilgrims, not in the three-dimensional world, but in the fourth dimension of human thoughts and feelings. Such people are called yogis, candidates for Godhead. If one does not consciously start on this journey, one creates an atmosphere of suffering. If a man shuts his eyes when the sun is shining, is it the fault of the sun?

miśrasya-sattvasya bhavanti dharmās
tv amānitādyā niyamā yamādyāḥ
śraddhā ca bhaktiś ca mumukṣutā ca
daivī ca sampattir asan-nivṛttiḥ

> [120] 'The attributes of "mixed sattva" are the virtues such as absence of pride (Bhagavad Gītā 13.8-12), the general and particular laws of conduct (Yoga Sūtras 2.30 and 32), faith, devotion, deep desire for liberation, the six-fold spiritual wealth beginning with inner control (cp. verses 22 ff. above) and desistance from pursuit of the unreal.

The holy philosophy affirms that all sufferings are terminable and that there is only one way to end suffering. It is to arouse the sleeping seeds of Godhead in our mind. Anthropology in its researches into human nature has found that no man is entirely blind to goodness or to the inner light.

Man is classed as a gregarious being. How otherwise can one account for friendship, dislike of loneliness and so forth? Why this craving to know? What is the object of it all? The answer is that man wants to grow, physically, mentally and spiritually. Spiritual growth is essential, and without it other growth is destructive and leads man to a state of restlessness, sometimes developing into a power complex which makes him a danger to the society in which he functions. Those friends are time-killers who do not uplift our mind. Those amusements that only make us laugh and do not also uplift the soul are a waste of time and life. That type of reading is useless which does not uplift the soul to God.

viśuddha-sattvasya guṇāḥ prasādaḥ
svātmānubhūtiḥ paramā praśāntiḥ
tṛptiḥ praharṣaḥ paramātma-niṣṭhā
yayā sad ānanda-rasaṃ samṛcchati

> [121] 'The attributes of pure sattva are radiance, direct experience of the Self, supreme peace, satisfaction, joy, sustained devotion to the supreme Self, whereby one attains the savour of eternal bliss.

Good, the supreme good, is nothing but the outer expression of godliness. No one can be really good unless he is godly. If he is not godly, one cannot be sure of his goodness; his mind may sink to lower levels at any time and this will show itself in his actions. Holy Christ said, 'Be ye perfect even as your Father in heaven is perfect'; that is what man is here for. The implications of this dictum are immense and affect every branch of society. Instead of power, cultivate goodness; then a real society can be formed but not otherwise.

This is Yoga. It is the *summum bonum* of human life.

20. The causal body

avyaktam etat tri-guṇair niruktaṃ
tat kāraṇaṃ nāma śarīram ātmanaḥ
suṣuptir etasya vibhakty-avasthā
pralīna-sarvendriya-buddhi-vṛttiḥ

[122] 'This is "the unmanifest", described according to its three constituents. It is "the causal body" of the Self. Its particular state is dreamless sleep when all the modifications of the mind and senses are dissolved.

sarva-prakāra-pramiti-praśāntir
bījātmanā 'vasthitir eva buddheḥ
suṣuptir etasya kila pratītiḥ
kiñcin na vedmīti jagat-prasiddheḥ

[123] 'Dreamless sleep is the cessation of all forms of knowledge with the mind in its seed state. Here, as everyone knows, there is the idea "I know nothing".

I know of no philosophy in the West in which you find any mention of the dreamless sleep state, although we are in it every day and we cannot do without it. Here comes the question which is not touched on at all in the Greek, German, French or English philosophy. No memory is possible without an experience. You remember only those things which you have experienced; if you have never experienced a thing you won't have a memory of it. This is very easy to accept, nobody can deny it. When you wake up from dreamless sleep you say: 'I slept so well I did not remember anything. It was such a peaceful sleep'. In so doing, you are describing by memory an experience which you have had. There was something you experienced during the state of dreamless sleep, the memory of which you later describe to your friend.

21. The not-self

dehendriya-prāṇa-mano-'hamādayaḥ
sarve vikārā viṣayāḥ sukhādayaḥ
vyomādi-bhūtāny akhilaṃ ca viśvam
avyakta-paryantam idaṃ hy anātmā

> [124] 'All this that we perceive, beginning with the body, senses, vital energy and ego, and including all modifications such as objects and feeling-states of the mind like pleasure, including even the whole universe from the elements like the ether up to "the unmanifest"—all this is not-self.

Man is a compound of shadow and substance, matter and Spirit. There is a feeling, desiring entity in man, and there is the spiritual reality. When this entity, by direct knowledge of its own nature, comes to the Lord and acquires His nature, then man is complete. When he detaches Self from not-self, letting the cognizing power act on his own nature rather than on the not-self, then he is free.

What is the not-self from which the Self should separate itself? It is the body, senses, vitality, mind, ego and so forth. All these are not-self. The not-self is not the medium of freedom. These are the things which constitute the limiting adjunct called Maya, and the Self of man has to know that it is distinct from them. Let us not make the mistake of the early fathers of the Christian Church. Do not kill the senses, but let the soul realize its separateness from these things.

māyā māyā-kāryaṃ sarvaṃ mahad-ādi-deha-paryantam
asad idam anātmakam tvaṃ viddhi maru-marīcikā-kalpam

[125] 'Know that Māyā and all its effects from the cosmic intellect (mahat) to the body are not-self and are as unreal as a mirage.

The cosmic intellect means the totality of all intellects, past, present and future. From that cosmic intellect to a blade of grass, all is a modification of the limiting adjunct Maya. All these and their cause, Maya, the limiting force, are not-self and therefore unreal like a mirage in the desert. Let us not make the mistake of running away from Maya. There are two choices: to run after it as real, or to think how wonderful are the works of the Lord and enjoy it without identification. Only by being a detached spectator can one really enjoy. A sober man is the real enjoyer in a drinking house. In this world, where ignorance and error are common, there is no use in quarrelling and hating those who do not know; enjoy it all as a spectator. It is all to be considered as illusion—that is, let there be no attachment to it. When we see a rainbow which disappears in a few minutes, we do not cry over it.

22. The Self

atha te saṃpravakṣyāmi svarūpaṃ paramātmanaḥ
yad vijñāya naro bandhān muktaḥ kaivalyam aśnute

[126] 'Now I will tell you the nature of the supreme Self, on knowing which a person is released from bondage and attains transcendence.

What is the nature of the real Self or Spirit in man? What is God? A most important question. From God, the universal Spirit, the substratum of all phenomena, the indestructible, imperishable, all-pervasive Self, the reality whose nature is bliss, nobody can escape.

What liquidity is to water, brilliance to the sun, fragrance to a flower, sincerity to a gentleman, God is to the universe. Nothing is so self-evident as the Lord, but only they will find Him who are tired of sense-pleasures and are searching for the haven of eternal peace and bliss. Those who look for sense-pleasures and at the same time want to find God are setting themselves an impossible problem which they will be unable to solve. If atheism has a long history, theism has a much longer one. Theism is as old as grave-digging and human tears. The imprint of the immanence of the Lord can be seen by the eye of knowledge. The truth of His existence is immediate, according to Spinoza.

asti kaścit svayaṃ nityam ahaṃ-pratyaya-lambanaḥ
avasthā-traya-sākṣī san pañca-kośa-vilakṣaṇaḥ

[127] 'There is a certain self-existent eternal principle, the basis of the notion "I", which is the Witness of the three states of waking, dream and dreamless sleep and is different from the five "sheaths".

The four proofs of the existence of God as formulated by St Anselm of Canterbury—teleological, cosmological, ontological and ethical—are hackneyed proofs and none of them is convincing. We cannot make the holy name of the Lord a matter of fashionable discussion. Unless a man loves, how can he know the sweetness of love? Unless a man makes friends, how can he know the delights of friendship as delineated by Cicero? Unless a man is a sincere candidate for the joy that does not terminate, how can he know the Lord? Unless you come to know the real cause of the bondage of suffering, how can you know freedom? Study with reverence the words of the holy Acharya and you will have proof of this truth and you will know God. To know God means to have the highest knowledge. 'Seek ye first the Kingdom of Heaven' is the divine injunction.

The human personality consists of five sheaths, under which is shining the light of Self (see verses 156-212). That light passes through the mind to the senses, and man is said to know, love, move, discriminate and so forth. Everything in the universe has its opposite—water-fire, light-darkness, life-death. What is the opposite of the relative? The Absolute. If you do not accept the Absolute as a hypothesis, the idea of God falls to the ground. The five sheaths—physical, vital, mental, intellectual and causal (see verses 156-190)—are all relative, passing, ever-changing. Their opposite is the substratum 'I am'. I once asked a man whose legs had been amputated whether he felt that his 'I' had undergone a reduction. The answer was 'No'. 'Do you feel 20% or 30% less?' 'No'. There is no breach of continuity under an anaesthetic or in a coma, and man realizes that there has been no break. On waking up from deep sleep one does not say 'I was annihilated for several hours'.

If the five sheaths are objects, what is their subject? It is the ultimate principle of Consciousness in us, the innermost Self, which knows: 'This is a brother, mother, flower, plate and so forth'. It implies that I am distinct from what I possess. So, likewise, when I say: 'My body, my mind, my life, my intellect'. When I subtract these, what remains is 'I', and that 'I' is God. He who knows all that happens in the waking, dreaming and dreamless states of consciousness, who is aware of the presence and absence of the functions of the mind; that substratum, 'I', is He, that is God, that is Brahman.

yo vijānāti sakalaṃ jāgrat-svapna-suṣuptiṣu
buddhi-tad-vṛtti-sad-bhāvam abhāvam aham ity ayam

> [128] 'It is that which has the feeling "I" and takes note of the mind and the presence and absence of all its modifications in waking, dream and dreamless sleep.

People ask: 'Where is God?' The rationalist, proud of the capacity of his intellect, wants to understand God. The scientist wants to measure Him—for scientific knowledge is all measurement. To a lover of power, He is domination. To a yogi, God *is*—and this is what He is. He is everywhere, but you can find Him only in your own being.

Of what does the being of man consist? Egoism (the 'I am' in the philosophical sense), the three states of consciousness (waking, dreaming and dreamless sleep) and the five sheaths (of food, vital energy, mind, knowledge and bliss or the causal body) which cover the light of God. These are the nine constituents of the human personality. God is the subject or Witness of the nine. The Acharya calls Him the substratum of the human 'I'.

Everything has an appearance and a substratum. 'I' is both the appearance and the substratum. The Witness of the five sheaths and the three states is in the human personality and is both the eternal, infinite, causeless cause of the whole universe and the substratum of the ego. Are you or are you not? Are you the body, are you the mind? Are you not rather the support of ego to whom God is directly known? He who is aware of the functions of the mind, or of the absence of those functions, he who says: 'My mind is dull today!', that is the substratum of the ego, the supreme Self (paramatman), or God. To apply the Aristotelean principle, the subject must be different from the object. There is a Witness of the subconscious functions of the mind. The mind is a perishable entity. Everything in the world is perishable. God is the imperishable element in the mind.

yaḥ paśyati svayaṃ sarvaṃ yaṃ na paśyati kaścana
yaś cetayati buddhyādiṃ na tu yaṃ cetayaty ayam

[129] 'He is the one who himself sees all, while no one sees him. He is the one who illumines the mind and so on through his light, but whom they do not illumine.

He is the one who sees all or knows all—the trees, the river, the hills—whom none sees. The body, senses, mind and intellect cannot see the Self; no appliance, scientific or otherwise, can see Him. It is He who animates the mind. Unless the mind is animated by a supramental force, it is dead.

yena viśvam idaṃ vyāptaṃ yaṃ na vyāpnoti kiñcana
ābhā-rūpam idaṃ sarvaṃ yaṃ bhāntam anubhāty ayam

[130] 'He is the one who pervades all this universe while nothing pervades Him. He is that luminous principle who illumines the whole world as His reflection.

He who pervades the universe is not pervaded by anything, even by time and space. Einstein's theory of relativity implies that space is limited and time is the fourth dimension. By His reflection the whole universe shines, just as the moon becomes luminous by acquiring a certain position in the firmament. That by whom all the solar systems, all the stars and nebulae of greatest magnitude are illumined, that is He, the Lord omniscient and omnipotent, whom Christ called 'Our Father in Heaven'.

yasya sannidhi-mātreṇa dehendriya-mano-dhiyaḥ
viṣayeṣu svakīyeṣu vartante preritā iva

[131] 'He is the one through whose mere proximity the body, senses and lower and higher mind operate amidst their appropriate objects, as if impelled.

ahaṃkārādi-dehāntā viṣayāś ca sukhādayaḥ
vedyante ghaṭa-vad yena nitya-bodha-svarūpiṇā

[132] 'He is the one, of the nature of constant and eternal knowledge, by whom objects as well as happiness and other feeling-states of the mind, are known as clearly as a pot standing in front.

eṣo 'ntar-ātmā puruṣaḥ purāṇo
nirantarākhaṇḍa-sukhānubhūtiḥ
sadaika-rūpaḥ pratibodha-mātro
yeneṣitā vāg-asavaś caranti

> [133] 'He is the inner Self, the ancient primordial Spirit, by nature unbroken experience of joy, ever the same, of the nature of pure knowledge, under whose impulsion speech and the various forms of the vital energy perform their functions.

He is the inmost Self. My fingers depend on the mind, mind depends on Him, He depends on nothing.

He is the essence of infinite bliss. Before 1868 the Emperor of Japan was a mere figurehead and took no part in the government. People asked: 'What did he do?' and the answer was: 'He enjoyed'. So we can say that the supreme Self (paramatman) is in constant enjoyment of His own nature.

If Desdemona had survived the strangling by Othello and had gone to a wise man and asked him: 'How was it that I loved him?', the wise man would have said: 'You were wrong to love a changeable man. That which changes is never reliable'. The only relationship which does not change is to be found with the supreme Self (paramatman), commanded by whom the spheres revolve and the atoms dance round their nuclei. When the earth was separated from the sun it was He who said: 'Thus far and no farther'. He is your Self, seated in the hearts of all of us as well as being the Self of the whole universe.

atraiva sattvātmani dhī-guhāyām
avyākṛtākāśa uru-prakāśaḥ
ākāśa uccai ravivat prakāśate
sva-tejasā viśvam idaṃ prakāśayan

> [134] 'He is the great light present in the ether concealed in the cave of the higher mind composed of sattva, illumining the whole world with its light like the sun shining on high.

Today this is just an expression, but one day you will be able to verify it in your own experience if you continue as students of this holy Yoga in all earnestness. A teacher of physics describes the *aurora borealis*, but only when you have seen its real glory for yourself will you understand what it is actually like. So also, when the casket of your mind, in which the Lord of Love dwells, is opened by the Guru, then you will see Him.

Where to look for the Lord? If we want to look at the planet Neptune we require a telescope. That telescope by which you see the Lord as your Self is 'a mind composed of sattva'. Why 'cave' or secret chamber? Because at present it is unknown to you. There sits your true Self (atman). As the *Brihadaranyaka Upanishad* says: 'He is the honey of all living beings' (2.5.12). Such is the Lord seated in the cave of the intellect manifesting in His light the universe.

jñātā mano-'haṃkṛti-vikriyāṇāṃ
dehendriya-prāṇa-kṛtakriyāṇām
ayo- 'gni-vat tān anuvartamāno
na ceṣṭate no vikaroti kiñcana

[135] 'He is the one who takes cognizance of the modifications of the mind and ego-sense and of the changes undergone by the body, senses and vital energy. He conforms to their changes, like the fire in a red-hot ball of iron, without himself acting or undergoing change.

He is that principle in you which knows that your mind is dull, brilliant or confused, and knows the changes in the ego and the activities of the body: 'I am walking, sitting and so forth'. He is that which cognizes all these in you, that which apparently adopts these forms. The body walks, not you. Can you imagine any action on the part of space? Action takes place in space, but space does not act. Anything which, like space, is all-pervasive, can have no activity—a subtle point in the philosophy—and therefore in the Self (atman) there is no activity.

Some people are horrified when they hear this. Yet if you attribute action to the all-pervasive Self you make it mortal. According to Aristotle there is no action in a thing without an impact from without.

Self (atman) is actionless (akriya), there is no action in Him and also no change.

na jāyate no mriyate na vardhate
na kṣīyate no vikaroti nityaḥ
vilīyamāne 'pi vapuṣy amuṣmin
na līyate kumbha ivāmbaraṃ svayam

[136] 'He is not born. He does not die. He neither increases nor diminishes nor undergoes any form of change. He is constantly and eternally the same. He no more dissolves when this body dissolves than the ether apparently enclosed in the pot dissolves on the destruction of the pot.

That which is subject to change is finite and mortal. It is not the Absolute–in Whom according to Christianity the Trinity inheres as Father, Son and Holy Ghost—who becomes. We are talking now of the region far beyond the Trinity. There are no modifications in Him. The holy philosophy is not pantheism (the theory of the reality of the modification—that God has become the world). It is not so. He does not cease to exist when the body is destroyed. He is independent.

prakṛti-vikṛti-bhinnaḥ śuddha-bodha-svabhāvaḥ
sad asad idam aśeṣaṃ bhāsayan nirviśeṣaḥ
vilasati paramātmā jāgradādiṣv avasthāsv
aham-aham iti sākṣāt sākṣi-rūpeṇa buddheḥ

[137] 'Of the nature of pure Consciousness, different from Nature and its modifications, illumining all this world and showing what does and what does not exist, itself without particular characteristics, the supreme Self shines throughout waking, dream and dreamless sleep, immediately evident as "I", the witness of the mind.

Here 'pure' means neither good nor bad, but Knowledge and Knowledge alone. He pervades and also manifests the gross and subtle universe. The gross universe is perceived by the senses; the subtle universe is perceived by the mental and psychic faculties. He is called the supreme Self (paramatman) when spoken of in relation to the body and mind, but He is different from matter and also from the modifications of matter.

niyamita-manasāmuṃ tvaṃ svam ātmānam ātmany
ayam aham iti sākṣād viddhi buddhi-prasādāt
jani-maraṇa-taraṅgāpāra-saṃsāra-sindhuṃ
pratara bhava kṛtārtho brahma-rūpeṇa saṃsthaḥ

[138] 'Control your mind and obtain, through the radiance of your higher mind, immediate knowledge of your own true Self in yourself in the form "This I am". Cross over the shoreless ocean of worldly life with its waves of birth and death. Establish yourself in the Absolute and gain your highest end.

Do we say with real feeling, 'Thy kingdom come'—that is, may purity (sattva), truth, love, kindness, liberality and one-pointed devotion come into our hearts? That is the one thing needful. Unless the heart is reformed, reform of parliament, voting, social order and so forth will not take us very far. Thus the first thing is to realize the supreme importance of a knowledge of God and then to search for it intensively.

Our ability to live happily in society and family is in proportion to the keeping of certain conditions, without which there can be no true friendship.

First let us be refined, which means to be scornful of anything vulgar—anything against the laws of truth and divine love. Then there must be a regulated, controlled mind, a mind functioning according to a certain code and not just as it likes, otherwise it becomes unreliable to one's own self as well as to others. There is a law or code which is given here: 'Practise that which is of a sattvic nature'. As T.H.Green puts it, this means 'to live so that by each act we add to the worth of our personalities'. This philosophy is not for comfort-lovers, but for lovers of truth, the pure in heart, whose goal, realization of Godhead, alone fills the mind. For them the mind has become a controlled horse, going according to the direction they give it.

A third condition is a purified intellect which has only the highest, purest desires. A man is what his desires are. They should be pure, not like those of a child: 'I want to be a Rockefeller, a Duke of Wellington': these are humbugs of desires. The right desire is 'I want to be a saint of God and His servant', and it should be kept before the mind constantly. Why is the worship of saints recommended by the Roman Catholic Church? Because if you keep your mind filled with the example and love of saints, you will mould your life according to their mode.

When these three things have been accomplished, then find out your real Self, your 'I', and identify it with the Lord. This 'I' is His gift. Through the gift, trace the Giver. Find your way to Him to merge in Him who is Love and the Controller of the universe in which everything other than Him is changing.

Change implies something which is immutable. At the back of our consciousness of change, there is an intuitive knowledge of that which does not change. Change is the ocean of becoming made up of the hard and dashing waves of repeated birth and death. If a man is satisfied with this changeful existence, he is a lunatic doomed to be shut up behind the prison bars of his desires and their consequences.

You will understand this philosophy if you understand that birth and death are limitations and that to be above them and beyond them is to contact a consciousness in which they do not exist. Such an understanding is a gift of God and when you have thus identified your 'I' with the Infinite, then you will be established for ever in great bliss and peace. And then you will be really blessed.

23. Superimposition

atrānātmany aham iti matir bandha eṣo 'sya puṃsaḥ
prāpto 'jñānāj janana-maraṇa-kleśa-saṃpāta-hetuḥ
yenaivāyaṃ vapur idam asat satyam ity ātma-buddhyā
puṣyaty ukṣaty avati viṣayais tantubhiḥ kośa-kṛd-vat

[139] 'Here in the world, it is the notion of "I" in relation to the not-self that constitutes bondage. It arises from ignorance and is the source of the whole collection of evils of birth and death. It is the cause whereby the soul takes this unreal body to be real and identifies itself with it, nourishes it, bathes it and pampers it with objects, like a caterpillar surrounding itself with the threads of its cocoon.

What is bondage? The conception of this not-self, this body, being 'I'. How does bondage come? Through ignorance. Suppose I am invited by a benevolent king to his palace where there is kindness and full liberty but, under the influence of some kind of self-hypnosis, I believe that the floor is a lake of water and cry out and cannot advance. Who has created this illusion? Who creates the snake in the rope? You who shout and make a noise! God has not created your illusion. It is your ignorance alone which conceals the true state of affairs. Some say: 'I don't believe this, I am a rationalist, a dialectician, or a materialist'—big, fine-sounding names! Others say: 'I do not know'. This is the evidence of ignorance. Who does not say this at times?

Ignorance brings in its train the miseries of birth and death and all that is sandwiched in-between. It is on account of ignorance that we think the ever-changing body to be eternal. A visitor came to me five years ago who told me she was sure that she would never grow old. 'Send me a post-card after fifty years', I replied. If a man tries to straighten the tail of a dog, he never will. The age of a crow is said to be three hundred years; a man kept one because he wanted to see whether this was so!

And just because we identify our body with the Self (atman), we nourish it, bathe it and preserve it in complete forgetfulness of God within us, and so we weave a cocoon for our souls.

atasmiṅs tad-buddhiḥ prabhavati vimūḍhasya tamasā
vivekābhāvād vai sphurati bhujage rajju-dhiṣaṇā
tato 'nartha-vrāto nipatati samādātur adhikas
tato yo 'sad-grāhaḥ sa hi bhavati bandhaḥ śṛṇu sakhe

[140 'He who is bemused by the constituent tamas misconceives one thing as another. It is through absence of the power to discriminate that one misconceives a snake for a rope; then a host of evils falls on the one who goes to pick it up. So listen, my friend, it is misconception that is bondage.

To see a thing as it is not is the effect of ignorance. In the classic of Cervantes, Don Quixote sees sheep coming towards him. He exclaims: 'These are demons, I must fight them!' It is the absence of discrimination which causes one to take a rope for a snake, to take the Self for the body and to take passionate words of love as pledges of love—when a pledge is asked for or given it is shop-keeping!

A great danger follows those who are in this condition of ignorance.

akhaṇḍa-nityādvaya-bodha-śaktyā
sphurantam ātmānam ananta-vaibhavam
samāvṛṇoty āvṛti-śaktir eṣā
tamo-mayī rāhur ivārka-bimbam

[141] 'This power of concealment (āvṛti-śakti), formed of darkness (tamas), obscures (even) the Self of infinite glory, which manifests itself through its power of unbroken and eternal non-dual consciousness—even as the eclipse obscures the face of the sun.

The glories of the Self of man are infinite, but they can only be made manifest through knowledge, because through ignorance they are veiled. The Self is eternal and one without a second, but it is veiled by ignorance. As the shadow of the moon (called Rahu in the Upanishads) veils the shining disc of the sun at the time of an eclipse, so this ignorance, or Maya, veils Eternity. Maya hides the power and glory of the Self. It can be dispelled by knowledge of God alone and by no other means. A man cannot acquire this knowledge without the grace of God, which becomes accessible through purity in thought, word and deed. No volition can take place without the power of God, and this comes by prayer and meditation.

tirobhūte svātmany amalatara-tejovati pumān
anātmānaṃ mohād aham iti śarīraṃ kalayati
tataḥ kāma-krodha-prabhṛtibhir amuṃ bandhana-guṇaiḥ
paraṃ vikṣepākhyā rajasa uru-śaktir vyathayati

[142] 'When the Self of pure light has been obscured, the soul begins through delusion to identify itself with the body. And then the great power of projection in rajas begins to trouble it with the bonds of lust, anger and so on.

These are the consequences which follow loss of discrimination between the Self and the not-self. The point to be noted is that forgetfulness of the Holy of holies in our mind makes us victims to the feeling of mental activity called rajas. Then follow ambition, passion, greed and the desire to subdue and control others. And the soul pays dearly for all such experiences.

mahā-moha-grāha-grasana-galitātmāvagamano
dhiyo nānāvasthāḥ svayam abhinayaṃs tad guṇatayā
apāre saṃsāre viṣaya-viṣa-pūre jala-nidhau
nimajjyonmaj jyāyaṃ bhramati kumatiḥ kutsita-gatiḥ

[143] 'And then he begins to wander about scarred in mind and warped in his ways, bobbing up and down in the

> shoreless ocean of the poison of sense-objects called worldly life. His sense of the true nature of his Self has been swallowed up by the great shark of metaphysical delusion, and he subjects himself and conforms blindly to the series of states that come over his mind.

When the intellect of man changes, the whole man changes; when the intellect is perverted, nothing helps. The poet Sur Dasa was blind, but his soul was lit with the light of God. Homer was blind also, but his mind was lit with rajas and he portrayed heroes, devotion to whom spreads havoc in one's own life and the lives of those around. When the intellect is perverted, a man is unaware of it, as the drunken man does not know that he is drunk. Once an Indian Christian preacher said to the writer: 'You are a believer in the *Gita*. Look at yourself. You have no shoes, your shirt needs mending! Look at the European nations, Christian nations. How prosperous they are! Why don't you worship Christ?' I answered: 'Christ had no shirt. What did He mean when He said: "Foxes have holes, and the birds of the air have nests; but the Son of man hath not where to lay his head"?' (*Matthew* 8.20) We parted company. His intellect was perverted.

Why does one want a confessor in the Church and a teacher in Yoga? Because they love you and will help. Others only flatter. It matters not whether the face is powdered and rouged, whether the dress fits, whether the hat was bought in Bond Street; but it does matter if the intellect is perverted. By the perpetual remembrance of the name of the Guru or God, one keeps the intellect unperverted. The happiest man is he who knows how to love.

He whose intellect is perverted is swallowed up by the shark of ignorance and he begins to imitate the states of his intellect, as a man under hypnosis imitates whatever the hypnotist wishes. If the intellect says: 'By any means be the most powerful man in the world', a man will shoot his dearest friend and wife mercilessly in his own home. When rajas takes possession of the intellect, man drifts along in the ocean of worldly life (sansara) full of the poison of sense-enjoyment.

Any attempt to enjoy the pleasures of the senses is fraught with the possibility of deadly poison. Whenever sense-enjoyment passes beyond the bounds of necessity, it becomes a poison. The fate of Emma Hamilton is well-known. When a man thinks only of sense-enjoyments, he becomes a stranger to greatness, peace and tranquillity.

People say: 'Why does not the Lord intervene?' Did He not intervene when He came as Christ? What more do they want? Did they listen to Him then? Only twelve followed and at the crucial moment they deserted Him. He intervenes as the holy saints of God and the holy teachers. How many hear and, hearing, believe and belong to Him wholly and solely? They are taken to the river to drink like horses dying of thirst, but they do not drink and only cry out: 'Why does no one help us?' God helps at every moment. These verses are the words of a holy teacher. Hear them and some day the seeds of truth they contain will germinate.

bhānu-prabhā saṃjanitābhra-paṅktir
  bhānuṃ tirodhāya vijṛmbhate yathā
ātmoditāhaṃkṛtir ātma-tattvaṃ
  tathā tirodhāya vijṛmbhate svayam

> [144] 'As a layer of cloud that has collected under the force of the sun spreads out and hides the sun, so does the ego-sense, which proceeds from the Self, spread forth of its own accord and hide the Self.

If you ask an ordinary man who he is, he replies by giving you a description of his ego: 'I am John Brown', 'I am Chinese', 'I am this', 'I am that'. It is said that one day, when Schopenhauer was deep in thought, he met someone who asked him, 'Who are you?' He replied, 'I will give you half the world if you can tell me!' This false egoism, such as 'I am a beauty', 'I am very rich', is due to forgetfulness of the presence of the Lord in our hearts.

Egoism is a cloud generated by want of adequate knowledge of God, and under it is hidden the universal Sun. By means of prayer, devotion and meditation you dissolve the cloud and find that you are the Sun itself, God. And then you become a saint of God.

24. The powers of concealment and projection

kavalita-dina-nāthe dur-dine sāndra-meghair
vyathayati hima-jhañjhā-vāyur ugro yathaitān
avirata-tamasātmany āvṛte mūḍha-buddhiṃ
kṣapayati bahu-duḥkhais tīvra-vikṣepa-śaktiḥ

[145] 'As on a stormy day, when the sun has been swallowed up by thick clouds, fierce squalls of icy wind will drive those clouds hither and thither, so does the pitiless power of projection drive a person of deluded mind this way and that, when the Self has been concealed by continuous ignorance.

etābhyām eva śaktibhyāṃ bandhaḥ puṃsaḥ samāgataḥ
yābhyāṃ vimohito dehaṃ matvā ''tmānaṃ bhramaty ayam

[146] 'A person's bondage comes verily through these two powers. Deluded by them he wanders about in error supposing himself to be the body.

25. Bondage

bījaṃ saṃsṛti-bhūmijasya tu tamo dehātma-dhīr aṅkuro
rāgaḥ pallavam ambu karma tu vapuḥ skandho 'savaḥ śākhikāḥ
agrāṇīndriya-saṃhatiś ca viṣayāḥ puṣpāṇi duḥkhaṃ phalaṃ
nānā-karma-samudbhavaṃ bahuvidhaṃ bhoktātra jīvaḥ khagaḥ

[147] 'Ignorance is the seed of the tree of reincarnation in worldly life, self-identification with the body the sprout, attachment the shoots, merit and demerit the sap, the body the trunk, the life-breaths the twigs, the various sense-organs their

tips, the sense-objects the tree's blossoms, pain its fruits, various in character arising from various deeds. And the bird enjoying experience on this tree is the soul.

ajñāna-mūlo 'yam anātma-bandho
naisargiko 'nādir ananta īritaḥ
janmāpyaya-vyādhi-jarādi-duḥkha-
pravāha-pātaṃ janayaty amuṣya

[148] 'This bondage of the not-self has its root in metaphysical ignorance, said to be uncaused, beginningless and endless (until removed by metaphysical knowledge). This is what brings on the flow of the sufferings of birth, death, disease and old-age.

Why has this situation arisen? Because the Sun of Spirit has been concealed under the cloud of ignorance. That ignorance is self-caused, it does not depend on any other cause. Time, space and the law of cause and effect are creations of ignorance.

Ignorance has no beginning because it did not presuppose the existence of time and space. But the link between cause and effect is terminable—it is not infinite. Causality operates only within time and space. The region beyond time and space is the subject of time and space, and there, cause and effect do not operate. When the cloud of egoism is dissipated and vanishes, ignorance ends.

The real cause of suffering is limitation. Wherever there are limitations there is suffering—it is a law. There is only one who is without limitations. That is the Lord, and He is within. By going to Him, we rise above limitations. The root cause of all evil is egoism. National egoism has led the world into its present plight. Alexander ruined Greece. He killed all culture, philosophy and art until the flame of knowledge was rekindled in Alexandria by the Ptolemies.

Man, conquer thyself, conquer thy limitations and ignorance! It is an uphill task, but make a beginning. Rub out all ignorance in the thought of the Lord. Flattery is a great offence because it exaggerates our ego. He who only dittos our limitations and prejudices is merely a worshipper of ignorance and no more. He is our friend who helps us to overcome them.

26. Discrimination of Self and not-self

nāstrair na śastrair anilena vahninā
chettuṃ na śakyo na ca karma-koṭibhiḥ
viveka-vijñāna-mahāsinā vinā
dhātuḥ prasādena śitena mañjunā

[149] 'This tree of reincarnation cannot be cut down by weapons, blown down by the wind, burnt down by fire or chopped down by millions of good deeds. It can be cut down only by the great shining sword of discriminative knowledge sharpened by the grace of the Lord.

How is ignorance cut down? Whatever makes the limitations seem real has to go. It is not cut by weapons, even by weapons upon which mantrams have been pronounced, as guns are blessed by the Churches! All wars and all education which extols wars are futile. Nor is ignorance destroyed by wind or fire or even by millions of good deeds. It is cut down only by the knowledge which comes through spiritual discrimination (viveka), sharpened by the grace of God—not by mere knowledge.

I cannot lift up this bell by my own power unless it is the power of God which lifts my hand. Nothing takes place without the power of God. How does this grace of God come? Through prayer, devotion and a life of fraternity in which love is the ruling power.

śruti-pramāṇaika-mateḥ sva-dharma-
niṣṭhā tayaivātma-viśuddhir asya
viśuddha-buddheḥ paramātma-vedanaṃ
tenaiva saṃsāra-sa-mūla-nāśaḥ

> [150] 'Devotion to spiritual duty comes only to him whose sole authority is the Veda, and there can only be purification of the mind through devotion to spiritual duty. Knowledge of the supreme Self comes only to him who has purified his mind, and there can only be cessation of repeated worldly life and its cause (metaphysical ignorance) through knowledge of the Self.

We are here in this life to listen, to learn, to discriminate, to grow in wisdom and in the end to become divinely inspired. The criterion of a philosopher is that when he is convinced, he is convinced once and for all and there is no more room for doubt. It is weak to be convinced and then to doubt again. Conviction comes through work and through purified clear thinking. Do not just hear and make philosophy a pastime, for you cannot play with anything holy. When Moses returned from Mount Sinai after having conversed with God, he said: 'Listen with reverence and then act upon it'. When Joshua was chosen as his successor, he never doubted his divine mission.

Yoga demands a full surrender which results in a complete life enriched by devotion to God. Then man becomes superconscious. Try every day to become superconscious, to expand your consciousness by identifying your interests with those of all living beings. Everybody is destined to become superconscious. Then why not try now to be what we are destined to be?

kośair anna-mayādyaiḥ pañcabhir ātmā na saṃvṛto bhāti
nija-śakti-samutpannaiḥ śaivāla-paṭalair ivāmbu vāpīstham

> [151] 'The Self does not manifest because it is covered over and concealed by the five sheaths beginning with the food sheath, like water in a well covered over and concealed by duck-weed of its own producing.

The ray of the light of the Lord becomes individualized, as it were, when it is covered by these five sheaths (to be described in verses 156 ff. below).

tac chaivālāpanaye samyak salilaṃ pratīyate śuddham
tṛṣṇā-santāpaharaṃ sadyaḥ saukhya-pradaṃ paraṃ puṃsaḥ

[152] 'When the duck-weed is removed, the pure water is clearly perceived. It quenches a man's thirst at once and renders him supremely happy.

pañcānām api kośānām apavāde vibhāty ayaṃ śuddhaḥ
nityānandaika-rasaḥ pratyag-rūpaḥ paraḥ svayaṃ-jyotiḥ

[153] 'In the same way, when the five sheaths have been negated, the supreme self-luminous principle shines out as the inmost reality, homogeneous as constant and eternal bliss.

The principle of limitation, or conditioning adjunct, is nescience, or erroneous interpretation (avidya). When it covers the reflection of the Lord in the individual (jiva), it forms five layers—one over the other. These layers are known as the five sheaths (koshas), and in them is encased the jewel of the reflection of the Lord. In the Tibetan mantram, 'Om mani padme hum', 'padme' is the lotus of man's mind in which 'mani', the jewel, is hidden. To discover this jewel is the object of Tibetan Yoga.

ātmānatma-vivekaḥ kartavyo bandha-muktaye viduṣā
tenaivānandī bhavati svaṃ vijñāya sac-cid-ānandam

[154] 'The wise person should effect the discrimination of the Self and the not-self for liberation from bondage. For it is only then that a person can know his own true nature as Existence, Consciousness and Bliss and be happy.

muñjād iṣīkām iva dṛśya-vargāt
pratyañcam ātmānam asaṅgam akriyam
vivicya tatra pravilāpya sarvaṃ
tadātmanā tiṣṭhati yaḥ sa muktaḥ

[155] 'He who discriminates his inmost Self, relationless and actionless, from the whole realm of objects, as one separates the inner stalk of a piece of muñja grass from its outer casing, dissolves the not-self and stands liberated as the Self.

Let us remember that nescience (avidya), the conditioning adjunct of which the sheaths are made, is made up of the three elements (gunas) of equilibrium (sattva), activity (rajas) and inertia (tamas). Rajas and tamas are the two poles; sattva, in the middle, keeps the balance between the two, otherwise the universe could not last.

27. The sheath of food (physical body)

deho 'yam anna-bhavano 'nna-mayas tu kośaś
cānnena jīvati vinaśyati tad-vihīnaḥ
tvak-carma-māṃsa-rudhirāsthi-purīṣa-rāśir
nāyaṃ svayaṃ bhavitum arhati nitya-śuddhaḥ

[156] 'This physical body, arising from food and consisting of food, is one sheath. It lives through food and perishes without it. It is a conglomeration of skin, flesh, blood, bones and excrement. It cannot be the eternal pure principle.

The first sheath is called the food-sheath (anna-maya kosha) and it is very opaque. It is called the food sheath because it is sustained by food. It is the food you eat that sustains this gross, physical body. If you do not eat, you become emaciated and wither away. So this visible body is called the food-sheath.

pūrvaṃ janer adhi mṛter api nāyam asti
jātaḥ kṣaṇaṃ kṣaṇa-guṇo 'niyata-svabhāvaḥ
naiko jaḍaś ca ghaṭavat paridṛśyamānaḥ
sv-ātmā kathaṃ bhavati bhāva-vikāra-vettā

[157] 'This physical body does not exist before its birth or after its death. Even after it is born, its nature is unstable and it changes from moment to moment. It is not a single entity, is

non-conscious and is an object of perception like a pot. How can it be one's own true Self, which is the knower of the (apparent) modifications undergone by Being?

pāṇi-pādādimān deho nātmā vyaṅge 'pi jīvanāt
tat-tac-chakter anāśāc ca na niyamyo niyāmakaḥ

[158] 'This body with its hands and feet cannot be the Self because it continues to live when some of its powers are retained after the loss of some of its limbs. As that which is subject to control, it cannot be the (Self as) controller.

deha-tad-dharma-tat-karma-tad-avasthādi-sākṣiṇaḥ
svata eva svataḥ siddhaṃ tad-vailakṣaṇyam ātmanaḥ

[159] 'The Self is the Witness of the body, its attributes and states. The existence of the Self is self-evident, and so is its difference from the body.

kulya-rāśir māṃsa-lipto mala-pūrṇo 'ti-kaśmalaḥ
kathaṃ bhaved ayaṃ vettā svayam etad-vilakṣaṇaḥ

[160] 'The body is a heap of bones smeared with flesh, full of impurities and thoroughly dirty. How can it be the self-existent one, who knows it as an object, different from it in kind?

tvaṅ-māṃsa-medo-'sthi-purīṣa-rāśāv
aham-matiṃ mūḍha-janaḥ karoti
vilakṣaṇaṃ vetti vicāra-śīlo
nija-svarūpaṃ paramārtha-bhūtam

[161] 'Those of confused mind identify themselves with a mass of bones, fat, flesh, skin and excrement. A reflective person will realize that in his true nature he is the supreme reality, different from the body.

deho 'ham ity eva jaḍasya buddhir
dehe ca jīve viduṣas tv ahaṃ-dhīḥ
viveka-vijñānavato mahātmano
brahmāham ity eva matiḥ sadā ''tmani

[162] 'A thoughtless person identifies himself with the body, an educated person identifies himself with body and soul, a great soul (mahātmā) possessed of discriminative knowledge ever has the conviction in himself "I am the Absolute".

atrātma-buddhiṃ tyaja mūḍha-buddhe
tvaṅ-māṃsa-medo-'sthi-purīṣa-rāśau
sarvātmani brahmaṇi nirvikalpe
kuruṣva śāntiṃ paramāṃ bhajasva

[163] 'Therefore, O man of confused mind, give up identifying yourself with a mass of skin, flesh, marrow, bones and excrement. Identify yourself with the Absolute, the Self of all, void of all fluctuations of the mind. Enjoy the supreme peace.

dehendriyādāv asati bhramoditāṃ
vidvān ahaṃtāṃ na jahāti yāvat
tāvan na tasyāsti vimukti-vārtā
'pyastv eṣa vedānta-nayānta-darśī

[164] 'One may be possessed of learning, but as long as one has not given up self-identification with the body and senses born of error, he will not acquire liberation, even though he be thoroughly acquainted with the texts of the Upanishads and the ethical teaching.

chāyā-śarīre pratibimba-gātre
yat svapna-dehe hṛdi kalpitāṅge
yathātma-buddhis tava nāsti kācij
jīvac-charīre ca tathaiva mā 'stu

[165] 'One does not identify oneself with one's shadow or reflection, one's dream-body, or one's body as imagined in the mind. And one should not identify oneself with one's living body either.

dehātma-dhīr eva nṛṇām asad-dhiyāṃ
janmādi-duḥkha-prabhavasya bījam
yatas tatas tvaṃ jahi tāṃ prayatnāt
tyakte tu citte na punar bhavāśā

[166] 'Self-identification with the body is the cause which produces the sufferings of birth, death, disease and so on, of people whose minds are set on the unreal. Hence you should make strenuous efforts to give up this self-identification. When one has done so, there is no question of further rebirth.

28. The sheath of the vital energy

The next sheath is the vital sheath (prana-maya kosha), made up of the five vital airs.

karmendriyaiḥ pañcabhir añcito 'yaṃ
prāṇo bhavet prāṇa-mayas tu kośaḥ
yenātmavān anna-mayo 'nna-pūrṇaḥ
pravartate 'sau sakala-kriyāsu

[167] 'The sheath of the vital energy is the vital energy associated with the five powers of action (speaking, holding, moving about, excretion and procreation). It is that which ensouls the physical body, filled with food, and enables it to engage in all its actions.

This is called the sheath of vital energy (prana-maya kosha) because it is constantly moving, constantly acting (it is 60% rajas and, say,

20% sattva and the remaining 20% tamas). The blood, cells and heart are all in constant silent motion, and this is carried on by the five vital airs in conjunction with the five organs of action, which together constitute the vital sheath.

naivātmā 'pi prāṇa-mayo vāyu-vikāro
gantā ''gantā vāyu-vad antar bahir eṣaḥ
yasmāt kiñcit kvāpi na vettīṣṭam aniṣṭaṃ
svaṃ vānyaṃ vā kiñcana nityaṃ paratantraḥ

[168] 'The sheath of vital energy is not the Self either. It is a modification of the wind-element, which comes and goes in and out of the body. It has no knowledge anywhere of anything desirable or undesirable, no knowledge either of itself or of another, ever under others' control.

29. The sheath of the lower mind

jñānendriyāṇi ca manaś ca mano-mayaḥ syāt
kośo mamāham iti vastu-vikalpa-hetuḥ
saṃjñādi-bheda-kalanā-kalito balīyāṃs
tat-pūrva-kośam abhipūrya vijṛmbhate yaḥ

[169] 'The sense-organs and the lower mind form the sheath of the lower mind which produces various ideas about things, associating them with the ideas of "I" and "mine". It has the power of introducing differentiation through names and so on, is powerful, and expands to fill the sheath of vital energy from within.

After the vital sheath comes the mental sheath (mano-maya kosha), the (lower) mind. You may say: 'In the lower forms of life, mind cannot be distinguished from vitality. In the amoeba, there is only motion, and even fishes have no mind'. But this is difficult to prove and it is a fallacy to assume that there can be life where there is no mind—the mental sheath (mano-maya kosha) is also there. In man, this is the thinking principle which contains the five organs of perception. Remember that without the senses of sight and hearing, the eyes do not see and the ears do not hear. When you are cooking, the process goes on in a pot, but the pot is not the process of cooking; similarly, it is the mind that receives the reports of the senses. The reports come through the eyes and ears and go to the mind, called the inner sense (antahkarana) in contrast to the eyes, ears and so forth which constitute the outer senses.

The ray of the light of the Lord becomes individualized when it is covered by the five sheaths. The mental sheath—the mind together with the senses—is the cause of diversity, because individualization means both loss of feeling one's identity with the supreme Spirit and also false identification with one's environment: 'I am this or that', 'I am Chinese, a learned man, a rich man' and so on.

The Lord says in the *Gita*: 'The mind is powerful' (6.35). It is powerful in creating obstructions, but also in removing them. It can create as well as destroy. Wrongly used, it produces harmful poisons; but when correctly used, it becomes a mighty liberating force. It manifests itself by permeating the vital sheath and expressing itself through life.

pañcendriyaiḥ pañcabhir eva hotṛbhiḥ
pracīyamāno viṣayājya-dhārayā
jājvalyamāno bahu-vāsanendhanair
mano-mayāgnir dahati prapañcam

[170] 'The sheath of the lower mind is a sacrificial fire burning up (dahati) the world (or 'supporting the world', reading vahati), its flames rising high through the various kinds of impressions (vāsanās) as fuel, stoked up with a flow of objects for sacrificial butter by the five sense-organs as priests.

To plunge into any lust is equivalent to throwing hay into a burning fire; the flames become momentarily stifled, but then they blaze up again with greater intensity and fury.

Just as the mind creates variety, so it can also create unity and non-duality. The use we make of the mind is responsible for the production of joys and sufferings.

na hy asty avidyā manaso 'tiriktā
mano hy avidyā bhava-bandha-hetuḥ
tasmin vinaṣṭe sakalaṃ vinaṣṭaṃ
vijṛmbhite 'smin sakalaṃ vijṛmbhate

[171] 'For there is no ignorance apart from the mind; the mind is that ignorance which causes the bondage of repeated births in the world. When the mind is destroyed, all else is destroyed, and when the mind continues to manifest, all else manifests.

The mind is not destroyed in the way in which the body is destroyed, but reincarnates. When the mind manifests, all manifests. 'When mind is destroyed, all else is destroyed' means that the mind can be evaporated by being exposed to the light of God. In the rules of warfare laid down by the traditional texts (smriti), it says: 'When the enemy turns his back and runs away, do not follow him. Do not strike the aged. Do not deprive the enemy of his means of livelihood, and when he surrenders, treat him as your child'. When the mind is 'destroyed', the instinctive part is withdrawn into the intellect (buddhi). There it becomes more rarefied, and is absorbed, becoming united with cosmic nescience (mulavidya). It ceases to exist as a separate entity, and the ray—which believed itself bound—becomes free. 'Destruction' of the mind means surrender of the mind to the Lord.

This is what is happening in the waking state. But there are three states through which man passes every day—waking, dreaming and dreamless sleep. We have to account for what happens in the dreaming and dreamless sleep states also.

svapne 'rtha-śūnye sṛjati sva-śaktyā
bhoktrādi-viśvaṃ mana eva sarvaṃ
tathaiva jāgraty api no viśeṣas
tat sarvam etan manaso vijṛmbhaṇam

> [172] 'In the dream-state, where there are no external objects, the mind alone projects a whole world, beginning with an experiencer and including his experience and its objects. And there is no difference in the waking state. Everything there also is the play of the mind.

In sleep, the mind, having no actual contact with the outer world, creates a whole dream universe. And in each and every dream you, the dreamer, are a participator, an actor. Who creates the dream world? The mind. So, in the waking condition also, the mind creates this world. From the spiritual point of view there is no difference. All this creation by the mind, of virtue and vice, gods and temples, religions and other things, is no better than a dream.

When do you know that a dream was a dream? When you are awake again. So also, when we awaken in samadhi, we come to know this experience of all the sages. You will come to know this.

All this phenomenal universe is a projection of the mind. It is the mind which creates a picture in which these passing phenomena are called friends and foes. Where is the late King George V today? Where is the gaiety of pre-war London? Nothing but a dream!

The spiritual life begins with the assumption that there is no real difference between the waking and dream states.

suṣupti-kāle manasi pralīne
naivāsti kiñcit sakala-prasiddheḥ
ato manaḥ-kalpita eva puṃsaḥ
saṃsāra etasya na vastuto 'sti

> [173] 'At the time of dreamless sleep, the mind is dissolved, and, as everyone knows, nothing (external) then exists. Hence man's world of experience in reincarnation is imagined by the mind and does not really exist.

In dreamless sleep the mind is absorbed in its cause and the world disappears. If the objects of the world were real, they would appear also in dreamless sleep. They do not, hence they are a creation of the mind.

vāyunā ''nīyate meghaḥ punas tenaiva nīyate
manasā kalpyate bandho mokṣas tenaiva kalpyate

[174] 'A cloud is first brought by the wind and then led away by the wind. In the same way, bondage is first imagined by the mind and then liberation is imagined by the mind.

The wind gathers clouds together and the wind dispels them; similarly, the mind creates bondage and the mind gives freedom. All concepts of God (Christ, holiness and so forth) are creations of the mind and nothing more.

How this is done is explained in the following stanzas.

dehādi-sarva-viṣaye parikalpya rāgaṃ
badhnāti tena puruṣaṃ paśuvad guṇena
vairasyam atra viṣavat suvidhāya paścād
enaṃ vimocayati tan mana eva bandhāt

[175] 'First the mind contrives attachment for the body and all objects. In this way, it binds the soul as an animal is bound by a leash. Then afterwards, the mind creates distaste for the objects, as if they were poison, and thereby releases the soul from bondage.

In Shakespeare's *Othello*, Desdemona, while hearing the perorations of the Moor, created attachment for him, becoming his slave. The same hand given to her in marriage asphyxiated her on the bridal bed. If you want to make a man your enemy, harbour attachment for him. Show him: 'I can't do without you' if you want to be maltreated and cast into the quagmire of despair. The same mind creates attraction and distaste for the objects of the senses. As a fly is caught in honey, so the mind is caught in attractions; and then the mind begins to feel reaction and to think they are poison because it finds itself in bondage.

The Spirit, the light behind the mind, is merely the Witness of the drama. Before discovering this, you have to do some solid thinking and you may not like it; but an enquirer into truth has to put away likes and dislikes. Truth is irrespective of likes and dislikes. A would-be enquirer into truth must put his likes and dislikes in a casket and lock it, and then only can he become an enquirer.

What is the result of all this reasoning?

tasmān manaḥ kāraṇam asya jantor
bandhasya mokṣasya ca vā vidhāne
bandhasya hetur malinaṃ rajo-guṇair
mokṣasya śuddhaṃ virajas-tamaskam

> [176] 'Thus it is the mind which brings about the soul's bondage and also its release. It is the cause of bondage when it is sullied by the attributes (or bonds)[1] of rajas, and a cause of liberation when it is pure and free from rajas and tamas.

Do we like to be bound? You will say 'No'. If you have read Aeschylus' drama *Prometheus Bound*, would any of you like to exchange places with Prometheus? Who would be a Hamlet? No one. You would rather be a Romeo. But each Romeo and Juliet may become a Samson and Delilah. A mind overpowered by lethargy and by desires, by tamas and rajas, constitutes a bondage.

Lethargy towards what? Knowledge of truth. I wonder if, when death holds you by the hair and drags you to the abyss, you will say: 'I must go to the office'? There is time for everything except coming to God! This is tamas. The great enemy of man is inertia, always to find an excuse to run away from devotion, meditation and study.

Desires for what? For more money, power, conquest of fresh fields every day. That is the second great enemy. One desire leads to another, until death comes, from whom you cannot escape.

1 guṇa means both 'attribute' and 'that which binds'. cp. commentary to v.112.

viveka-vairāgya-guṇātirekāc
 chuddhatvam āsādya mano vimuktyai
bhavaty ato buddhimato mumukṣos
 tābhyāṃ dṛḍhābhyāṃ bhavitavyam agre

[177] 'When the mind is pure through an abundance of the attributes of discrimination and detachment, it makes for liberation. So the wise and sincere seeker of liberation pursues firm discrimination and detachment as his first task.

In order for Spirit to realize itself, the rays of the Spirit passing through the mind assume the characteristics of the mind, just as the light of the sun passing through differently coloured glasses becomes red, blue and so forth. There is no difference in the ray, only in the medium. So also, fundamentally, there is no difference between a saint and a sinner; the difference is in the mode of expression of the divine ray in the mind. All differences are due to the quality of the mind. In *Yoga Vasishtha*, holy Vasishtha says: 'O Ramaji, the world is a creation of the mind and it shares the qualities and characteristics of the mind'.

Why is one a saint and another a sinner? The answer is, one has a purified mind in which equanimity (sattva) predominates and the other an impure mind ruled by passion (rajas) and inertia (tamas). Through one the spiritual light flows remaining untainted, through the other it becomes tainted and limited.

What should we do? How should we live? The answer is: purify your mind. Avoid any association, any friendship, any book which is useless or harmful. Welcome any association according to its beneficial effect on the mind, the extent to which it purifies and uplifts the mind, makes it independent of the senses and sense-joys and lets it rise above the trivial joys of love of power and sex and so forth.

You cannot write a letter on horse-back and you cannot purify the mind unless it is stilled. A mind that has no depth, longs for company and is stupid, must be transformed through tranquillization. The emperor Napoleon is reported to have said: 'My mind is like a chest full of drawers which I can open and close at will'. Thus should we be masters of our minds.

The mind can be taught at any age. The writer had a friend in China who began the study of medicine at the age of sixty. After five years he passed his examinations, coming out first. All we have to do is to make a resolution and to keep to it. This must be undertaken whole-heartedly. Nothing can be achieved by being luke-warm or by saying: 'It is so difficult!' Courage is that modification of the mind which loves to wrestle with impediments and rejoices in overcoming them.

If we want to live life spiritually we must still the mind, then purify it, and then the ray of the Lord will reflect itself clearly. Then a man becomes a man of peace and wisdom, a saint, a rishi. How shall we purify it? Curtailment of desires, harbouring only spiritual ones, is the way to purification of the mind. Annihilation of all desires by exercising the power of spiritual discrimination (viveka) brings about the achievement of sainthood.

Our life should be consciously directed towards the lighthouse of divine knowledge. Such a life must have a lantern and a staff. The lantern is discrimination (viveka), the staff is detachment (vairagya). Vairagya means indifference to the objects of the world, the conviction that the spiritual truth is a fact and that the objects of the world are illusory. In the *Ramayana* we are told how the whole capital of Ayodhya was ablaze with light to welcome the installation of holy Rama as Emperor of India. Yet overnight he went into banishment for fourteen years, living on roots and fruits, sleeping on banks and never entering a town. Tulsi Dasa says: 'Reverence to the holy feet of Rama, who in all conditions remained the same, unmoved, unagitated'. This is detachment (vairagya).

mano nāma mahā-vyāghro viṣayāraṇya-bhūmiṣu
caraty atra na gacchantu sādhavo ye mumukṣavaḥ

> [178] 'The mind is like a great tiger prowling about in the glades of the forest of sense-objects. Therefore good souls who seek liberation should not visit that forest.

The meaning is, let not the wise—those who want to watch their minds—wander in the forest of sense-pleasures where there is no clear track. Let them beware, and not be associated with such a mind.

manaḥ prasūte viṣayān aśeṣān
sthūlātmanā sūksmatayā ca bhoktuḥ
śarīra-varṇāśrama-jāti-bhedān
guṇa-kriyā-hetu-phalāni nityam

> [179] 'It is the mind that ever brings forth for the experiencer all objects, gross and subtle, along with his body, differing in each case according to caste, stage of life and clan—as well as all causes and effects, acts and attributes.

What is the world, this table, friend, wife, anything objective? What is subject? Subject is subject only if face to face with objects. If everything objective is removed, then subject becomes the light of Consciousness or Spirit and the objects a form of illusion superimposed on it.

The subject is but a conditioned form of Consciousness. The divine ray in the human mind becomes all you see, just as the light in a magic-lantern shows the impressions of objects on a canvas screen, revealing rocks, mountains and so on. Are these objects really on the canvas? No. They are projected onto the canvas and the canvas reveals them, but is untouched by them. The canvas represents the light of Consciousness on which the mind, when lit by it, projects the pictures, or impressions, of causes and effects, acts and attributes. The mind is the magic-lantern, the intellect is the slide inserted, and the experiencer of the impressions is the individualized form of the divine light.

The divine ray in man, the Spirit, is the real subject, the

experiencer of joy and sorrow, of the sea of calm and storm. All these pictures created by the mind are lit by the ray of Consciousness or Spirit, and the mind reports them to the Spirit. As Vasishtha says: 'The whole world is a creation of the mind', but only a purified mind will understand it thus. A drunken man's judgement is unreliable, and the mind, when it is intoxicated with nescience, is even less reliable.

The mind creates 'all objects, gross and subtle', that is, whether experienced in the waking or the dreaming condition. Metaphysically there is very little difference between the two: both are temporary and passing. During the dreaming condition, mountains and other objects appear real, but on awakening they are known to be dreams. During the waking condition, objects appear real, eternal, but in samadhi or ecstasy—the condition of spiritual enlightenment—the world is seen in its true light, its true nature. Plotinus experienced it seven times—it is a state of super-consciousness.

A few seconds before death the mind realizes: 'All I have heard was a novel, fiction, all I have seen was a magic show'. The Quran says: 'All is unreal except Allah'. The name and the named are the same. Such ideas as 'I am learned, he is foolish' are meaningless and have no reality attached to them. Therefore wake up! See the fifth and sixth dimensions, the super-normal condition, samadhi or 'the Kingdom of Heaven'. Then the truth will be known and the world (jagat), being passing and transient, will be realized to be a creation of the mind.

asaṅga-cid-rūpam amuṃ vimohya
dehendriya-prāṇa-guṇair nibadhya
ahaṃ mameti bhramayaty ajasraṃ
manaḥ sva-kṛtyeṣu phalopabhuktiṣu

[180] 'The mind puts this pure relationless Consciousness under delusion and binds it with the thongs of body, senses and vital energy. It keeps the soul wandering in error, experiencing the karmic results of its former deeds with the feelings of "I" and "mine".

Why does the Spirit make this mistake? It is not the Spirit but the mind which does so. Suppose you were to see a sunset, say in Mongolia, seeing glorious colours and shapes and experiencing a wonderful peace and stillness. What is their origin? The sun might say: 'It is I who am setting!' Yet it never sets. So it is with the mind. It is deluded due to nescience (avidya). This is a fact which cannot be disputed.

Nescience expresses itself through the greatest philosophers as well as through the simplest souls as: 'I do not know'. Newton, one of the greatest intellects, said: 'I seem to have been only like a boy, playing on the sea-shore, and diverting myself in now and then finding a smoother pebble or a prettier shell than ordinary, while the great ocean of truth lay all undiscovered before me'. The more we know, the more we discover that we do not know. So is the individualized consciousness deluded by nescience.

The holy Acharya reminds us again and again that the chief medium through which the divine life expresses itself is the mind and that as the mind is, so is life. If the mind is impure, thoughts are impure and actions confused. An impure mind is full of desires. The chief function of the mind is finding the means of fulfilling these desires. Even some good desires may produce disharmony; all desires, as such, are impediments to freedom. Impelled by desires, one performs actions and accumulates karma. Many desires are unconscious. Though asleep, they may revive at a particular moment and sprout forth. The subconscious or causal body contains millions of impressions, called in the psychology of Freud 'repressions'. According to the Lord in the *Gita*, desire is the greatest enemy of man (3.37).

You will say: 'What about the desire to help others?' It is the Lord who helps, and the duty of man is to make himself a fit instrument to be used by the Lord. To have no individual expectations, hopes or desires is the way to happiness. Therefore the spiritual life begins with subduing harmful lower desires, prompted by passion (rajas) and lethargy (tamas), by means of higher sattvic desires. The only object of goodness (sattva) is to prevent evil in the form of sloth and inertia, passion and ambition. A pure mind is one which has fewer and fewer desires. In the holy philosophy, purification of the mind means to say 'No' to harmful desires and to dedicate the heart to the Lord. Then all desires take wings.

adhyāsa-doṣāt puruṣasya saṃsṛtir
adhyāsa-bandhas tv amunaiva kalpitaḥ
rajas-tamo-doṣavato 'vivekino
janmādi-duḥkhasya nidānam etat

[181] 'Man's reincarnation is due to the error of superimposition, and the bondage of superimposition is imagined by the mind alone. This is the cause of the sufferings of birth, death, disease and so on in the case of one who lacks discrimination and is afflicted with the evils "rajas" and "tamas".

It is said that unless a man refines, elevates and purifies his life, he will be born again and again as a man or an animal. Man's transmigration is due to superimposition, which means to see a thing differently from what it is. The world is fundamentally nothing but electro-magnetic flashes of consciousness and to think of it as something belonging to us, something to acquire and so forth, is a delusion and the cause of rebirth.

ataḥ prāhur mano 'vidyāṃ paṇḍitās tattva-darśinaḥ
yenaiva bhrāmyate viśvaṃ vāyunevābhra-maṇḍalam

[182] 'That is why the wise who know the metaphysical truth say that the mind is that metaphysical ignorance whereby the world is kept in motion, as the wind drives on the clouds in the sky.

Where does the error lie? In the mind, in ignorance, want of discrimination. Wherever this discrimination is absent, it causes frustration of the evolution of the soul, which is thrust back to learn further lessons.

tan manaḥ-śodhanaṃ kāryaṃ prayatnena mumukṣuṇā
viśuddhe sati caitasmin muktiḥ kara-phalayate

> [183] 'Therefore the one who truly desires liberation should make strenuous efforts to purify his mind. When the mind is purified, liberation will come to him like a fruit held in the palm of his hand.

At school we are taught to have ambitions, to become owners of fleets of ships and so forth. Let education change and let man be taught wisdom—purification, not repression, of desires. When desires, instead of being repressed, are sublimated, then we learn how to live well. Let us understand that mind is a detail, and learn how to live for the grand purpose of life by finding the Lord within through devotion and knowledge.

mokṣaika-saktyā viṣayeṣu rāgaṃ
nirmūlya saṃnyasya ca sarva-karma
sac-chraddhayā yaḥ śravaṇādi-niṣṭho
rajaḥ-svabhāvaṃ sa dhunoti buddheḥ

> [184] 'He who roots out attachment for objects through becoming attached solely to the pursuit of liberation, and who gives up all self-interested action, entirely absorbed in hearing, pondering over and sustained meditation on the metaphysical texts of the Veda in a spirit of true faith, rids the mind of its character of rajas.

There should be a perpetual and dominating yearning to be free, not just a mere desire. We live in order to be free. The corollary is that we must give up all love for sense-objects whilst recognizing our need of them for adequate maintenance of the body. Why? Because otherwise the energy which is to be transformed into a liberating force is wasted in devotion to their pursuit and we become more attached and so bound tighter and tighter to them.

There must be a yearning for freedom producing a conquest of the love for sense-objects. This is its negative aspect. Its positive aspect is to be devoted with faith to the teachings of the scriptures. Attendance at meetings is useless and life is a show of hypocrisy, if we restrict it to merely hearing the truth and do not let it affect the soul and live accordingly. No salvation is possible through mere hearing; no hungry man can appease his hunger by eating an imaginary dinner of seventy courses.

Doubts are legitimate up to a point, but when they are resolved they should not be considered again. If they crop up again, they should be dispelled with determination and no further argument. Shri Shankara says: 'When once conviction is reached about the path, the teacher and the discipline, let all doubts go and do not let the mind be swayed again'. A vacillating mind acquires nothing in this life. Where one allows doubts and suspicions, there one digs one's own grave. Poise and balance is indicative of peace and of a mind devoted to wisdom. Love is the expression of a mind in its normal condition. The perfect state of mind is one of peace, poise and ceaseless contemplation, in quietude, of the highest principle, God.

Desires are born of the attribute of rajas and constitute heavy chains which bind the soul, and do not let the tiny ray of inner light transform itself into the conflagration of omniscience. No lasting rest and satisfaction is possible to a mind which is uncontrolled and has not been purged of desires and restlessness. We should live for freedom for everybody, not only for ourselves at the expense of others. The one great difference between the philosophy of Socrates and of those Greek philosophers who came before him was that Socrates insisted on purity of the heart and intellect, and on virtue. That alone is knowledge which inclines our hearts to the good of all.

mano-mayo nāpi bhavet parātmā
hy ādy-anta-vattvāt pariṇāmi-bhāvāt
duḥkhātmakatvād viṣayatva-hetor
draṣṭā hi dṛśyātmatayā na dṛṣṭaḥ

[185] 'Indeed, the sheath of the lower mind could never be the supreme Self. It has a beginning and an end. It is subject to change. It is of the nature of pain. It is a perceived object. The seer (the ultimate Witness) can never be perceived as an object.

A great error prevails in the West. They think that mind is Spirit. Shri Shankara in his commentaries produces strong arguments to show that the mind is a tool in the hands of the individual soul (jiva). The transcendent Self (atman) is not the mind because the mind is an object of the inner Consciousness, an evolute of matter which is mortal and is constantly changing. The mind is naturally the womb of pain since all that is changeable is painful. Those depending on the mind are like people living in a house of soot who constantly get soiled by soot. Whose mind has ever brought him peace? There is only one principle which is above change and that is the ultimate Reality. In Him alone is perfect peace and rest. Bliss is the nature of the Self (atman). Sometimes a ray of it passes through the realm of mind, and the soul experiences a passing joy or pleasure. Peace comes from the Lord alone, and unless the mind is directed towards Him through self-control, devotion and meditation, peace is a fugitive bird which never really materializes, and our life is a series of expectant moments and no more.

30. The sheath of the higher mind

buddhir buddhīndriyaiḥ sārdhaṃ sa-vṛttiḥ kartṛ-lakṣaṇaḥ
vijñāna-maya-kośaḥ syāt puṃsaḥ saṃsāra-kāraṇam

[186] 'The sheath of the higher mind consists of the higher mind itself with its modifications, along with the sense-organs and their modifications. It is the performer of action and the cause of the soul's reincarnation.

What is the transmigrating element in the human personality? What is it that leaves the body at death? What is the cause of transmigratory life (sansara), that which is constantly changing? It is the spiritual element or higher part of the mind called buddhi. This is the peak of the intellect closest to the conscious Self (atman), along with its modifications, egoism and so forth, and the organs of knowledge, which appears to be an agent and forms the knowledge-sheath (vijnana-maya kosha).

anuvrajac-cit-pratibimba-śaktir
vijñāna-saṃjñaḥ prakṛter vikāraḥ
jñāna-kriyāvān aham ity ajasraṃ
dehendriyādiṣv abhimanyate bhṛśam

[187] 'It is a modification of Nature called 'knowledge' (vijñāna), being a power of knowledge consisting of a reflection of Consciousness in the higher mind, to whose modifications it conforms. It is continually identified with the body, the sense-organs and so on, with the stark feeling "I am the one who has this knowledge" and "I am the one who does this action".

Now comes the question: who is bound and who is freed? God is not bound or deluded. What is that element that has suffered this illusion and imagines itself bound? The reply is as follows:

Imagine a million patches of cloud stretching from horizon to horizon, each patch having five layers in which each layer is finer than the one below. Imagine the rays of the sun illumining and penetrating these clouds, endowing each patch with movement—mental as well as physical—and you have a picture of the relation of beings to the Lord omniscient and omnipotent. The shining forth of the light of the sun in each patch of cloud, though it is not different from the sun, depends for its manifestation on the cloud; if there were no cloud there would be no shining forth. That which thinks through the mind, desires and wills, enjoys and suffers, sleeps and awakens, is a ray of the divine Sun which is temporarily deluded and identifies itself with the five layers or sheaths through which it shines forth. The fourth layer or sheath is made up of intellect which, on account of its rarefied state, produces an intelligence of its own.

anādi-kālo 'yam ahaṃ-svabhāvo
 jīvaḥ samasta-vyavahāra-voḍhā
karoti karmāṇy api pūrva-vāsanaḥ
 puṇyāny apuṇyāni ca tat-phalāni

> [188] 'It is indeed the individual soul, beginningless in time, of the nature of (an individual) "I", the one who effects all practical dealings. Conditioned by impressions from previous lives, it performs meritorious and non-meritorious deeds and experiences their karmic results.

The individual soul (jiva) is the complex created by the light of the Sun on the fourth layer or sheath of cloud which assumes a vitality and movement of its own. St Paul says that man is a triple alliance of body, mind and spirit, and this knowledge-sheath is what he calls 'spirit' and what, in common parlance, is called the soul. It is without beginning because the Lord, whose ray it is, is beyond time and space.

The soul has one power, that of identifying itself with objects or disidentifying itself from them. It is its nature to be identified with something; this is the meaning of 'falling in love', becoming identified with an object of love. So the soul can identify itself either with a modification of Nature (prakriti) or with the Lord, but it cannot remain disidentified. The wise man is he who is identified with art and beauty and with the Lord. The climax of love is when the lover and beloved are one, for love admits of no difference. For a sentient being, self-identification is natural.

What is the characteristic of the soul? Egoism (ahamkara). It carries out all its functions on the relative plane, performing good and evil actions and experiencing their results. Whatever we think, say and hear leaves a photographic impression, or samskara, on this sheath, and man's character-to-be is the aggregate of these impressions. Therefore we must be extremely careful as to what we think and do. Nothing is wasted, and the Lord is the dispenser of this karma. When the body becomes unfit, the soul leaves it and, after a long process, it transmigrates again, as described in the third chapter of the *Vedanta Sutras*.

bhuṅkte vicitrāsv api yoniṣu vrajann
āyāti niryāty adha ūrdhvam eṣaḥ
asyaiva vijñāna-mayasya jāgrat-
svapnādy-avasthāḥ sukha-duḥkha-bhogaḥ

[189] 'It comes and goes in different lives, rising up or sinking down in variegated wombs. To this sheath of higher knowledge belong the states of waking, dream and so on (including dreamless sleep, mystical trance and swoon). It is the one who experiences pleasure and pain.

Through desires and actions, the soul comes and goes in various bodies, human or animal, and it is through this knowledge-sheath that the individual soul experiences grief and joy, sleeps and awakens.

dehādi-niṣṭhāśrama-dharma-karma-
guṇābhimānaṃ satataṃ mameti
vijñāna-kośo 'yam ati-prakāśaḥ
prakṛṣṭa-sānnidhya-vaśāt parātmanaḥ
ato bhavaty eṣa upādhir asya
yad-ātma-dhīḥ saṃsarati bhrameṇa

[190] 'The sheath of the higher mind always identifies itself with the duties, rituals and attributes of the various stages of life, which in fact pertain to the body. Because of its extreme proximity to the highest Self, it is highly luminous. It is the natural apparent conditioning adjunct of the Self, by identifying with which a person undergoes reincarnation through error.

It is through this sheath that the soul either runs after passing things or comes to Yoga to be freed. Freedom can only be effected in this world. Therefore let the soul rise from slavery to the senses, race prejudice and so forth, and look up to the Lord.

31. How the Self is untouched by its apparent conditioning adjuncts (upādhi)

yo 'yam vijñāna-mayaḥ prāṇeṣu hṛdi sphurat-svayaṃ-jyotiḥ
kūṭasthaḥ sann ātmā kartā bhoktā bhavaty upādhi-sthaḥ

[191] 'That self-luminous principle of Consciousness, manifesting in the midst of the sense-organs in the heart, though the rock-firm and changeless Self, becomes (apparently) a performer of action and an individual experiencer in the midst of the apparent conditioning adjuncts.

There are three worlds: matter, mind and Spirit. God in His totality is called Spirit, and in the individual form, He is the human soul. It is one and the same thing. As the Atlantic Ocean narrowed between England and France is called 'the Channel', so the Lord omniscient, omnipotent and ever-compassionate, is called the individual soul (jiva) when He apparently limits Himself.

The world of matter is in a state of constant flux—this is the meaning of its Sanskrit name 'sansara', the ever-changing. The Greek philosopher Heraclitus said that you cannot bathe in the same river twice. Where are the holy saints of the past, the authors of great systems of philosophy such as Kant, the great composers like Beethoven?

These three worlds of matter, mind and Spirit are not like layers; they interpenetrate one another. The world of the mind observes through the senses the world of matter and creates out of it new horizons, earths and heavens. It consists of our desires, thoughts, loves, hates, ideals and urges or impulses. The world of Spirit is a world of light under which matter is seen and mind observed—not physical light but 'That Light which lights up the mind, by whose power the mind functions, who dwells in the mind and whom the mind does not know' (*Brihadaranyaka Upanishad* 3.7.22). That is the Lord omniscient, omnipotent and omnipresent, the world of Spirit.

svayaṃ paricchedam upetya buddhes
tādātmya-doṣeṇa paraṃ mṛṣātmanaḥ
sarvātmakaḥ sann api vīkṣate svayaṃ
svataḥ pṛthaktvena mṛdo ghaṭān iva

> [192] 'Assuming limitation through the error of self-identification with that totally unreal entity the higher mind, the Self, though in truth the Self of all, sees itself as different from itself, as if it were seeing pots and supposing them to be different from the clay from which they were made.

The soul (jiva) is entangled with the mind. The soul has self-consciousness; the mind is not self-conscious. 'I am' is the self-consciousness of the soul and it is attributable to the Self (atman).

How is this tangle between the soul and the mind to be resolved? Who can free us from our sufferings once and for ever? We ourselves. Of course the deciding factor is the grace of God; but that grace is available to all who make serious, sustained and determined attempts to free themselves from lust.

Forgetfulness of the important fact that 'I am the Spirit' creates the phantoms of suffering, limitations and a world which grinds the soul into the powder of lassitude and want of faith. A man is dead when he has no faith, not necessarily when the heart ceases to beat. There must be faith in oneself—in the holy truth that 'I am Spirit; the body and mind are my instruments and not my Self'. How this faith can be verified is the burden of the true philosophy called Yoga or, in a wider sense, religion.

upādhi-sambandha-vaśāt parātmā
hy upādhi-dharmān anu bhāti tad-guṇaḥ
ayo-vikārān avikāri vahnivat

sadaika-rūpo 'pi paraḥ svabhāvāt

[193] 'Through seeming to be related to its apparent limiting adjuncts, the supreme Self appears to conform to their nature and assume their attributes. Though the supreme ever remains the same in its true nature, it appears to conform to the nature of its changing conditioning adjuncts as the fire in a red-hot lump of iron appears to undergo the changes undergone by the lump (while remaining unaltered in its true nature as fire)'.

As the *Brihadaranyaka Upanishad* says: 'A man is what he thinks himself to be' (4.4.5). If he believes himself to be weak, mortal and perishable—which, fundamentally, he can never be—then he is weak, mortal and a prey to all sufferings. Spiritual ignorance (avidya) is not want of knowledge, but erroneous knowledge. Lack of knowledge is not hurtful, but erroneous knowledge is.

Now you will understand why we say: 'Remember God'. It is most vital that we should do so. Epictetus said: 'Think of God more often than you breathe!' In Him there are no afflictions or suffering, but perennial bliss that we cannot experience except by His grace. Remember Him in your heart. All other forms of remembrance are preliminary, but if you feel and meditate on Him in the form 'Thou art my own Self', you will one day feel the throb of Infinity and be free.

The real life is the life of the saints of God who, by controlling their passions, lusts and emotions, have created a vacuum in the mind, uniting themselves with the cosmic Self—the ray uniting itself with the Sun.

32. Self-knowledge is the sole means to liberation

śiṣya uvāca
bhrameṇāpy anyathā vā 'stu jīva-bhāvaḥ parātmanaḥ
tad-upādher anāditvān nānāder nāśa iṣyate

[194] The pupil said: 'Whether it is by delusion or otherwise

that the supreme Self assumes the form of the individual soul, its conditioning adjunct is beginningless, and it is generally maintained that what is beginningless cannot be destroyed.

ato 'sya jīva-bhāvo 'pi nityā bhavati saṃsṛtiḥ
na nivarteta tan-mokṣaḥ kathaṃ me śrī-guro vada

[195] 'So the state of the Self as individual soul is eternal reincarnation. It will never come to an end. Tell me, O revered Teacher, how can I attain liberation from this state?'

Our life, our view of history, our understanding of the law of cause and effect are dismally incomplete before our heart is lit by the discovery of God. Our whole life is a tangle which we have to unravel. If I tie a knot around my finger with this handkerchief, I am forming a knot between the sentient (my finger) and the insentient (my handkerchief). Such is our life: a knot is formed between the mind and God. Under this knot, the ray of God, which is the essence of the human personality and is perfect and imperishable, is tied by the mind, which in itself is insentient, finite and full of suffering.

Speaking philosophically, this is called superimposition. Man imposes on his own nature, which is infinity and bliss, the mind which is finite and restless. If it is accepted that this illusion is beginningless and consequently without an end, must not the separate individuality (jivahood) of the soul continue for ever?

śrī-gurur uvāca
samyak pṛṣṭaṃ tvayā vidvan sāvadhānena tac chṛṇu
prāmāṇikī na bhavati bhrāntyā mohita-kalpanā

[196] The Guru replied: 'Your question was a good one, O wise soul. Listen carefully while I give you the answer. A piece of imagination wrought through error in delusion can never count as authoritative knowledge.

bhrāntiṃ vinā tv asaṅgasya niṣkriyasya nirākṛteḥ
na ghaṭetārtha-sambandho nabhaso nīlatādi-vat

[197] 'The relationless, actionless, formless Self cannot enter into relation with an object except through some error, like the colourless ether of the sky appearing blue.

The Absolute (brahman) has never become the individual (jiva). If it were a fact that God had forgotten His nature and thought Himself bound, the objection would be valid, but it is not so. It is merely imagined, and an imagined condition is not a fact. Suppose you put Herbert Spencer under hypnosis and told him he was a dog and he barked; the barking is not real because he has not in fact become a dog. Similarly God has not become bound in reality. There can be no real connection between that which is formless, unattached and untainted and the objective world, just as space has no real connection with the illusory blueness we see in it. The Self of man is never really bound; it is our intellect (buddhi) which considers itself bound or free, just as it is our eyes which conjure up the illusion that the sky is blue.

svasya draṣṭur nirguṇasyākriyasya
pratyag-bodhānanda-rūpasya buddheḥ
bhrāntyā prāpto jīva-bhāvo na satyo
mohāpāye nāsty avastu-svabhāvāt

[198] 'The Self, the Witness, actionless and without empirical attributes, of the nature of inmost Consciousness and Bliss, appears to have assumed the form of an individual soul on account of an error on the part of the mind. This form is unreal and, being unreal, no longer exists when metaphysical ignorance has been removed.

Bondage lies in the individual soul and 'individual soul' (jiva) means the intellect animated by the presence of the Lord. Suppose someone drew a dwarf or a goblin on these walls, it would only be revealed if the light were allowed to enter the room. Even so do these hallucinations of bondage and freedom appear in the intellect when it is animated by the divine ray of the Lord.

> yāvad bhrāntis tāvad evāsya sattā
> mithyājñānojjṛmbhitasya pramādāt
> rajjvāṃ sarpo bhrānti-kālīna eva
> bhrānter nāśe naiva sarpo 'pi tad-vat

> [199] 'It exists only as long as the error exists. It is a manifestation of erroneous knowledge arising from inattention to the truth. As the snake only lasts as long as one is in error over the rope and no longer exists when the error is removed, so does the individual soul cease to exist when there is knowledge of the Self.

A shepherd once found a newly-littered lion cub and cared for it, bringing it up with his sheep. It behaved like a sheep, bleating and eating grass, until one day a full-grown lion saw it. The lion took the cub to a well, showed it its reflection and convinced it of its real nature, whereupon the young lion began to roar and plunged into the forest and thereafter lived like its own kind. So the divine ray enclosed in the human personality, identifying itself with the mind, takes on itself the mind's changes and is unhappy. What is the object of philosophy and religion? The enlightenment of the divine ray in man so that it ceases to think 'I am a sheep' and knows itself to be a lion. The lion, which is the Divine, imagines itself to be a sheep, the mind; but by following certain practices it will realize that it is not.

What are those practices? They are called Adhyatma Yoga.

> anāditvam avidyāyāḥ kāryasyāpi tatheṣyate
> utpannāyāṃ tu vidyāyām āvidyakam anādy api
> prabodhe svapna-vat sarvaṃ saha-mūlaṃ vinaśyati
>
> anādy apīdaṃ no nityaṃ prāg-abhāva iva sphuṭaṃ
> anāder api vidhvaṃsaḥ prāg-abhāvasya vīkṣitaḥ

[200-201] 'Metaphysical ignorance and its effects are said to be beginningless. But when metaphysical knowledge has come, everything to do with ignorance, along with ignorance itself, comes to an end, like a dream after one wakes up. Though the state of being an individual soul is beginningless, it is clear that it is like the "non-existence before production" (of the Vaiśeṣikas). For a thing's non-existence before production, though beginningless, is seen to come to an end with the production of the thing.

yad buddhy-upādhi-sambandhāt parikalpitam ātmani
jīvatvaṃ na tato 'nyat tu svarūpeṇa vilakṣaṇam

[202] 'The state of being an individual soul is imagined in regard to the Self on account of a connection with the mind and other factors of the individual organism. But in its true nature the soul is not anything different[1] from the Self.

sambandhaḥ svātmano buddhyā mithyā-jñāna-puraḥsaraḥ
vinivṛttir bhavet tasya samyag-jñānena nānyathā

[203] 'The connection of the Self with the mind depends on erroneous knowledge, and that can be brought to an end by right knowledge only, and not otherwise.

brahmātmaikatva-vijñānaṃ samyag-jñānaṃ śruter matam

[204] 'It is the teaching of the Veda that knowledge of the identity of the Self with the Absolute is right knowledge.[2]

1 Reading 'anyat' and 'vilakṣaṇam' with Muni Lāl and Bhāgavat for 'anyas' and 'vilakṣaṇaḥ' of Mādhavānanda.

2 *Śvetāśvatara Upanishad* 6.15, etc.

tad ātmānātmanoḥ samyag-vivekenaiva sidhyati
tato vivekaḥ kartavyaḥ pratyagātmāsadātmanoḥ[1]

[205] 'That metaphysical knowledge comes only through a correct discrimination of Self and not-self. Therefore one should make a discrimination between the inmost Self and the unreal self.

jalaṃ paṅkavad atyantaṃ paṅkāpāye jalaṃ sphuṭam
yathā bhāti tathātmāpi doṣābhāve sphuṭa-prabhaḥ

[206] 'As muddy water is seen clearly to be water only when the mud has been removed, so does the Self shine out clearly when faulty views have been eliminated.

What is the mud? Ignorance—that is, erroneous knowledge. To say 'This is my house' or 'This is my relative' is ignorance. What is knowledge? That which is opposed to it. The way to tranquillize the mind is to cut out all selfishness and all anger and then to render it taintless.

asan-nivṛttau tu sadātmanā sphuṭaṃ
pratītir etasya bhavet pratīcaḥ
tato nirāsaḥ karaṇīya evā
'sad-ātmanaḥ sādhv ahamādi-vastunaḥ

[207] 'With the elimination of the untrue, this inmost Self manifests as the true Self. One must therefore thoroughly extirpate the unreal self,[2] beginning with the ego.

Intellect (buddhi) is the faculty of critical reflection and

1 'ātmāsad' = ātma + asad. Mādhavānanda reads 'sad' by what appears to be a rare slip.

2 Reading 'asad' for 'sad' with Muni Lāl and H.R. Bhāgavat.

discrimination, and the Self is reflected in it clearly. Self-analysis through introspection (vichara) is possible in the intellect, which leads ultimately to the cognition of identity. Purification of the intellect by study and practice of non-attachment (vairagya) and meditation is a great means to divine cognition.

ato nāyaṃ parātmā syād vijñāna-maya-śabda-bhāk
vikāritvāj jaḍatvāc ca paricchinnatva-hetutaḥ
dṛśyatvād vyabhicāritvān nānityo nitya iṣyate

[208] 'And so that which is called the sheath of the higher mind is not the supreme Self, because it is subject to change, because it is non-conscious and limited, because it is an object and because it is not invariably present. The impermanent should not be taken for the eternal.

The vital sheath (prana-maya kosha), mental sheath (mano-maya kosha) and knowledge sheath (vijnana-maya kosha) together form the subtle body.

33. The sheath of bliss

ānanda-pratibimba-cumbita-tanur vṛttis tamo-jṛmbhitā
syād ānanda-mayaḥ priyādi-guṇakaḥ sveṣṭārtha-lābhodayaḥ
puṇyasyānubhave vibhāti kṛtinām ānanda-rūpaḥ svayam
bhūtvā nandati yatra sādhu tanu-bhṛn-mātraḥ prayatnaṃ vinā

[209] 'The sheath of bliss is a modification of ignorance tinted (lit. kissed) by a reflection of the true bliss of the Absolute. It has the characteristics of joy, etc. (Taittirīya Upanishad 2.5) It arises on the acquisition of a desired object. Of the nature of bliss, it manifests in the case of fortunate souls when they experience the results of their meritorious actions. When it emerges, every embodied soul can feel true joy without effort.

Behind the bliss sheath is the innermost principle of all beings, Brahman (the Absolute), in its complete integrity. It is infinite peace and bliss. Through the impress of nescience (avidya) this innermost existence, the supreme Self, identified apparently with its outer coverings, or sheaths, appears as the seat of will, power and knowledge. But the Self (atman) within is pure Consciousness.

ānanda-maya-kośasya suṣuptau sphūrtir utkaṭā
svapna-jāgarayor īṣad iṣṭa-saṃdarśanādinā

[210] 'The sheath of bliss manifests pre-eminently in dreamless sleep. There is a slight manifestation of it in dream and waking at the vision of desirable objects and so on.

There is knowledge even in dreamless sleep. Just as you might say, 'I saw a performance of Hamlet today and the death of Ophelia was so touching', in the same way you are describing an experience when you say on waking up from dreamless sleep 'I slept so well, it was so very peaceful, I remember nothing'.

naivāyam ānanda-mayaḥ parātmā
sopādhikatvāt prakṛter vikārāt
kāryatva-hetoḥ sukṛta-kriyāyā
vikāra-saṅghāta-samāhitatvāt

[211] 'This sheath of bliss is not the supreme Self—because it is based on a merely apparent conditioning adjunct (upādhi), because it is a modification of Nature, because it is an effect, being the result of one's previous meritorious deeds, and because it is part of a complex of modifications (i.e., it is one of the series of sheaths, all of which are material, impermanent and so on).

pañcānām api kośānāṃ niṣedhe yuktitaḥ śruteḥ
tan-niṣedhāvadhiḥ sākṣī bodha-rūpo 'vaśiṣyate

[212] 'When the five sheaths have been negated by reasoning based on Vedic revelation, the point at which that negation has to stop is the Witness, which is left over standing as Consciousness.

We must go behind each of the sheaths to see the true Self (atman)—even behind the intellect and beyond our bliss consciousness in dreamless sleep. Bliss (ananda) is the *summum bonum*. It is not an attribute of Self; it is the being of Self. Bliss and Consciousness are one and the same.

yo 'yam ātmā svayaṃ-jyotiḥ pañca-kośa-vilakṣaṇaḥ
avasthā-traya-sākṣī san nirvikāro nirañjanaḥ
sadā ''nandaḥ sa vijñeyaḥ svātmatvena vipaścitā

[213] 'This self-luminous Self, different from the five sheaths, the Witness of the three states of waking, dream and dreamless sleep, changeless, taintless, eternal joy—that is what the wise person should realize to be his true Self'.

Bliss is identical with fullness of being. The conception of bliss is not psychological; it is metaphysical—to use the word in the sense of Aristotle. Bliss appears as divided when the expression of the Self (atman) is incomplete. It is not at all determined by the external senses; it is wholly and totally independent of matter (prakriti). 'Self is bliss' is declared by Shruti (the Upanishads).

The psychological experience of the not-self is the source of conditioned delight which passes away like the shadow of a cloud on the green hill. The Self is the source of unconditioned joy. It needs no object to give rise to it and no object to continue it. When the clouds of ignorance (avidya) have disappeared, it shines for ever. The Knower of Self (jnani) feels, 'I have been bliss always. What a joke that I thought I was not bliss!' To seek for the nature of the Self is to seek for bliss. Try this experiment now, and with determination.

34. The true nature of the Self

śisya uvāca

mithyātvena niṣiddheṣu kośeṣv eteṣu pañcasu
sarvābhāvaṃ vinā kiñcin na paśyāmy atra he guro
vijñeyam kimu vastv asti svātmanā ''tma-vipaścitā

[214] The pupil said: 'O Teacher, when the five sheaths have been rejected as unreal, I see nothing left over but the non-existence of all. What knowable reality remains with which the knower of the Self can identify?'

śrī-gurur uvāca

satyam uktaṃ tvayā vidvan nipuṇo 'si vicāraṇe-
aham-ādi-vikārās te tad-abhāvo 'yam apy anu

sarve yenānubhūyante yaḥ svayaṃ nānubhūyate
tam ātmānaṃ veditāraṃ viddhi buddhyā susūkṣmayā

[215-216] The Guru replied: 'Your question is excellent, my learned one. You are good at reasoning. You must perceive by the most subtle thinking that the principle by which all your different states, such as ego-feeling and the rest, as well as their absence (in dreamless sleep), are experienced, but which is itself not an object of experience, is the Self, the ultimate knower.

An intelligent man must be neither credulous nor unduly sceptical. Logic is not the whole of the life of man and does not always lead to inner satisfaction. The problem addressed by Yoga is not logical but ontological—that is, ascertaining the truth of an object or statement in the immediacy of human consciousness, irrespective of its appearance. For instance, this plate is red, round and smooth — this is its appearance. Ontology means: 'What is its essence?'

According to the yogic philosophy, that indefinable, infinite substance or essence is God, the abode of all goodness, truth and beauty, from which the whole cosmos has come forth, in which it abides and to which it goes back. In the Upanishads, the sages ask: What is That from which all this has come, which maintains all and to which all returns?

If a man wishes to study the Greek or German philosophers, he can buy a book or go to a teacher, but if you want to study this Yoga, you have to prove your competence to do so. The claim of this philosophy is to make you consciously immortal and give you peace and satisfaction for ever—eternal fellowship with love in the infinitude of God, freedom for ever and in every possible way: 'O Arjuna, I shall fully teach thee this knowledge which is a matter of experience and when it is known subjectively and spiritually, nothing remains unattained' (*Gita* 7.2). The same claim is made in the words of holy Jesus: 'Whosoever drinketh of the (living) water that I shall give shall never thirst; but the water that I shall give him shall be in him a well of water springing up into everlasting life' (*John* 4.13-14). These are statements made by two seers of Truth, one Jewish, the other Indian. So it is not enough just to take a book and study; let us be practical. This problem will only be solved by you when your mind has been stilled and enlightened.

tat-sākṣikaṃ bhavet tat tad yad yad yenānubhūyate
kasyāpy ananubhūtārthe sākṣitvaṃ nopayujyate

asau sva-sākṣiko bhāvo yataḥ svenānubhūyate
ataḥ paraṃ svayaṃ sākṣāt pratyag-ātmā na cetaraḥ

[217-218] 'By whatever anything is experienced, that is its witness. In the case of a thing which has not been experienced, nothing can be spoken of as its "witness". The Self is its own witness because it is experienced by itself. Hence it alone is itself the Absolute, the inmost immediate Self.

This light of God is 'I am'. To see 'I am' you need no other light. This is a matter to be thought of in absolute silence and the greatest faith.

How do we know? Are the five senses of perception the instruments of true knowledge? We say we see the blue sky, but is the sky really blue? We say we see the vault of heaven as an inverted bowl, but is it really so? Chocolate to one is bitter, to others delectable; beer is an elixir to some, to others it is poison. The reports of our senses are unreliable. Our senses tell us of the veil in which the sensations are wrapped up, but tell us nothing of reality. Where is the Truth that will make us free? How shall we know about it?

According to the *Mundaka Upanishad* (3.1.1) the human personality is like a tree on which are seated two birds. One bird is happy in and by itself, it has no wants: true happiness must come without an object, by itself. The other bird, on a lower branch, is busy eating the fruits of the tree. It nibbles a glossy fruit or a seed and, being disappointed, tries another, repeating the experiment endlessly. When the lower bird gets tired of this experimenting, it looks up to the golden bird above and thinks: 'How can I be so perfect, so desireless as this golden bird?' When its resolution to be like the upper bird is strong and its concentration on the upper bird is complete, a miracle happens, and this is called intuition. The lower bird realizes it has no existence of its own and is united with the upper bird; doubts come to an end, sufferings cease, there is nothing but delight, the universe is seen, the truth is realized. Then follows a life of perfect freedom, joy and identity with God.

In order to know the truth and be free, we have first to banish pleasures from the realm of our life. In place of lower pleasures arising out of sensations, we have to plant seeds of benevolence, harmlessness, rigid self-control, adoration and devotion to the Lord. Thus adorned, the garden of our soul becomes a fit abode for the manifestation of the Most High in ourselves, and this new experience is ecstasy (samadhi).

Both Bergson and Kant unanimously condemn the life of the senses as being incompetent to lead the soul to the desired end. Every worldly desire is a chain which prevents the soul's upward flight. Do not give your love to the unreal, the perishable, but to the real, the imperishable. The imperishable is hidden in all that is perishable. It is the unpurified intellect which distorts. When self-control has been practised, when the pursuit of pleasure is over and God becomes our bread, our meat and our highest desire, the taint is removed and the higher Self takes the place of the lower self. Then the problem of life is solved for ever.

> jāgrat-svapna-suṣuptiṣu sphuṭataraṃ yo 'sau samujjṛmbhate
> pratyag-rūpatayā sadāham aham ity antaḥ sphuran naikadhā
> nānākāra-vikāra-bhāgina imān paśyann ahaṃ-dhī-mukhān
> nityānanda-cidātmanā sphurati taṃ viddhi svam etaṃ hṛdi

> [219] 'Become aware of that which is present in your own heart as the Self. It manifests clearly within as the inmost Self throughout waking, dream and dreamless sleep. It always asserts itself as "I", "I" in various forms. It assumes the ego-sense and so on, and assumes their various modifications. It manifests with the nature of eternal Bliss and Consciousness.

Sometimes a single man in silence and tranquillity can achieve what changes the whole aspect of Nature. It was in silence and tranquillity that Galileo changed the whole conception of astronomy, not by drum-beating and flag-flying methods.

I am sitting in my room and a wave of pessimism passes over my mind: the walls seem to say, 'Thou hast failed!'; the past years seem to hiss 'worthless! worthless!' and mental pictures assume the forms of titans, fearful shapes about to swallow one whose very breath spells danger and depression. In the midst of this, a golden shadow flits across the room and all is changed: the walls cry, 'Blessed art thou!', the hideous forms become angels, there is peace everywhere. This is a common experience. What has brought about the change? Life colours the mind with different hues.

Complaints, grumbles and difficulties change under the influence of silence and tranquillity. These two words contain more wisdom than all the works of Plato and Schopenhauer. Silence means silence of the demands of the five senses. It is the eyes, ears, tongue and other senses that have raised the clamour. The eyes say 'I must see this and that', the ears 'I must hear this and that' and so forth. Real life begins when we can rule the senses and there is the silence and peace we speak of here.

Everything in life seems to be unfolding something out of its inner being. The seed becomes a plant, the plant becomes flowers, the flowers become more seeds again. A specific organism changes from a lower to a higher form and acquires more complex forms. It seems that there is something in every atom, seed and grain of dust and in every mind which is struggling to unfold. St Paul has said that Christ is present in the heart of all. In Mahayana Buddhism it is stated that the heart of Buddha is latent in every heart. And in the *Gita,* the Creator of the universe has said: 'O Arjuna, know Me to be the eternal seed of all beings' (7.10). This means that there is a divine light unfolding itself in every object and in every mind. Bergson has called this process 'creative evolution' and his name for this creative force is 'consciousness unfolding itself'.

We begin to deteriorate physically, psychologically and spiritually when we stop this creative unfolding of our own being. Who likes a parasite? We become social parasites if we only take advantage of the labour of others and do not leave behind us something created by ourselves for the benefit of humanity in the form of good deeds, philosophy, science and so forth. What is the ultimate end of this unfoldment? What is the purpose of our life? To know God, to acquire the attributes of Godhead.

We become what we love. If we love to hate, we become subjects of hate; if we love beauty, we become beautiful; if we love good, we become good and if we love God we will acquire Godhead.

This is the end and purpose of life. If you do not fulfil this purpose in this life you will be born again and yet again. Slowly, silently, with resolution, apply the yogic principles and this life can be converted from a dream of beauty into actual beauty. Let us have so much love for the Lord and His truth that our whole life is coloured by it.

ghaṭodake bimbitam arka-bimbam
ālokya mūḍho ravim eva manyate
tathā cid-ābhāsam upādhi-saṃsthaṃ
bhrāntyāham ity eva jaḍo 'bhimanyate

[220] 'Just as an utterly deluded person might suppose he was looking at the sun when he beheld its reflection in the water of a water-pot, so a stupid person erroneously thinks "That is verily myself" when identifying himself with the reflection of Consciousness in the apparent conditioning adjunct of the individual organism.

Water has the capacity to reflect the sun in every drop, similarly the human mind, by virtue of the presence of the constituent (guna) of sattva in it, has the capacity to reflect the Lord of the universe in it. The reflection, together with the Lord Himself, its substratum, and the mind, form the individual soul or jiva. The personality of man is thus a composite, being made up of a part which is mortal and destructible, and a part which is immortal, indestructible and bliss. It is rather unfortunate that we devote so much of our time to associations which have only to do with the perishable and temporal part, neglecting that which is eternal, imperishable and all-bliss.

If man were indeed all matter and nothing more, he would never have such deep urges to immortality, infinity and self-transcendence. Where is the man who does not feel at times that he has contacted a realm in his own being which far transcends the temporal one? A man in love, a man enjoying the highest beauty in contemplation of Nature, like Wordsworth, transcends himself and becomes a seer. No man is satisfied with his present state. We think that a man of worldly eminence is happy, but when we probe into his soul we find him less happy than a man who lives in a basement. The writer has contacted many such men and has found them bankrupt in real satisfaction and hemmed in by walls of fear and disappointment.

ghaṭaṃ jalaṃ tad-gatam arka-bimbaṃ
vihāya sarvaṃ vinirīkṣyate 'rkaḥ
taṭa-stha etat-tritayāvabhāsakaḥ
svayaṃ-prakāśo viduṣā yathā tathā

[221] 'A wise person will disregard the pot and the water and the reflection of the sun in the water and will behold the sun which is its own light and which illumines the triad of the pot, the water and the reflection, while itself remaining separate from them.

When you are able to take leave of your five senses of action, your five senses of cognition and also of your mind, then what remains is the Lord, God. Those who want to enjoy the fragrance of a rose need not analyse the flower nor study the chemical analysis of its petals; and those who want the perfume of inner peace, freedom and delight are invited to come to their Maker within themselves without arguments and without too much of the how and why of temporary objects. Let us take every day, for one hour or more, a voluntary holiday from our senses and mind and the world, which is a misrepresentation of God as seen through those finite and unreliable organs; otherwise we remain shuttlecocks between a tear and a smile and remain bound.

dehaṃ dhiyaṃ cit-pratibimbam evaṃ
visrjya buddhau nihitaṃ guhāyām
draṣṭāram ātmānam akhaṇḍa-bodhaṃ
sarva-prakāśaṃ sad-asad-vilakṣaṇam

[222] 'Even so will the wise person reject the body and the mind and the reflection of Consciousness in the higher mind, and will behold, in the secret recesses of the higher mind, in the heart, the Self, the Witness, unbroken Consciousness, the illuminator of all, different both from the manifest and the unmanifest.

The pragmatic materialistic philosophy abolishes the immortality of the soul, spiritual idealism and devotion to God or His incarnations and believes only in action and 'changing the environment'. In the spiritual philosophy represented by Krishna, Christ, Buddha and Lao Tzu, the chief object of life is contemplation, and action is only an accessory to it. St Thomas Aquinas says: 'Action should be undertaken only in so far as it helps the life of contemplation'.

The argument of the contemplative philosophers is: 'We do believe in action, but you must perform the right action, that action which will bring inner peace (shanti), freedom, delight and real prosperity'. It is said in the *Gita* (5.10) that our action must be an offering to the Lord. Unless you contact the Lord through contemplation, you will never truly evaluate your action and you are liable to commit terrible blunders. Is not the road to hell paved with good intentions? It is a yogic dictum that mind-culture must precede our action.

There are two objectives in the world, the real and the unreal. The unreal is that which is ever changing and uncertain. The pursuit of the real brings everlasting peace and delight. Choose which you like.

There are two 'I's of man, the empirical 'I' and the transcendental 'I'. The empirical self is mortal, ever-changing, unreliable; truth can be known only by the transcendental Self. It is that inner 'I' which is the ray of God. Try to know this divine ray, the real 'I', through prayer, devotion, contemplation, study and by keeping away from those not similarly minded; then every one of your actions will be an example which will influence the world. Alexis Carrel says: 'Live with those who are similarly minded', hence the importance of centres and groups which foster a life of study, devotion and mutual affection.

Once when I was in Peking, an epidemic of cholera broke out and I was advised to leave the city, which I did. As I was running away, I said to myself: 'I have left the physical bacteria of cholera. I must now leave the bacteria of hate, anger, prejudice and fear. Verily these inner bacteria are more subtle in their effects and their attacks than the outer ones of cholera'. When we live in a good mental climate of renunciation, knowledge and devotion, the outer climate will not matter much. St Francis of Assisi, having renounced wealth and comfort, was seen kissing the wounds of lepers and, by his whole way of living, announcing his sojourn in the right inner climate.

nityaṃ vibhuṃ sarva-gataṃ susūkṣmam
antar-bahiḥ-śūnyam ananyam ātmanaḥ
vijñāya samyaṅ-nija-rūpam etat
pumān vipāpmā virajo vimṛtyuḥ

[223] 'When a person has become rightly aware of his own true nature as eternal, all-pervading, very subtle, having nothing either outside it or inside it, and which is not other than the Self, then he is free from evil, free from taint, immortal.

When the empirical self is completely silenced, then you will see the transcendental Self, the ray of God. When it is realized, then man is free and blissful.

viśoka ānanda-ghano vipaścit
svayaṃ kutaścin na bibheti kaścit
nānyo 'sti panthā bhava-bandha-mukter
vinā sva-tattvāvagamaṃ mumukṣoḥ

[224] 'Such a wise person grieves not. He is himself bliss, all-bliss everywhere (lit. "a mass of bliss"). He has nothing to fear from any quarter. There is no other way to liberation from bondage to reincarnation except that one truly desirous of liberation should come to know the true nature of his own Self.

brahmābhinnatva-vijñānaṃ bhava-mokṣasya kāraṇam
yenādvitīyam ānandaṃ brahma sampadyate budhaiḥ

[225] 'The means to liberation from reincarnation is direct awareness that one is non-different from the Absolute. Through this, the wise attain to the Absolute as bliss, one without a second.

In certain great moments of life the Self, through one object, speaks to the Self in man, like a ray of spiritual light radiating from one individual and affecting the other kindred soul. Truly fortunate are they who have this faculty developed in them. This recognition endures through incarnations, and under its influence that soul has a vision of spiritual freedom (moksha).

brahma-bhūtas tu saṃsṛtyai vidvān nāvartate punaḥ
vijñātavyam ataḥ samyag brahmābhinnatvam ātmanaḥ

> [226] 'When the enlightened person has realized the Absolute, he does not return again for reincarnation in the world. Therefore one should acquire direct realization of one's own non-difference from the Absolute.

To awaken this faculty of cognition in one's own self is the purpose of yogic association with the spiritually minded and proximity to the Teacher. How blessed is one who acquires this spiritual cognition. It is an undisputed fact of experience that when there is enduring faith and all-absorbing love of an image of God, He will be revealed through it to the devotee.

satyaṃ jñānam anantaṃ brahma
viśuddhaṃ paraṃ svataḥ-siddham
nityānandaikarasaṃ pratyag-
abhinnaṃ nirantaraṃ jayati

> [227] 'The Absolute is the real, knowledge, the infinite, pure, transcendent, self-established, ever of the one savour of eternal bliss, non-different from the inmost Self—that Absolute is ever supreme.

35. The world is non-different from the Absolute

sad idaṃ paramādvaitaṃ svasmād anyasya vastuno 'bhāvāt
na hy anyad asti kiñcit samyak-paramārtha-tattva-bodhe hi

[228] 'This supreme non-dual principle is real because nothing apart from it exists. For when one awakens to a right knowledge of the supreme principle, one finds that nothing else exists.

Is our psychological life mechanical or something else? Is the mind just a machine? No, definitely not. A machine has no purpose—a typewriter does not type on its own—but psychological life has a purpose. 'Purpose' means that there is some constructive end in view. Mental life is constructive; its progress cannot be infinite, as some unscientific thinkers like Madame Blavatsky and Alice Bailey hold; the invalidity of this conception is obvious. If progressive evolution was infinite it could only move in a circle and thus return to the beginning, since a straight line extended to infinity becomes a circle.

Happiness and misery are constructions of the mind. The Upanishads declare that mind is the cause of both freedom and bondage (*Amritabindu Upanishad* 2). Happiness is the expression of freedom; misery of bondage. Freedom is immortality, light; bondage is death, darkness—both are created by the mind.

What is the end? What is the end of a cloud? It condenses into rain, which becomes a river which flows to and ends in the sea. So the little self finally expands into infinity. And if the mind engages in activities other than those intended for it by destiny, it suffers.

What is true of the individual mind (microcosmos) is true of the sum total of human minds (macrocosmos). Christ came, Buddha came, Shri Dada came like meteors to tell not only individuals but the whole of humanity to direct, purify and still the mind, tried under the fire of selfless benevolence and discharge of duty, and so to direct it towards Godhead.

The Bible says that Christ came to abolish death. The Upanishads say, 'Those who see Him in the cavity of their hearts become immortal. There is no other way to happiness'. These last two statements are identical. Sainthood is not only for the few but for the whole of society.

yad idaṃ sakalaṃ viśvaṃ nānārūpaṃ pratītam ajñānāt
tat sarvaṃ brahmaiva pratyastāśeṣa-bhāvanā-doṣam

[229] 'This whole universe with all its variegated forms is only perceived through ignorance. When all false ideas are rejected, all that variety is seen to be (in truth) the (homogeneous) Absolute alone.

People who have an inadequate and superficial acquaintance with the Advaita philosophy of Shri Shankara, often misunderstand the expression: 'The world is unreal'. They run away with the conclusion that, according to Shri Shankara, it has no basic existence at all. The fact is otherwise.

Shri Shankara says in his great commentary that the world is not unreal in the sense in which a dream is unreal, or in the sense that a barren woman's son is unreal, or the appearance of a rainbow is unreal. The Sanskrit word translated as 'unreal' in the expression 'the world is unreal' (jagan mithya) is 'mithya'. As defined by the great metaphysician Sadananda Saraswati, 'mithya' literally means 'inexplicable'—that it can neither be called real nor unreal.

mṛt-kārya-bhūto 'pi mṛdo na bhinnaḥ
kumbho 'sti sarvatra tu mṛt-svarūpāt
na kumbha-rūpaṃ pṛthag asti kumbhaḥ
kuto mṛṣā kalpita-nāma-mātraḥ

[230] 'Though the clay pot is an effect of the clay, it is not different from the clay, as it is everywhere of the nature of clay. The pot-form is nothing separate from the clay. So why call it a pot (except for practical purposes)? It is merely an erroneously imagined name (for what is in fact clay).

kenāpi mṛd-bhinnatayā svarūpaṃ
ghaṭasya saṃdarśayituṃ na śakyate
ato ghaṭaḥ kalpita eva mohān
mṛd eva satyaṃ paramārtha-bhūtam

[231] 'No one can demonstrate that the pot has a nature of its own, separate from the clay. So the pot is merely imagined through error. Only the clay is real in the last resort.

Any object consists of five aspects: name, form, existence, awareness and blissfulness. Name and form are equally unreal. They change perpetually, and forms are called by different names in different countries. But the basic fact of an object is its existence. That does not change. It is always the same.

sad-brahma-kāryaṃ sakalaṃ sadaiva
tan-mātram etan na tato 'nyad asti
astīti yo vakti na tasya moho
vinirgato nidrita-vat prajalpaḥ

[232] 'All effects of reality, the Absolute, are simply that reality and nothing else. Nothing else exists. He who affirms that anything else does exist has not yet lost his delusion. He is like one talking in his sleep.

The world, according to the system of Advaita, has no independent existence. It exists by virtue of the existence of the Spirit, or God, and cannot be separated from It. This is not the Hegelian doctrine of the phenomenal world and the Absolute, nor that of Spinoza. Both of them take matter and the realm of name and form as real. But Shri Shankara, in his Advaita doctrine, makes it clear that only the appearance of the object is unexplainable; the substance is existence (sat) or God.

brahmaivedaṃ viśvam ity eva vāṇī
śrautī brūte 'tharva-niṣṭhā variṣṭhā

tasmād etad brahma-mātraṃ hi viśvaṃ
nādhiṣṭhānād bhinnatāropitasya

[233] 'We have that fine text from the Atharva Veda, "All this variegated universe is in truth only the Absolute" (Muṇḍāka Upanishad 2.2.11). Therefore this variegated universe is in truth only the Absolute. For that which is superimposed is non-different from the substratum onto which it is superimposed (e.g., the mirage water is non-different from the desert sand).

satyaṃ yadi syāj jagad etad ātmano
'nantatva-hānir nigamāpramāṇatā
asatya-vāditvam apīśituḥ syān
naitat trayaṃ sādhu hitaṃ mahātmanām

[234] 'If this world were real, it would follow that the Self was not infinite, and that would undermine the validity of the Veda (as it would contradict Taittirīya Upanishad 2.1). And it would imply that the Lord spoke untruthfully (cp. the next verse below). These three points are not good or approved by great souls.

īśvaro vastu-tattva-jño na cāhaṃ teṣv avasthitaḥ
na ca matsthāni bhūtānīty evam eva vyacīkḷpat

[235] 'The Lord knows the nature of reality, and His conception was the same when He said, "I am not in the creatures, and neither are they in me" (Gītā 9.4-5).

yadi satyaṃ bhaved viśvaṃ suṣuptāv upalabhyatām
yan nopalabhyate kiñcid ato 'sat svapna-van mṛṣā

[236] 'If the world were real, it would be perceived in dreamless sleep. But it is not so perceived, and so it is unreal like a dream.

Many people will say that in dreamless sleep the consciousness is totally destroyed and that nothing remains. But if this is really the case, you will have to say that when we wake up, a new consciousness is born in us, and if it is a new consciousness, how is it able to repeat or know the things of the past? What is it that has continuity of consciousness? When you wake up from dreamless sleep, you recognize your wife and children, and so forth; you do not ask your wife who she is. A person who awakes from sound sleep has the consciousness that during that state he was perfectly ignorant of everything. What is experienced in dreamless sleep is a complete absence of knowledge of anything in the world. If the whole consciousness was nullified and destroyed at that time, you would have no such experience at all.

atah̤ pr̥thaṅ nāsti jagat parātmanah̤
  pr̥thak pratītis tu mr̥ṣā guṇādi-vat
āropitasyāsti kim arthavattā
  'dhiṣṭhānam ābhāti tathā bhrameṇa

[237] 'So the world is not separate from the supreme Self. The notion that it is so is erroneous, like the notion that attributes are separate from the substances in which they inhere (i.e., as if "blue" could exist independently of something which was blue). Does anything superimposed have any real existence? It is simply an erroneous appearance of the substratum.

The world consists of the primordial substance, which is supported on the existence of God and which is neither different from God nor yet identical with Him. This substance consists of the three modes (gunas) of inertia, activity and light. In order to realize God, one has to overcome inertia and agitation by the practice of virtue (dharma), prayer, devotion, meditation, charity and philanthrophy on a non-sectarian and universal basis.

Thus it will be seen that in Vedanta there is infinite scope for the practice of virtue, prayer, devotion and all the good deeds that uplift the soul from the region of darkness to the region of light.

bhrāntasya yad yad bhramataḥ pratītaṃ
brahmaiva tat tad rajataṃ hi śuktiḥ
idaṃtayā brahma sadaiva rūpyate
tvāropitaṃ brahmaṇi nāma-mātram

[238] 'Whatever is seen in error by anyone in delusion is in fact only the Absolute. Indeed the (falsely seen) silver is really only mother-of-pearl. It is always the Absolute that is falsely conceived as this or that; but what is superimposed onto the Absolute is only a name (and not a reality—as the clay elephant is only clay and not an elephant).

36. The nature of the Absolute

ataḥ paraṃ brahma sad advitīyaṃ
viśuddha-vijñāna-ghanaṃ nirañjanam
praśāntam ādy-anta-vihīnam akriyaṃ
nirantarānanda-rasa-svarūpam

[239] 'And so the supreme Absolute is real, one without a second, a homogeneous mass of pure Consciousness, taintless, peaceful, beginningless and endless, actionless and of the nature of the savour of unbroken bliss.

The only solution to the problem of life—which means limitation and suffering—is the cognition of the nature of one's own Self or, metaphysically speaking, knowledge of God, ultimate Reality: 'Know the truth, and the truth shall make you free' (*John* 8.32). Ultimately the riddle of life is solved by knowledge, and knowledge alone—knowledge of the real nature of one's own Self or, metaphysically speaking, knowledge of God or ultimate Reality.

nirasta-māyākṛta-sarva-bhedaṃ
nityaṃ sukhaṃ niṣkalam aprameyam
arūpam avyaktam anākhyam avyayaṃ
jyotiḥ svayaṃ kiñcid idaṃ cakāsti

[240] 'It is void of all the distinctions set up by Māyā. It is constant and eternal joy, partless and not subject to cognition as an object through the authoritative means of knowledge. It is formless, unmanifest, nameless, not subject to diminution or destruction. It shines as a strange, self-luminous light.

jñātṛ-jñeya-jñāna-śūnyam anantaṃ nirvikalpakam
kevalākhaṇḍa-cinmātraṃ paraṃ tattvaṃ vidur budhāḥ

[241] 'It is infinite and without the distinction into subject, object and subject-object knowledge. It does not fluctuate. It is pure, unbroken Consciousness. That is the supreme principle known to the enlightened ones.

aheyam anupādeyaṃ mano-vācām agocaram
aprameyam anādy-antaṃ brahma pūrṇaṃ mahan mahaḥ

[242] 'The Absolute is beyond either rejection or acceptance. It is inaccessible to mind or words. It is not subject to cognition by an authoritative means of knowledge. It has no beginning or end. It is a great infinite light.

That light of God is 'I am'. This is a matter to be thought of in absolute silence and the greatest faith. Gandhi has said: 'Put the Lord on your lips and He will find His way into your heart'. In moments of absolute silence, every day think 'I am He, I am He'.

Can we have knowledge of God or the nature of the Self in the present state of our mind? No! Can we see our reflection in a river which is muddy and dark? No, we cannot. A mistake often made by the so-called 'Swamis' and those who have not understood the holy mystery, is that they think that merely by reading *The Crest Jewel of Wisdom* or other scriptures, you will have abiding peace. Something more is necessary. In terms of the Christian doctrine, it is the grace of the Lord God infinite which will permit you to participate in His nature through His Son, provided the Holy Ghost (the holy Spirit) adorns your heart. Repetition of 'I am Brahman (the Absolute)' is useful, but if it is preceded by a disciplined mind, the light will dawn more quickly and we shall no longer be subject to fluctuating moods and relapses. In one of his Persian poems, Rama Tirtha says: 'I run after the light and am happy. It is withdrawn, and lo, I am again a man of the world. I cry and hear only my echo. Again I try to find the light and again I am happy'. Anyone who has practised mysticism or religion must be aware of this problem.

How can we have the state of mind in which our doubt about the existence of God in and through everything and everywhere is finally crushed? St Thomas Aquinas calls it: 'A conviction of the existence of the Lord and His ability to reward you'. Not by a mere intellectual conviction. The Lord is not a dead force. He is a living, loving, transcendent force within and through our soul. You cannot serve God and mammon (*Matthew* 6.24). The heart has a window, and if it is shut by devotion to earthly desires, the ray of light which comes from the Father in Heaven is shut out.

The grace of the Lord is not unconditional. What is the condition? St Thomas says: 'The practice of charity, in the sense meant by St Paul'. Charity means edification of the heart, general forgiveness, universal tolerance, to give our real affection to each and all, to cut out the word 'condemnation', to open our hearts to embrace all creatures of God as messengers from Him—all this and more is charity, called in the *Bhagavad Gita* 'the practice of sattva'.

37. The great texts of the Upanishads

tat-tvaṃ-padābhyām abhidhīyamānayor
brahmātmanoḥ śodhitayor yadīttham
śrutyā tayos tat tvam asīti samyag
ekatvam eva pratipādyate muhuḥ

[243] 'If the identity of the Absolute and the Self (of the enquirer) in their true form (śodita) is repeatedly[1] and rightly (samyag) taught by the Veda with the words "that" and "thou"—

aikyaṃ tayor lakṣitayor na vācyayor
nigadyate 'nyonya-viruddha-dharmiṇoḥ
khadyota-bhānvor iva rāja-bhṛtyayoḥ
kūpāmbu-rāśyoḥ paramāṇu-mervoḥ

[244] 'Then this identity is expressed by the implied not the literal meanings of "that" and "thou", which latter contain mutually contradictory elements (which have to be eliminated if the sentence is to make sense). One does not take literally sentences which identify a firefly (on account of its particular brilliance) with the sun, or a servant (e.g., a crown representative) with the king, or a well (of unusually large size) with the sea, or a minute particle (in sarcastic speech) with Mount Meru.

tayor virodho 'yam upādhi-kalpito
na vāstavaḥ kaścid upādhir eṣaḥ
īśasya māyā mahad-ādi kāraṇaṃ
jīvasya kāryaṃ śṛṇu pañca-kośam

[245] 'This contradictory element that arises in the meanings of "that" and "thou" (if they are taken literally) is imagined on account of apparent conditioning adjuncts. But no real

1 Nine times at *Chāndogya Upanishad* 6.8.7 and the succeeding passage.

conditioning factor exists. There are two illusory ones. There is (with regard to "that") the Māyā of the Lord, consisting of the cosmic intellect and other principles that go to make up the world of Nature and appear as a cause. And note well that there is the apparent conditioning adjunct (with regard to "thou") of the five sheaths of the individual soul, which appear as an effect.

etāv upādhī para-jīvayos tayoḥ
samyaṅ nirāse na paro na jīvaḥ
rājyaṃ narendrasya bhaṭasya kheṭakas
tayor apohe na bhaṭo na rājā

[246] 'The two apparent conditioning adjuncts (Nature and the five sheaths) appear to affect the Absolute and the individual soul respectively. When they are eliminated, there is no "Absolute" (as distinguished from the soul or from anything relative) and no "individual soul". It is the kingdom that makes the king, and the shield that makes the common soldier; take away the kingdom and the shield, and there is no king or soldier.

athāta ādeśa iti śrutiḥ svayaṃ
niṣedhati brahmaṇi kalpitaṃ dvayam
śruti-pramāṇānugṛhīta-bodhāt
tayor nirāsaḥ karaṇīya eva

[247] 'And so the Veda itself denies the reality of imagined duality in the words "And so there is the teaching 'Neither this nor that'" (Bṛhadāraṇyaka Upanishad 2.3.6). Therefore the two apparent conditioning adjuncts (Nature and the five sheaths) should be abolished through enlightenment based on the Veda as a means of knowledge.

This Yoga taught in the Veda is embodied in the *Gita,* the only reliable exponent of which is the holy teacher Shankara Acharya. Here is a simple definition: 'Yoga is a life directed to a definite goal, the goal being God-vision within'. In *The Crest Jewel of Wisdom,* the question raised is: 'What is the truest guide to the vision of God in our own being?' It is wisdom, and it demands as a spiritual force the whole personality of the one who possesses it. Wisdom is to pursue what is real in life and to be indifferent to what is unreal. That which we call real remains the same in the past, present and future; the unreal is that which is ever changing.

Wisdom is not achieved by devoting one hour a day to its pursuit. It demands the total effort of all our energies and passions in order to reach the highest goal of life. Let us not be like the man who said: 'On Sunday I am a religious man, on Monday I forget all about Church and religion and am a wise man!' Such notions of 'practical life' are stupid and dangerous. No practical life is worth a grain of sand which is not founded on contemplation. The outer life is only one expression of it and not the whole, because there is also the inner life.

Can we ever be too contemplative? Certainly not! The inner life is 95% of the real life of man. Do we not live mostly in our dreams, desires, motives and day-dreams when we are not sleeping? So how can we agree with those who say that practical life must constitute 99% of our life and only 1% of contemplation? All that you see today in scientific discovery and control of Nature is the outcome of the contemplation of one man, Aristotle. To contemplate is to refresh our mind in the cool waters of the inner life and to see things as they are.

nedaṃ nedaṃ kalpitatvān na satyaṃ
rajjau dṛṣṭa-vyāla-vat svapna-vac ca
itthaṃ dṛśyaṃ sādhu yuktyā vyapohya
jñeyaḥ paścād eka-bhāvas tayor yaḥ

[248] 'One must reject whatever is objectively perceived, through proper reasoning of the form "Not this, not this", "It cannot be real because it has been imagined like the snake falsely seen in a rope or like a dream". What will then remain is the identity of the Absolute and the Self, and that is what has to be known.

tatas tu tau lakṣaṇayā sulakṣyau
tayor akhaṇḍaika-rasatva-siddhaye
nālaṃ jahatyā na tathā 'jahatyā
kintūbhayārthātmikayaiva bhāvyam

[249] 'Then the two words "that" and "thou" must be properly interpreted according to their implied meanings, in order to establish their purport of undifferentiated unity. It will not do to interpret the two words with an implied meaning in such a way that the primary meanings are either totally lost or wholly retained; they should be interpreted by an implied meaning that also partly includes the primary meaning.

sa devadatto 'yam itīha caikatā
viruddha-dharmāṃśam apāsya kathyate
yathā tathā tat tvam asīti vākye
viruddha-dharmān ubhayatra hitvā

[250] 'When we say "This is that Devadatta", we assert identity with rejection of contradictory features (e.g., younger, wearing a hat, etc.). In the same way, "That thou art" is an assertion of identity between the Absolute and the Self, rejecting the contradictory features (apparent association with Nature on the part of the Absolute, apparent association with the five sheaths on the part of the Self).

saṃlakṣya cinmātratayā sad-ātmanor
akhaṇḍa-bhāvaḥ paricīyate budhaiḥ
evaṃ mahāvākya-śatena kathyate
brahmātmanor aikyam akhaṇḍa-bhāvaḥ

[251] 'In this way enlightened souls recognize as pure Consciousness the undifferentiated identity of the Absolute (sat) and the Self. And there are hundreds of great texts in the Veda which assert the undifferentiated identity of the Absolute and the Self.

38. Meditation on the Absolute

asthūlam ity etad asan nirasya
siddhaṃ svato vyoma-vad apratarkyam
ato mṛṣā-mātram idaṃ pratītaṃ
jahīhi yat svātmatayā gṛhītam
brahmāham ity eva viśuddha-buddhyā
viddhi svam ātmānam akhaṇḍa-bodham

> [252] 'When the unreal has been eliminated by the processes implicit in such texts as "Not gross nor minute..." (Bṛhadāraṇyaka Upanishad 3.8.8), then the Self asserts its existence independently, like the all-pervading ether in a way that cannot be contradicted by mere logic. And so you must give up this mere illusory appearance that you have perceived and accepted as being your own Self. Awaken to your own Self as undifferentiated Consciousness, feeling with your mind, "Verily, I am the Absolute".

In our mind there are three chambers: a chamber of alchemy, a chamber of illusion and a chamber of association or identification. The chamber of identification is with the sense-objects. The chamber of illusion is the chamber of desires; each and every desire is an illusion. You will say: 'How about the desire to know God?' The word 'desire' does not apply to it; neither Shankara Acharya nor St Thomas Aquinas call it a desire. A desire means a yearning for an object which we do not possess, and God—the ultimate Self—is ever-achieved. There is a chamber of alchemy in the mind in which you can transmute your lower nature—the sensual nature which you have in common with the lower animals—into a brilliant light of the knowledge of God that is a unity of awareness. Worldly love is an illusion, worldly knowledge is an illusion; being, and what follows being, is called experience. In this region, all those illusions can be transmuted into brilliant light. You transmute all the material of the two lower regions which clings to your mind as residue. The only thing that matters there is the grace of

God in the form of the holy Spirit. God the Absolute, as God the Father, is the creator, governor and sustainer. As God the Son, He takes birth in His incarnations. As God the illuminator of the inner region, the giver of light, the breaker of bonds, He is called the holy Spirit. And the presence of the holy Spirit is called the grace of God.

Let us be very clear about our goal in life. The purpose of human life is one and only one, to know God, not as an object but as an integral and ultimate principle of your personality called the Self. The teacher does not promise anything at all. He says: 'I give you a matchbox and you already have a candle. Strike the match and light the candle, then go ahead yourself'. The match-box that he gives is called the holy Yoga—that is, unselfish benevolence, devotion and higher knowledge. That is all. If you keep the match-box and do not strike the match for fifty million years, you will remain in darkness, for neither God nor any saint will do it for you. St Thomas is very positive on this point.

'Work for your salvation diligently' are the words of the holy Buddha. As he also says, the problem is very simple. We suffer; we want to get out of suffering; we are in sorrow; we want to cross the river of sorrow for ever. The path whereby this is done is called Adhyatma Yoga.

mṛt-kāryaṃ sakalaṃ ghaṭādi satataṃ
    mṛn-mātram evābhitas
tadvat saj-janitaṃ sad-ātmakam idaṃ
    san-mātram evākhilam
yasmān nāsti sataḥ paraṃ kimapi tat
    satyaṃ sa ātmā svayaṃ
tasmāt tat tvam asi praśāntam amalam
    brahmādvayaṃ yat param

[253] 'As pots and everything else made of clay are just clay and nothing else, so is this world, born of Being and having Being for its true nature, nothing but pure Being. Since nothing other than Being exists, everything is that, including the Self

itself. Therefore you yourself are the non-dual, transcendent Absolute, profoundly peaceful and pure.

Clay is the cause of a jar; it is made out of clay. Waves, bubbles and foam are produced out of water and are not different from the water. The law that the effect is not different from its cause must be understood. The cause of all is the Lord (ishvara), and I am that Lord. This form of meditation is called laya dhyana.

nidrā-kalpita-deśa-kāla-viṣaya-
jñātrādi sarvaṃ yathā
mithyā tad-vad ihāpi jāgrati jagat
svājñāna-kāryatvataḥ
yasmād evam idaṃ śarīra-karaṇa-
prāṇāham-ādy apy asat
tasmāt tat tvam asi praśāntam amalaṃ
brahmādvayam yat param

[254] 'Just as in dream, space, time, objects, the individual experiencer himself and so on are all falsely imagined, so are they also here in waking, where they result from ignorance of the Self. Since this body, organs, vital energy, ego and so on are unreal, the truth therefore is that you are that transcendent non-dual Absolute, profoundly peaceful and pure.

If the dream world is said to have an existence at all, it is not different from the dreaming consciousness. What are the garden, the palace in the garden, the library, the zoo, the lake and the springs seen in a dream? They are all nothing but the dream consciousness. Similarly, the world in the waking state is nothing but God, and that God is the Spirit in man.

jāti-nīti-kula-gotra-dūragaṃ
nāma-rūpa-guṇa-doṣa-varjitam
deśa-kāla-viṣayātivarti yad
brahma tat tvam asi bhāvayātmani

[255] 'You are that Absolute which is above caste, code of conduct, family and tribe, which is without name or form, without virtues or defects, which transcends space, time and objects—meditate on this in your mind.

yat paraṃ sakala-vāg-agocaraṃ
gocaraṃ vimala-bodha-cakṣuṣaḥ
śuddha-cid-ghanam anādi vastu yad
brahma tat tvam asi bhāvayātmani

[256] 'You are that supreme Absolute which transcends the range of all speech but which can be known through the pure eye of enlightenment, the beginningless reality, a homogeneous mass of pure Consciousness—meditate on this in your mind.

ṣaḍbhir ūrmibhir ayogi yogihṛd-
bhāvitaṃ na karaṇair vibhāvitam
buddhy-avedyam anavadya-bhūti yad
brahma tat tvam asi bhāvayātmani

[257] 'You are that Absolute which is untouched by the six waves of misery (hunger and thirst, grief and delusion, decrepitude and death), which is the object of meditation of the yogis in their hearts, which cannot be grasped by the senses or known by the mind, which is of flawless grandeur[1] —meditate on this in your mind.

bhrānti-kalpita-jagat-kalāśrayaṃ
svāśrayaṃ ca sad asad vilakṣaṇam
niṣkalaṃ nirupamānam ṛddhi-mad
brahma tat tvam asi bhāvayātmani

1 Reading 'anavadya-bhūti' with Muni Lāl and Bhāgavat.

[258] 'You are that Absolute which is the substratum of the various phases of the falsely imagined world, which is its own support, which cannot be labelled as either being or non-being, partless, incomparable, possessed of unfathomable powers —meditate on this in your mind.

janma-vṛddhi-pariṇaty-apakṣaya-
 vyādhi-nāśana-vihīnam avyayam
viśva-sṛṣṭy-avana-ghāta-kāraṇaṃ
 brahma tat tvam asi bhāvayātmani

[259] 'You are that Absolute which is indestructible, free from birth, growth, development, decay, disease and death, the cause of the projection, maintenance and dissolution of the world—meditate on this in your mind.

asta-bhedam anapāsta-lakṣaṇaṃ
 nistaraṅga-jala-rāśi-niścalaṃ
nitya-muktam avibhakta-mūrti yad
 brahma tat tvam asi bhāvayātmani

[260] 'You are that Absolute which has no distinctions, whose essential nature remains ever unchanged, which is motionless like a waveless ocean, which is ever free, which is incapable of undergoing division—meditate on this in your mind.

ekam eva sad aneka-kāraṇaṃ
 kāraṇāntara-nirāsa-kāraṇam
kārya-kāraṇa-vilakṣaṇaṃ svayaṃ
 brahma tat tvam asi bhāvayātmani

[261] 'You are that Absolute which is one but which is the cause of many and the cause of the destruction of other causes, which is in itself different in nature from either cause or effect— meditate on this in your mind.

nirvikalpakam analpam akṣaraṃ
yat kṣarākṣara-vilakṣaṇam param
nityam avyaya-sukhaṃ nirañjanaṃ
brahma tat tvam asi bhāvayātmani

[262] 'You are that Absolute which does not fluctuate, vast and indestructible, indeed transcendent, beyond either destruction or non-destruction, eternal changeless joy, taintless—meditate on this in your mind.

yad vibhāti sad anekadhā bhramān
nāma-rūpa-guṇa-vikriyātmanā
hema-vat svayam avikriyaṃ sadā
brahma tat tvam asi bhāvayātmani

[263] 'You are that Absolute that is real but which appears in different forms due to error, undergoing apparent modification as name, form and attribute while being in its true nature ever without modification, like gold (which remains unchanged in essence when wrought into the forms of different animals)—meditate on this in your mind.

yac cakāsty anaparaṃ parātparaṃ
pratyag-eka-rasam ātma-lakṣaṇam
satya-cit-sukham anantam avyayaṃ
brahma tat tvam asi bhāvayātmani

[264] 'You are that Absolute which shines with nothing beyond it and which is beyond the beyond, which has the one homogeneous feeling of interiority, which is identical with the Self, which is infinite reality-consciousness-joy and indestructible—meditate on this in your mind.

uktam artham imam ātmani svayaṃ
bhāvaya prathita-yuktibhir dhiyā

saṃśayādi-rahitaṃ karāmbuvat
tena tattva-nigamo bhaviṣyati

[265] 'Meditate in your mind on these points as here stated using the traditional arguments. Thereby you will lose your doubts and other difficulties and you will see the truth of the teachings as clearly as water held cupped in the hand.

svam bodha-mātraṃ pariśuddha-tattvaṃ
vijñāya saṅghe nṛpavac ca sainye
tadā ''tmanaivātmani sarvadā sthito
vilāpaya brahmaṇi dṛśya-jātam

[266] 'Pick out your own Self, Consciousness only and of extremely pure nature, from the other factors in your empirical personality, as you might pick out a king from amidst his army. Then ever stand firm in that Self, realizing your identity with it and dissolve the whole realm of objects.

buddhau guhāyāṃ sad-asad-vilakṣaṇaṃ
brahmāsti satyaṃ param advitīyam
tad-ātmanā yo 'tra vased guhāyāṃ
punar na tasyāṅga-guhā-praveśaḥ

[267] 'The Absolute, the supreme non-dual principle, neither being nor non-being in the empirical sense, is present in the cave of the heart (buddhi). He who dwells in that cave, identifying himself with that, never again enters the hovel of the body.

39. Renunciation of the subtle impressions

jnāte vastuny api balavatī vāsanā 'nādir eṣā
kartā bhoktāpy aham iti dṛḍhā yāsya saṃsāra-hetuḥ
pratyag-dṛṣṭy-ātmani nivasatā sāpaneyā prayatnān
muktiṃ prāhus tad iha munayo vāsanā-tānavaṃ yat

[268] 'Even when the real has been known, the powerful impression current from beginningless time in the form "I am an individual performing action and enjoying experiences" and causing reincarnation in the world, has to be removed with care by the one dwelling in and identifying himself with the Self as inmost Witness. For it is that conquest [lit. weakening] of the subtle impressions that the sages call liberation in this very life.

Subtle impressions (vasanas) are the latent desires formed in the past which have gone deep into the mind and are not felt, but are subject to revival under favourable conditions. Shri Vishvamitra while practising austerity (tapas) lost his heart to the nymph Menaka on a spring afternoon. The subtle impression (vasana) was revived. No one is safe from the assault of nescience (avidya). Therefore watch your mind and see that it is filled with faith and devotion (sattva), and pray.

Cultivate vichara (spiritual introspection) and dosha-drishti (seeing the defects in sense-objects). Vichara is the intellectual understanding of the truth, 'I am Self (atman)'; to crush all scepticism by reasoning is vichara; to talk calmly about the holy philosophy to strengthen your conviction, 'I am Self (atman)', is vichara.

To see the inherent defects of suffering, instability and so forth in the outwardly pleasing sense-objects is dosha-drishti. Shri Vishvamitra did not exercise dosha-drishti when the nymph approached him. He was not prudent and did not see the destruction of his austerity (tapas) through his dalliance with her.

In the *Gita* the two paths of occupation with the world (sansara) and retirement from the world—pravritti and nivritti—are called 'action' and 'inaction'. On either path, vichara and dosha-drishti are helpful.

To be in the world and to belong to the world are different matters. Devotion and knowledge of Truth (jnana) will complete the life-work of the soul (jiva).

aham mameti yo bhāvo dehākṣādāv anātmani
adhyāso 'yaṃ nirastavyo viduṣā svātma-niṣṭhayā

[269] 'This superimposition of the notions "I" and "mine" onto the body and senses and other aspects of the not-self has to be halted by a wise person through concentration on the Self.

jñātva svaṃ pratyag-ātmānaṃ buddhi-tad-vṛtti-sākṣiṇam
so 'ham ity eva sad-vṛttyā 'nātmany ātma-matiṃ jahi

[270] 'Having first gained a knowledge of the inmost Self, the Witness of the mind and its activities, give up self-identification with the not-self through concentration on the true notion "I am That" (viz., "I am the inmost Self").

There is an imaginary enemy and that enemy is the human mind. There is no friend in the world and no enemy except our own mind. To the extent that we have governed our mind, it becomes our friend. Another way of saying the same thing is to say that the greatest enemy of man is ignorance. Where does ignorance dwell? In the mind—it dwells in us. Man has two selves, the empirical self and the transcendental self. It is by sublimating the empirical self that man comes to the transcendental Self. What is the way by which we can sublimate the mind and come to the realization of God? One who has not sat at the holy feet of a man of God and has no faith in holy revelation will not be able to solve this riddle.

What can lead one to God is not a great intellect but purity of mind attained by means of control—a mind free from agitation and devoted to God. It is not necessary to foster our mind but to sublimate it. The mind is not something to be killed; it is an instrument to be refined and rightly used.

The holy Acharya says that the following three propensities of the mind are to be overcome:

lokānuvartanaṃ tyaktvā tyaktvā dehānuvartanam
śāstrānuvartanaṃ tyaktvā svādhyāsāpanayaṃ kuru

> [271] 'Giving up slavery to the world, giving up slavery to the body, giving up slavery to traditional texts, get rid of your superimpositions.

We are not to be the slaves of social formalities and observances (this implies any physical conditions imposed on us by others—divine ethics are quite different from social ethics).

Can we do anything worthwhile when we devote three hours a day to the welfare of the body? Unless we become unconcerned with trimming the body, and give all our attention to the devotion of the soul, our life is wasted. The body's needs have to be relegated to their proper position.

Many people think that by much learning of secular knowledge they can know God. That is a great mistake. Only so much of secular learning is useful as will enable us to establish the holy truth on a rational basis.

loka-vāsanayā jantoḥ śāstra-vāsanayāpi ca
deha-vāsanayā jñānaṃ yathāvan naiva jāyate

> [272] 'It is through over-attachment to the world, to study of the traditional texts and to the body, that right metaphysical knowledge fails to arise.

The desire to walk according to the inclinations of society is a great impediment. The Lord Christ was known as a man who associated with sinners and publicans.

God alone is real and all else unreal. When you have heard this, a study of Aristotle and Galileo is no longer needed. 'The Kingdom of

Heaven is within you.' Many great lives have been lost through so-called 'scholarship'.

Many people have a body mania in their desire to keep the body fit and comfortable, but we should try to rise above consciousness of our bodies.

> saṃsāra-kārāgṛha-mokṣam icchor
> ayo-mayam pāda-nibaddha-śṛṅkhalam
> vadanti taj-jñāḥ paṭu-vāsanā-trayaṃ
> yo 'smād vimuktaḥ samupaiti muktim

[273] 'The experts say that the keen impressions generated by over-attachment to the world, to study of the traditional texts and to the body are the iron fetters that bind the feet of the one desirous of liberation to the prison-house of repeated worldly lives. He who escapes these impressions attains liberation.

A prison is a place where our activities are limited. There are small and large prisons in the world, and there is also the 'Kingdom of Heaven'—the region of liberty and real freedom. Let those who want deliverance from the prisons get over these three great impediments.

> jalādi-samparka-vaśāt prabhūta-
> durgandha-dhūtā ''garu-divya-vāsanā
> saṅgharṣaṇenaiva vibhāti samyag
> vidhūyamāne sati bāhya-gandhe

[274] 'When the heavenly odour (vāsanā with pun on "subtle impression") of fragrant aloe-wood has been lost through the evil odour arising through contamination with water or other liquid, its true fragrance can only be restored by grinding it afresh and thereby eliminating the odour that had come from without.

antaḥ-śritānanta-duranta-vāsanā-
dhūlī-viliptā paramātma-vāsanā
prajñā 'tisaṅgharṣaṇato viśuddhā
pratīyate candana-gandhavat sphuṭā

[275] 'Similarly, the bliss of the Self is filmed over by the dust of endless faulty impressions. When these have been worn away through the friction of repeated re-orientation (of the mind inwards), then the bliss of the Self manifests clearly like sweet sandalwood incense.

anātma-vāsanā-jālais tirobhūtātma-vāsanā
nityātma-niṣṭhayā teṣāṃ nāśe bhāti svayaṃ sphuṭā

[276] 'The impression of the true Self is hidden by the web of impressions of the not-self. When the latter have been destroyed by constant attention to the Self, the Self manifests clearly of its own accord.

yathā yathā pratyag-avasthitaṃ manas
tathā tathā muñcati bāhya-vāsanāḥ
niḥśeṣa-mokṣe sati vāsanānām
ātmānubhūtiḥ pratibandha-śūnyā

[277] 'The more the mind turns within, the more it escapes the impressions derived from without. When one's escape from the subtle impressions is complete, direct experience of the Self reigns without hindrance.

The mind's function is to receive, co-ordinate and pigeon-hole impressions in pursuit of the discovery of truth. If the mind is not purified, it can make terrible mistakes as, for instance, Nobel, who discovered explosives but had no idea that they would be used for any but humanitarian purposes. Why has this been so? Because the intellect when dissociated from the holy Spirit is unfit for social service.

In the mystic life there are outer rituals and there is inner experience. Rituals are meant to train our speech, sight, hands and feet so that they may not lead the soul astray in the empirical realm (sansara). Tulsi Dasa says that the five senses can be messengers of peace if ruled by a heart stayed in the presence of God, but that otherwise they become robbers. When the senses are unsanctified by the contemplation of the Lord, they become unworthy, unreliable instruments. A mixed life—seven hours sleep, one hour for God and the rest of the day spent on external pursuits—is no use. Let us live in such a way that each action is an auxiliary of contemplation.

Does *The Crest Jewel of Wisdom* advocate monasticism? No. Monasticism is only meant for the very few, not for the majority. Shri Dada lived an exemplary life; his nights were passed in devotion, his days in serving the Untouchables. St Augustine practised great contemplation, yet what an active life his was! In philosophy, sociology and other branches of learning, St Augustine introduced great light. The life of St Bernard is another example. What contemplation is in the inner life, charity expresses in the outer. Gandhi was also a great contemplative. A soldier who contemplates can fight better; Arjuna in the *Gita* is such an example. So where is the idea of inaction?

40. Giving up superimposition

svātmany eva sadā sthityā mano naśyati yoginaḥ
vāsanānāṃ kṣayaś cātaḥ svādhyāsāpanayaṃ kuru

> [278] 'The mind of the yogi dissolves (lit. "is destroyed") through his continuous concentration on his true Self, and the subtle impressions wane. Therefore put an end to your superimpositions.

No phrase is used so much by the Lord in the *Gita* as 'with mind fixed on no other object but Me'. You may say: 'How can I fix my mind on God when I am eating, walking and so forth?' But is He not the breeze who caresses you, the road you walk on and the pedestrian?

One sentence of a beggar changed the heart of St Francis. Was the beggar, perhaps, Christ who came to call His saint back to Him? Has He not taught in the form of birds, a wife, a friend?

In contemplation the yogi shares the divine secrets. He induces on the creaturely level the divine vision, while still gazing internally into his own Self, God. Contemplation is superior to action in the beginning; contemplation is a superior motion of the intellect (buddhi). Through the light of wisdom and love, we become His co-workers in the divine plan. There is no need to be anxious. The Lord will use His servants as He sees fit.

tamo dvābhyāṃ rajaḥ sattvāt sattvaṃ śuddhena naśyati
tasmāt sattvam avaṣṭabhya svādhyāsāpanayaṃ kuru

> [279] 'Tamas is overcome by rajas and sattva. Rajas is overcome by sattva. Sattva dissolves of its own accord when pure. Therefore establish yourself in sattva and put an end to your superimposition.

The mind consists of these three elements. Tamas means inertia, laziness and love of comfort; rajas means activity, passions, desire; sattva means light and reason.

Nothing degrades a man so much as love of physical comforts. Rome was destroyed by it, and a good deal of what this country is suffering now is attributable to it. The tamas constituent of the mind, laziness, has to be overcome by wise activity.

There are two kinds of activity, right and wrong. When we are acting unselfishly for the good of others and act as prescribed in the holy scriptures, that is right action. It is most difficult to know what is good and what is not good, and we must go to the scriptures for guidance. Prayer, devotion, service of our fellows, rigid guarding of our lips and our mind constitute right action.

Sattva means pursuit of right discrimination, meditation on the Lord as our Self and expansion of the whole personality in sympathy and light. When tamas and rajas have been overcome by sattva, sattva dies of itself. An Acharya has said, 'I lit a flame with great care to illumine my heart and now the flame is also subsiding and I have no need to blow it out!' When you have reached this topmost rung of the ladder, you enter into the chamber of alchemy, the chamber of light. That is all.

prārabdhaṃ puṣyati vapur iti niścitya niścalaḥ
dhairyam ālambya yatnena svādhyāsāpanayaṃ kuru

[280] 'Acquire the firm conviction that once the body has begun, it will inevitably continue, and resort scrupulously to patience. Strive hard to put an end to your superimpositions.

nāham jīvaḥ paraṃ brahmety atad-vyāvṛtti-pūrvakam
vāsanā-vegataḥ prāpta-svādhyāsāpanayaṃ kuru

[281] 'Put an end to your superimpositions that arise through the force of subtle impressions by turning away from the not-self with the affirmation "I am not the individual self: I am the Absolute, the supreme (para)".

śrutyā yuktyā svānubūtyā jñātvā sārvātmyam ātmanaḥ
kvacid ābhāsataḥ prāpta-svādhyāsāpanayaṃ kuru

[282] 'Realize that in your true nature you are the Self of all. Do this through listening to the Vedic texts, through pondering over them and through acquiring direct intuition. Put an end to any superimpositions that may arise through the lingering traces of false appearances.

Listening means hearing such texts as 'That thou art' (tat tvam asi) from a competent teacher—hearing of wisdom. Wisdom is of two kinds, supreme and relative. Turn your back on relative wisdom; hear the supreme wisdom as found on the pages of the *Gita*, the Upanishads and the holy Gospel of Christ. This hearing is called shravana.

Pondering (manana) means consideration of the correctness of the reasoning by which the identity of 'That' and 'thou' (in the above example) is established, i.e., that the divine ray in you is identical with the supreme Sun, Vasudeva, God. Pause and think whether the reasoning, by which you have come to know intellectually the identity of your soul with God, is correct; and that is done by you yourself with the help of the Guru.

When you are sure that your reasoning is correct and that the vital spark in you is really identical with the supreme Lord (and before you are convinced of it you must have flooded your heart with light) there must be profound and repeated meditation (nididhyasana) on the essence of it. Meditation is an effort by the most subtle and purest quality of the mind to understand by inner feeling the essence of holy sentences like 'That thou art'. There must be complete concentration of the mind directed towards that which is determined by the first two processes.

an-ādāna-visargābhyām īṣan nāsti kriyā muneḥ
tad-eka-niṣṭhayā nityaṃ svādhyāsāpanayaṃ kuru

[283] 'The true sage neither accepts nor rejects anything and so has no connection with action. Therefore concentrate continually on that "One" and put an end to your superimpositions.

tat tvam asy ādi vākyottha-brahmātmaikatva-bodhataḥ
brahmaṇy ātmatva-dārḍhyāya svādhyāsāpanayaṃ kuru

[284] 'Use the knowledge of your identity with the Absolute that comes from texts like "That thou art" (Chāndogya Upanishad 6.8.7, etc.) and put an end to your superimpositions in order to strengthen your sense of identity with the Absolute.

ahaṃ-bhāvasya dehe 'smin niḥśeṣa-vilayāvadhi
sāvadhānena yuktātmā svādhyāsāpanayaṃ kuru

[285] 'Discipline yourself and carry on with carefully putting

an end to your superimpositions until all sense of "I" in relation to the body has been dissolved.

pratītir jīva-jagatoḥ svapna-vad bhāti yāvatā
tāvan nirantaraṃ vidvan svādhyāsāpanayaṃ kuru

[286] 'As long as the appearance of an individual soul and a world remains manifesting like a dream, so long, O wise soul, should you continually repress your superimpositions.

nidrāyā loka-vārtāyāḥ śabdāder api vismṛteḥ
kvaccin nāvasaraṃ dattvā cintayātmānam ātmani

[287] 'Reflect continually on the Self in your mind. Do not allow a moment's scope for forgetfulness through sleep, worldly dealings or preoccupation with the sense-objects.

mātā-pitror malodbhūtaṃ mala-māṃsa-mayaṃ vapuḥ
tyaktvā cāṇḍāla-vad dūraṃ brahmībhūya kṛtī bhava

[288] 'Your body arose from the impurities of the bodies of your parents and is itself composed of flesh and impurities. Disown it and keep well away from it as if it were an outcaste. Realize the Absolute. Gain the final end of life.

ghaṭākāśaṃ mahākāśa ivātmānaṃ parātmani
vilāpyākhaṇḍa-bhāvena tūṣṇīṃ bhava sadā mune

[289] 'O sage! Through dwelling on unbroken Consciousness, dissolve your individual self in the supreme Self, as the space in the pot dissolves in universal space on the destruction of the pot. Then remain ever silent.

sva-prakāśam adhiṣṭhānaṃ svayaṃbhūya sad-ātmanā
brahmāṇḍam api piṇḍāṇḍaṃ tyajyatām mala-bhāṇḍa-vat

[290] 'Realize your true nature as the self-luminous substratum of the world-illusion. And, as that reality, give up the body and also the whole universe as a mere sink of impurities.

cid-ātmani sad-ānande dehārūḍhām ahaṃ-dhiyam
niveśya liṅgam utsṛjya kevalo bhava sarvadā

[291] 'Apply the "I-notion", at present fixed on the body, to the Self as Existence-Consciousness-Bliss. Give up the subtle body. Establish yourself eternally in transcendence.

The basis of life is Existence-Consciousness-Bliss (sat-chit-ananda). Whatever object you consider, you will find that it is based on this one infinite element. In the Vedanta phraseology we call it Brahman, which literally means 'majestic', 'infinite'. Existence (sat) is the principle of all that exists in any form, which retains its nature unchanged, unaltered during the three divisions of time—past, present and future. It is the names and forms which change and not the substance. Sometimes waves and sometimes ripples rise and fall in water, but the water, as water, does not change. Water corresponds to existence (sat), the waves, bubbles, foam and ripples resemble the changing names and forms of Maya.

Inanimate matter eventually evolves into animate forms. In the spring, the earth bursts out into plants and blossoms. There is some conscious force in nature which guides its evolution and which, in the course of time, appears as the sentient beings. Some internal principle which feels and responds to outer stimuli emerges from matter (it is already there or it could not emerge). This latent principle is called Consciousness (chit). It is the basis of matter and life; it is in the mind and it is also in life in general.

Every object in nature is dear to someone or other. Men whom the world hates, such as a Timur, Hulagu Khan or Caligula, are known to have been dearly loved by women. Every animal is susceptible to love. It is clear from these observations that the underlying reality in each and every object is an object of endearment. The Self of man is the object of the highest love. Real love and the bliss arising out of love mean that the object of our love is identified with our Self.

Self is Existence-Consciousness-Bliss (sat-chit-ananda). If the Self is bliss, why do we not experience bliss all the time? Because it is obscured by nescience (avidya). Existence (sat) and consciousness (chit) are evident, but bliss (ananda) is not. Nescience obscures only the bliss aspect of Brahman. The root cause of all misery is nescience.

The mind is the final evolute of nescience (avidya). It reveals and yet conceals the Self. The highest function of the mind is the sense of individuality, the separative sense. In love we lose our sense of individuality and therefore love is praised by poets and philosophers.

To experience the bliss aspect of the Self, the mind must be made no mind; the former impressions on the mind must be obliterated. Yoga is the psychological process by which we learn how to negate the mind, the cause of all grief and distraction. All ambitions, desires, urges and impulses go when the sense of individuality goes. How foolish it is to think that we are wise, that we know all, that we are superior to others. 'Thou art all, I am nothing' is the highest wisdom. 'The mind is the cause of bondage; the mind is also the cause of release', says the Upanishad (*Amritabindu Upanishad*. 2). This is the way to realize 'All is Brahman (the Absolute)'.

yatraiṣa jagad-ābhāso darpaṇāntaḥ puraṃ yathā
tad brahmāham iti jñātvā kṛta-kṛtyo bhaviṣyasi

[292] 'Once you have the firm conviction "I am that Absolute in which the world-appearance manifests like a city seen in a mirror", you will have achieved all that there is to achieve.

yat satya-bhūtaṃ nija-rūpam ādyaṃ
cid-advayānandam arūpam akriyam
tadetya mithyā-vapur utsṛjaitac
chailūṣa-vad veṣam upāttam ātmanaḥ

> [293] 'Go back to your own original primordial form of non-dual consciousness and bliss, void of form or action. Give up your illusory body, which you have only donned as an actor dons a costume.

An actor may be young yet on the stage he appears to be old. The spirit of man is innately good but under the impulse of ignorance he appears in many forms or states and is unhappy. We pass much of our time in useless struggle carrying fear and disappointment with us—this is a fact which cannot be denied. Knowledge is the only way to happiness—knowledge of the nature of the Self. Real happiness comes only through one means, the return of the soul to its true nature.

41. The 'I' as ego: rejection of ego-feeling

sarvātmanā dṛśyaṃ idaṃ mṛṣaiva
naivāham arthaḥ kṣaṇikatva-darśanāt
jānāmy ahaṃ sarvam iti pratītiḥ
kuto 'ham-ādeḥ kṣaṇikasya sidhyet

> [294] 'This whole realm of objects is illusory. The ego is not a reality, as it is seen to come and go momentarily. So how can one accept as true the notion "I know everything" when the ego and the rest are themselves momentary?

Shri Shankara says: 'What is this world? What is its nature? How is it born? Whither is it going? What is its purpose? Let not the wise think of these questions. Let the wise think this is all illusion (maya)'. If you are a spiritual student, then know the Self (atman) and you know all. Shri Vidyaranya Swami says, 'When the individual soul (jiva) has known his identity with Brahman (the Absolute), then for whose sake should he woo anxieties and worries?' (*Panchadashi* 7.1)

Both pessimism and optimism are modifications (vrittis) of the mind, so are joys and sufferings and also our hopes and disappointments. Each mental modification is followed by its opposite, and in each pair of opposites there is the trio of the seer, seen and seeing. Those who ride on a wave must necessarily be subject to ups and downs. What is called peace is not the total cessation of strife and there is no strife without a faint chance of peace.

These pairs of opposites refer to the waking condition, and most Western psychologists ignore two other important states of consciousness—dream and dreamless sleep. Life is not just a pendulum oscillating between a smile and a tear. Life in the pairs of opposites starts with the ego-conditioned self-consciousness; but religious leaders have experienced the source of life, the light of pure Consciousness. 'Impossible! Ridiculous!' the psychologist may say. But is your experience the limit of human experience, Mr Psychologist? What about the state of hypnosis? What about subliminal consciousness?

ahaṃ-padārthas tv ahaṃ-ādi-sākṣī
nityaṃ suṣuptāv api bhāva-darśanāt
brūte hy ajo nitya iti śrutiḥ svayaṃ
tat pratyag-ātmā sad-asad-vilakṣaṇaḥ

> [295] 'The "I" in the true sense of the word is the witness of the ego-sense and other modes of the mind. We know this, since its presence is always evident, even in dreamless sleep.[1] The Veda itself says that it is "unborn" and "eternal" (Kaṭha Upanishad 1.2.18). It is the inmost Self, different both from the manifest and the unmanifest.

The Vedic psychology affirms that there is a real phase of life which begins where the ego ends. Consciousness implies self-consciousness. That state is above the ego and is not a mental or thought (vritti) experience. There pure Consciousness (chit) experiences

1 See comment on verse 210, above.

Itself. This experience is not within the realm of the mind, though sometimes a particular tide of the sea of the mind has a partial experience of the state and terms it 'ecstasy'.

vikāriṇāṃ sarva-vikāra-vettā
nityo 'vikāro bhavituṃ samarhati
manoratha-svapna-suṣuptiṣu sphuṭaṃ
punaḥ punar dṛṣṭam asattvam etayoḥ

[296] 'That which takes cognisance of the modifications of all the things which undergo modification must itself be eternal and changeless and without modification. Again and again, we experience the absence of the physical body and the subtle body in day-dreaming, dream and dreamless sleep (i.e., the physical body disappears in day-dreaming and dream, the subtle body in dreamless sleep. Since they repeatedly disappear, they cannot be our "I" in the true sense of the word.).

ato 'bhimānaṃ tyaja māṃsa-piṇḍe
piṇḍābhimāniny api buddhi-kalpite
kāla-trayābādhyam akhaṇḍa-bodhaṃ
jñātvā svam ātmānam upaihi śāntim

[297] 'So give up your self-identification with the physical body of flesh, and also with that imagination of the mind that identifies itself with the physical body in the form of the ego. Realize as your own true Self that undifferentiated Consciousness that stands uncontradicted in past, present and future. Attain (eternal) peace.

A diamond is put into a handsome casket which is placed on a beautiful cushion. If a man only worships the cushion and does not open the casket, what will you say? 'How unfortunate that he does not see the Koh-i-Noor within!' Shri Dada says: 'Beloved ones, in you is encased the divine ray'. 'O Arjuna, I am seated in the hearts of all'

(*Gita* 15.15). If we care only for the body, we are really miserable. However much you care for the body, it will not care for you and you will have to leave it one day. Therefore the injunction of the holy saint is: 'Open the casket of your mind with the key of Yoga as given in the *Gita* and expounded by Shri Shankara, and grasp the jewel within, the Crest-Jewel, your own Self'.

tyajābhimānaṃ kula-gotra-nāma-
rūpāśrameṣv ārdra-śavāśriteṣu
liṅgasya dharmān api kartṛtādīṃs
tyaktvā bhavākhaṇḍa-sukha-svarūpaḥ

[298] 'Give up identification with (the physical body and its) family, clan, name, form and stage of life. These are based on nothing better than a rotting corpse. Give up also the attributes of the subtle body, such as the feeling that one does acts and enjoys individual experiences. Realize your true nature as undifferentiated unbroken bliss.

The real life begins where the ego ends. To contact that exalted state of Consciousness, which is called God in theology and chetana in the Vedic philosophy (e.g., in *Katha Upanishad* 2.2.13), it is essential that a picture of the exalted state in its psychological setting be impressed upon the mind, and that picture can only be a suggestion of the ideal. It is a thought-form which sets into motion the thought-life whose waves flow into the supra-psychological region. Concentration on that picture, excluding all other thought and emotional forms, is the necessary prelude to religious experience. The picture may be conceptual, based on the Absolute, i.e., 'I am Brahman', or it may be concrete, assuming the form of a Divine Incarnation such as Krishna, Christ or Buddha.

santy anye pratibandhāḥ puṃsaḥ saṃsāra-hetavo dṛṣṭāḥ
teṣām ekaṃ mūlaṃ prathama-vikāro bhavaty ahaṅkāraḥ

[299] 'Man is seen also to be faced by other obstacles which keep him in reincarnation. But they all have their common root in the first modification, the ego-sense.

yāvat syāt svasya sambandho 'haṅkāreṇa durātmanā
tāvan na leśa-mātrāpi mukti-vartā vilakṣaṇā

[300] 'As long as one is connected with the evil ego-sense, there is no question of liberation, which is totally different in kind.

Individualism will not allow man to live as a moral being or to know anything worthwhile. The close atmosphere of personal feelings shuts out all moral and humane feelings. To put oneself sympathetically in the place of another is essential to a moral life. The purpose of the life of knowledge, called the intellectual life, is to get away from the things which are, as Aristotle says, 'first for us'.

The immediate apprehensions of the senses, the direct appearances, are most delusive. The confused Ptolemaic system, which seems evident, leads us to account for everything, however complex and different, on the supposition that the universe revolves around our individual selves. But science confirms the Copernican system, changing our point of view to that of the sun, the universal centre around which all things really revolve.

Can we easily get out of ourselves, away from the environment and our nature as individuals? This problem troubled Aristotle at the dawn of Western psychology. He solved it by attributing a universal capacity to intelligence: 'It is able to master all objects, that is, to understand them'. In the intelligible world intelligence is not one thing among others, it is a principle in reference to which alone the world exists. The thinking subject appears to be an individual among other individuals but, as a thinking subject, it is free from the world and from the limitations of its own being. The individuality of a self-conscious being rests on universality. In the language of Aristotle, the self has all the qualities or it has none. It is capable of relating itself to all and so of making them parts of its own life. The self of man is universal and, as such, is capable of rising above all limitations and conditions.

ahaṅkāra-grahān muktaḥ svarūpam upapadyate
candra-vad vimalaḥ pūrṇaḥ sadā ''nandaḥ svayaṃprabhaḥ

[301] 'When one is free from the "eclipse" of the ego-sense, one attains one's true nature, pure, infinite, self-luminous eternal bliss, like the moon when the eclipse is over.

yo vā pure so 'ham iti pratīto
buddhyā viklṛptas tamasā 'timūḍhayā
tasyaiva niḥśeṣatayā vināśe
brahmātma-bhāvaḥ pratibandha-śūnyaḥ

[302] 'That which was formerly imagined[1] by the mind, thoroughly deluded through ignorance, as "I am such and such", realizes without any further obstacle that its true Self is the Absolute when all such wrong ideas have been removed.

Through one-pointed devotion of the heart, the aspirant realizes the illusory character of the experience of the pairs of opposites. It is an essential preparation. The mind can see God only in the state of equanimity (samata). This is the ideal state of the religious student. He must always remember that whatever is within the range of mental conception or sense experience is not the Self (atman). The yogi turns his back on expectations and disappointments and heads the barque of his life through the narrow strait of the ego to the tideless sea of Consciousness (chit).

brahmānanda-nidhir mahā-balavatā
'haṅkāra-ghorāhinā
saṃveṣṭyātmani rakṣyate guṇa-mayaiś
caṇḍais tribhir mastakaiḥ

1 Reading 'viklṛptas'.

vijñānākhya-mahā-'sinā dyuti-matā
vicchidya śīrṣa-trayaṃ
nirmūlyāhim imaṃ nidhiṃ sukha-karaṃ
dhīro 'nubhoktuṃ kṣamaḥ

[303] 'The treasure of the bliss of the Absolute is wrapped round and guarded for its own use by the fearsome snake of the ego-sense, with its three vicious hoods representing the three constituents (guṇa). If a hero cuts off these three heads with the great gleaming sword of knowledge and destroys the ego, then he can enjoy the delightful treasure.

yāvad vā yat kiñcid viṣa-doṣa-sphūrtir asti ced dehe
katham ārogyāya bhavet tadvad ahantāpi yogino muktyai

[304] 'A body cannot be fit as long as even a drop of poison remains inside it. Similarly, the yogi cannot attain liberation as long as he harbours any ego-feeling at all.

The doctrine of the holy *Gita Shastra* is that our egoism is meant to be sacrificed in the service of man, God and Truth.

ahamo 'tyanta-nivṛttyā tat-kṛta-nānāvikalpa-saṃhṛtyā
pratyak-tattva-vivekād ayam aham asmīti vindate tattvam

[305] 'When the ego-sense itself is totally brought to an end, the various false imaginations it throws up are brought to an end with it. Then one is able to discriminate the inmost Self and to discover reality with the conviction "This am I".

Just as when you burn sandalwood, though the sandalwood is consumed it emits a fragrance which fills the whole room and your whole being is filled with it; so, if our egoism—our sense of individuality, petty possession and self-importance—is burnt in love of truth, devotion and inner silence, then we get the spiritual Truth.

ahaṅkartary asminn aham iti matiṃ muñca sahasā
vikārātmany ātma-pratiphala-juṣi sva-sthiti-muṣi
yad-adhyāsāt prāptā jani-mṛti-jarā-duḥkha-bahulā
pratīcaś cinmūrtes tava sukha-tanoḥ saṃsṛtir iyam

[306] 'Quickly abandon your identification with the ego-sense, which is subject to change, possesses no more than a reflection of the Self and robs you of your true nature. For your life in reincarnation, with its many sufferings through birth, death and decrepitude, arises from your superimposition of the ego-sense onto your true nature, which is the inmost Self, of the form of joy.

sadaika-rūpasya cid-ātmano vibhor
ānanda-mūrter anavadya-kīrteḥ
naivānyathā kvāpy avikāriṇas te
vinā 'ham-adhyāsam amuṣya saṃsṛtiḥ

[307] 'In your true nature you are the Self as pure Consciousness, ever homogeneous and unchanging, all-pervading, of the nature of bliss, irreproachable in any way. Changeless as you are, you could not undergo reincarnation except as an appearance resulting from superimposition of the ego-sense.

tasmād ahaṅkāram imaṃ sva-śatruṃ
bhoktur gale kaṇṭaka-vat pratītam
vicchidya vijñāna-mahā-'sinā sphuṭaṃ
bhuṅkṣvātma-sāmrājya-sukhaṃ yatheṣṭam

[308] 'This ego-sense is your enemy and is like a thorn in the throat of one trying to eat. So cut it out with the sword of knowledge and enjoy [lit. "eat"] at will the pleasure of the sovereignty of your own true Self.

tato 'ham āder vinivartya vṛttiṃ
santyakta-rāgaḥ paramārtha-lābhāt
tūṣṇīṃ samāssv'ātma-sukhānubhūtyā
pūrṇātmanā brahmaṇi nirvikalpaḥ

[309] 'And so, having rejected the notion of ego, etc., and having rid oneself of attachment through realizing the supreme Self, you should sit (samāssva) quietly in the Absolute with the experience of the joy of the Self, being free from all wrong imagination on account of (having realized) one's infinite Self.

sa-mūla-kṛtto 'pi mahān ahaṃ punar
vyullekhitaḥ syād yadi cetasā kṣaṇam
sañjīvya vikṣepa-śataṃ karoti
nabhasvatā prāvṛṣi vārido yathā

[310] 'But even after being obliterated together with its source, this great ego will return to life and assume hundreds of new forms if there appear even a momentary suggestion of it in the mind, like a cloud propelled by the wind in the rainy season.

42. Giving up self-interested action, anxiety and subtle impressions

nigṛhya śatror ahamo 'vakāśaḥ
kvacin na deyo viṣayānucintayā
sa eva sañjīvana-hetur asya
prakṣīṇa-jambīra-taror ivāmbu

[311] 'Once this enemy, your ego, has been firmly restrained, you should allow it no opportunity for thinking of pleasurable sense-objects, for this is just what brings it back to life, as water revives a parched citron tree.[1]

1 Cp. verse 268, above.

Man is subject to fear and the lunacy of greed, egoism, anger and aversion, so long as he clings to the unnatural raft of individuation in the sea of Consciousness. Contemplation of God as the universal essence, Shri Vasudeva, is the real life—to feel at-one-ment with Him who, by His innate power of compassion controls ignorance.

dehātmanā saṃsthita eva kāmī
vilakṣaṇaḥ kāmayitā kathaṃ syāt
ato 'rtha-sandhāna-paratvam eva
bheda-prasaktyā bhava-bandha-hetuḥ

[312] 'It is only he who identifies himself with the body who feels lust for sense-objects. How could this occur in one dissociated from the body? And so it is dwelling on objects that is the cause of repeated births, as it brings attachment to the realm of distinctions.

The mental action is more important than physical actions. The effect of an action is not on the organ but on the mind.

kārya-pravardhanād bīja-pravṛddiḥ paridṛśyate
kārya-nāśād bīja-nāśas tasmāt kāryaṃ nirodhayet

[313] 'In the case of the subtle impressions and their results, the cause is found to expand with the expansion of the effect, and to be eliminated with the elimination of the effect. So one should work to eliminate the effect.

Our actions once performed are not annihilated. A hard word or a kind word leaves its corresponding record on the tablet of the mind. The aggregate of these impressions is called our character. There is some truth in the statement of psychoanalysts that a large part of our mind works unconsciously. The play of vicarious desires is called unconscious urges.

vāsanā-vṛddhitaḥ kāryaṃ kārya-vṛddhyā ca vāsanā
vardhate sarvathā puṃsaḥ saṃsāro na nivartate

[314] 'The effects of the subtle impressions increase with the increase of the impressions, and the impressions increase with the increase of their effects. (It seems that) there is no way in which a person's rebirth can come to an end.

Many people imagine things: 'I wish I were this or that!' It is a most harmful practice. Each and every desire is a seed which you have sown in your mind. Therefore be very careful what you desire. These unconscious desires are the latent deposits in your psychological stuff, not only of one but of many incarnations.

saṃsāra-bandha-vicchittyai tad dvayaṃ pradahed yatiḥ
vāsanā-vṛddhir etābhyāṃ cintayā kriyayā bahiḥ

[315] 'Therefore a person of self-control must burn up both the impressions and their results (in the form of self-interested activity) in order to root out the bondage of rebirth. The impressions wax stronger through dwelling on external objects and through action to secure them.

tābhyāṃ pravardhamānā sā sūte saṃsṛtim ātmanaḥ
trayāṇāṃ ca kṣayopāyaḥ sarvāvasthāsu sarvadā

[316] 'It is the impressions as fed and augmented by thought and action that produce further reincarnation for the soul. One has to apply the means for putting an end to impressions, thoughts and self-interested action, all three, continuously, in all stages of one's life.

sarvatra sarvataḥ sarvaṃ brahma-mātrā 'valokanam
sad-bhāva-vāsanā-dārḍhyāt tat trayaṃ layam aśnute

> [317] 'This means is to fix one's gaze always, everywhere and in every way on the Absolute alone. The three (enemies in the form of the impressions, and the thoughts and self-interested actions to which they give rise) are brought to an end through the strengthening of the counter-impression that in one's true nature one is the Absolute (lit. 'the real').

There are two kinds of desires, dominant and superficial. The superficial desires are suppressed by the dominant desires. If you have a dominant desire, other desires will not bother you so much. I am no extraordinary man, but in my life I have been able to avoid many evils by having the one dominant desire that I must be a Brahmin scholar. I have simply refused to entertain any desire other than the desire to have learning and a knowledge of philosophy. Take a man whose dominant desire is to play cards or to drink; every other desire he has will be suppressed by it. So let your dominant desire be to know the Lord and to be united with Him.

kriyā-nāśe bhavec cintā-nāśo 'smād vāsanā-kṣayaḥ
vāsanā-prakṣayo mokṣaḥ sā jīvan-muktir iṣyate

> [318] 'With desistance from self-interested action comes cessation of thoughts about objects, and with this comes exhaustion of the impressions. Exhaustion of the impressions is liberation, called (in this form) "liberation in life".

sad-vāsanā-sphūrti-vijṛmbhaṇe sati
hy aṣau vilīnā tv aham-ādi-vāsanā
atiprakṛṣṭāpy aruṇa-prabhāyāṃ
vilīyate sādhu yathā tamisrā

> [319] 'Just as even the thickest darkness is dispelled by the light of the sun, so the subtle impressions of the individual ego and the rest are dispelled when the counter-impression of truth manifests.

tamas tamaḥ kāryam anartha-jālaṃ
na dṛśyate saty udite dineśe
tathādvayānanda-rasānubhūtau
naivāsti bandho na ca duḥkha-gandhaḥ

[320] 'Just as darkness and all its evil concomitants (burglary and so on) vanish with the rise of the sun, so bondage and every speck of pain disappears when there is direct realization of non-dual bliss.

This state is called Self-realization, attainment of God, direct perception of Self. This light never dims, fluctuates nor disappears. It is the only abiding principle in the empirical world, and once it is realized, there is nothing further to be achieved or attempted. There is no further need for discipline and no duty to be performed. 'I am the associationless Consciousness. What have I to do with the world and its duties?' says Shri Vidyaranya.

There are no degrees or stages in the Absolute, which is, was and ever will be the Self of the individual soul (jiva). Self-realization is not progressive. It is absolute. 'He who thinks himself to be free is free; he who thinks himself to be bound is bound', says the *Ashtavakra Gita*.

This is the final truth. Neither science, religion, nor philosophy have any other message to give. It is immortality. It is the discovery of the ever-achieved.

43. The danger of carelessness

dṛśyaṃ pratītaṃ pravilāpayan svayaṃ
san mātram ānanda-ghanaṃ vibhāvayan
samāhitaḥ san bahir antaraṃ vā
kālaṃ nayethāḥ sati karma-bandhe

[321] 'As long as bondage to merit and demerit remains, one should pass one's time in strict concentration, meditating on pure

Being as massed bliss, causing the gradual dissolution of the whole objective realm, inner and outer.

pramādo brahma-niṣṭhāyāṃ na kartavyaḥ kadācana
pramādo mṛtyur ity āha bhagavān brahmaṇaḥ sutaḥ

[322] 'One should never be careless over one's continuous devotion to the Absolute. That holy son of Brahmā, Sanatkumāra, spoke of carelessness as death.

An evil which proves a very great obstacle in the advancement of matters secular or spiritual is what is called in Sanskrit, pramada. It means carelessness, want of full appreciation of the importance of a task taken in hand, postponement of a good project begun owing to certain obstacles. We have to guard against this evil with as much care as we can command. There is no achievement without surmounting obstacles. A good and moral life is a walk on a steep hill which you cannot climb without enduring fatigue and having a strong will to move on.

na pramādād anartho 'nyo jñāninaḥ sva-svarūpataḥ
tato mohas tato 'haṃ-dhīs tato bandhas tato vyathā

[323] 'For him who has attained metaphysical knowledge, there is no other evil apart from carelessness (in forgetting) about his own true nature. For delusion springs from it, and from delusion ego-sense, from ego-sense bondage, and from bondage suffering.

viṣayābhimukhaṃ dṛṣṭvā vidvāṃsam api vismṛtiḥ
vikṣepayati dhī-doṣair yoṣā jāram iva priyam

[324] 'Forgetfulness may bring about agitation even in the mind of a man of spiritual vision, if he turns towards objects, just as a woman may be the cause of agitation in the mind of her dear illicit lover due to his mental defects (like attachment, etc.).

yathā 'pakṛṣṭaṃ śaivālaṃ kṣaṇa-mātraṃ na tiṣṭhati
āvṛṇoti tathā māyā prājñaṃ vāpi parāṅmukham

[325] 'Just as duckweed on a pond returns immediately even when pushed away, so Māyā will cover over even a man of wisdom if he turns his attention away from the supreme.

lakṣya-cyutaṃ sad yadi cittam īṣad
bahir-mukhaṃ san nipatet tatas tataḥ
pramādataḥ pracyuta-keli-kandukaḥ
sopāna-paṅktau patito yathā tathā

[326] 'If the mind becomes even a little extrovertive and falls away from its true goal, then it drops down again and again as a ball dropped carelessly will bounce its way down a flight of steps.

viṣayeṣv āviśec cetaḥ saṅkalpayati tad-guṇān
samyak-saṅkalpanāt kāmaḥ kāmāt puṃsaḥ pravartanam

[327] 'If the mind turns to objects, it pictures to itself their attributes. From vigorous picturing springs desire, from desire springs self-interested activity.

tataḥ svarūpa-vibhraṃśo vibhraṣṭas tu pataty adhaḥ
patitasya vinā nāśaṃ punar nāroha īkṣyate
saṅkalpaṃ varjayet tasmāt sarvānarthasya kāraṇam

[328] 'From self-interested activity results a fall from one's true nature, and one who has fallen from his true nature sinks down low. One who falls in this way does not (usually) rise up but goes to destruction. Therefore one should avoid this process of picturing the attributes of objects, the cause of all evil.

There is some truth in what the Communists call dialectical

materialism, though the word 'dialectical' is Hegelian, not coined by Marx, and can be applied more to the moral and spiritual phase of life than to the social and economic conditions. It means progress through clashes of two opposing forces.

There is the quality of inertia, or tamas, in the mind of man and there is the opposing force of activity, called rajas. The quantity of tamas in our mind, which produces love of ease and comfort and the urge to extract pleasure from external objects without much struggle, ought to be reduced by the exercise of rajas of a higher order. Tamas first manifests itself in a slight tendency to postpone the performance of our duty or spiritual task. If it is not checked then, it gathers force.

A very simple habit which, when formed, is a great antidote to carelessness, is the two-fold habit of studying some spiritual classic every day and writing something every day to help us in our study and to help others. If these two practices are pursued every day, then carelessness will not dare to invade our heart, and its harmful suggestions will be nipped in the bud. If you want to be saved from many moral and spiritual difficulties, to have a sweet disposition, to be a diffuser of cheerfulness and goodwill, then be a student of the holy philosophy, both in the metaphysical and aesthetic senses.

ataḥ pramādān na paro 'sti mṛtyur
vivekino brahma-vidaḥ samādhau
samāhitaḥ siddhim upaiti samyak-
samāhitātmā bhava sāvadhānaḥ

[329] 'And so, for the person of discrimination who knows the Absolute, there is no other death apart from carelessness over concentration. He who practises (continuous) concentration achieves success. So be careful, be a man of concentration.

Carelessness (pramada) is like insidious poison analogous to the administration of unrefined mercury to your system injudiciously. Carelessness in little things, if not checked, leads to carelessness in big things. To wake up at an appointed time every morning stops the assaults of carelessness. But it is not enough to wake up and to go on day-dreaming. To expose the mind to the winds of thoughts which are irrelevant is also a form of carelessness. To be punctual in our appointments and in the performance of our daily allotted tasks has proved a great help in subduing carelessness. The best time to practise any virtue is the morning, and to meditate on it before going to sleep is to impress your consciousness with it.

44. Rejection of the unreal

jīvato yasya kaivalyaṃ videhe sa ca kevalaḥ
yat kiñcit paśyato bhedaṃ bhayaṃ brūte yajuḥ śrutiḥ

[330] 'He who attains transcendence while still alive is (surely) transcendent (kevala) on the fall of the body. The Yajur Veda (Taittirīya Upanishad 2.7) says that anyone who sees any distinctions whatever experiences fear.

yadā kadā vāpi vipaścid eṣa
brahmaṇy anante 'py aṇu-mātra-bhedam
paśyaty athāmuṣya bhayaṃ tadaiva
yad vīkṣitaṃ bhinnatayā pramādāt

[331] 'Whenever a wise person of this kind sees even a speck of difference in the infinite Absolute, then whatever he has seen through carelessness as different, immediately becomes a danger to him.

śruti-smṛti-nyāya-śatair niṣiddhe
dṛśye 'tra yaḥ svātma-matiṃ karoti
upaiti duḥkhopari duḥkha-jātaṃ
niṣiddha-kartā sa malimluco yathā

[332] 'He who identifies himself with anything perceptible,

against the teaching of the Veda and the tradition (smṛti), supported by hundreds of arguments, goes from misery to misery. He is a felon, like a thief.

satyābhisandhāna-rato vimukto
mahattvam ātmīyam upaiti nityam
mithyābhisandhāna-ratas tu naśyed
dṛṣṭaṃ tad etad yad acora-corayoḥ

[333] 'He who tells the truth is liberated and attains his true greatness; he who speaks what is untrue perishes. We see this in the case of trial by ordeal, which separates the innocent one from the thief.[1]

yatir asad anusandhiṃ bandha-hetuṃ vihāya
svayam ayam aham asmīty ātma-dṛṣṭyaiva tiṣṭhet
sukhayati nanu niṣṭhā brahmaṇi svānubhūtyā
harati param avidyā-kārya-duḥkhaṃ pratītam

[334] 'A man of discipline should withdraw from pursuit of the unreal, the cause of bondage. He should remain with his gaze fixed on the Self, thinking "This I am". Devotion to immediate apprehension of the Absolute gives joy and removes that terrible suffering that is undergone on account of metaphysical ignorance.

The knowledge of the Self is more important than fame, wealth and so forth. He will not be able to know the Self, or God, who still relishes the delights of the world. But he who knows that there is the sting of a bee in every drop of honey, that passing things bring only passing delight, he is qualified to know the Truth and thus to become free, above death and more stable than the pole-star.

1 Cp. *Chāndogya Upanishad* 6.16.1

bāhyānusandhiḥ parivardhayet phalaṃ
dur-vāsanām eva tatas tato 'dhikām
jñātvā vivekaiḥ parihṛtya bāhyaṃ
svātmānusandhiṃ vidadhīta nityam

[335] 'Attention to the external increases its essential result, bad subtle impressions, further and further the more it goes on. One should come to see this through making the various necessary acts of discrimination and should withdraw from the external and seek continually for the Self.

Our life is like a book, some pages of which are already written, but a good bit of which is not written. What is already written is our karma, the result of actions of the past with which we have come into the world. The impressions of all the past actions are treasured in a very minute form on the causal body, which is wrongly called 'the subconscious' or 'the unconscious' by the psychologists. There are many blank pages and many blank lines on every page of our daily life. It is for us to write on them, and what we write constitutes or conditions our bliss, our freedom.

Write benevolence, write tolerance, write self-conquest and write devotion to God in the book of your life every day. If you write new lines in a more vivid ink and with greater sweep, then you cancel a good bit of what is already written.

bāhye niruddhe manasaḥ prasannatā
manaḥ-prasāde paramātma-darśanam
tasmin sudṛṣṭe bhava-bandha-nāśo
bahir-nirodhaḥ padavī vimukteḥ

[336] 'When the external has been blocked out, the mind becomes clear. When the mind is clear, vision of the supreme Self ensues. When the supreme Self has been well and truly perceived, the bondage of worldly life comes to an end. Blocking out the external is thus the path to liberation.

kaḥ paṇḍitaḥ san sad-asad-vivekī
śruti-pramāṇaḥ paramārtha-darśī
jānan hi kuryād asato 'valambaṃ
sva-pāta-hetoḥ śiśu-van mumukṣuḥ

[337] 'What seeker of the Absolute, who was wise and able to discriminate the real from the unreal, and who, having accepted the Veda as his authority, had enjoyed direct vision of the final reality, would deliberately resort to the unreal, the cause of his fall, like a thoughtless child?

dehādi-saṃsakti-mato na muktir
muktasya dehādy-abhimaty-abhāvaḥ
suptasya no jāgaraṇaṃ na jāgrataḥ
svapnas tayor bhinna-guṇāśrayatvāt

[338] 'He who is attached to the body and so on cannot have liberation; and the liberated one cannot feel attachment for the body and so on. He who is asleep cannot have waking experience, nor can he who is awake enjoy sleep, as the two states have different attributes.

Yoga is not a set of practices which you can follow for a certain time and then live as you like. It is a way of life devoted to the fulfilment of our spiritual destiny, the unfoldment by each and every individual of this divine consciousness in himself to an unlimited extent. It means to come into contact with the indwelling reality called God, and to feel consciously immortal, consciously omniscient—to feel consciously that every living being, whether rich or poor, ignorant or learned, is the manifestation of the same divine being who manifests in us.

45. How to concentrate on the Self

antar bahiḥ svaṃ sthira-jaṅgameṣu
jñānātmanā ''dhāratayā vilokya
tyaktākhilopādhir akhaṇḍa-rūpaḥ
pūrṇātmanā yaḥ sthita eṣa muktaḥ

[339] 'He who has seen himself as Consciousness[1] standing as the support of all the moving and the fixed, both within and without, who has given up identification with any conditioning adjunct, who is without differentiation and stands as the infinite Self of all—he is liberated.

sarvātmatā bandha-vimukti-hetuḥ
sarvātma-bhāvān na paro 'sti kaścit
dṛśyāgrahe saty upapadyate 'sau
sarvātma-bhāvo 'sya sad-ātma-niṣṭhayā

[340] 'Becoming the Self of all[2] is the cause of liberation from bondage. There is nothing higher than realizing that one is the Self of all. This "being the Self of all" is only possible when devotion to the Self as the real is so intense that the objects of the world are not apprehended.[3]

dṛśyasyāgrahaṇaṃ kathaṃ nu ghaṭate dehātmanā tiṣṭhato
bāhyārthānubhava-prasakta-manasas tat-tat-kriyāṃ kurvataḥ
saṃnyastākhila-dharma-karma-viṣayair nityātma-niṣṭhā-parais
tattva-jñaiḥ karaṇīyam ātmani sad-ānandecchubhir yatnataḥ

1 Reading 'jñānātmanā' with Muni Lāl and Bhāgavat.

2 Reading 'sarvātmatā' according to the demands of the context.

3 'not apprehended as real', Muni Lāl.

> [341] 'How can the objects of the world not be apprehended on the part of one who remains identified with the body, whose mind is attached to the experience of external objects, and who performs various acts to attain them? This "non-apprehension" of objects is what has to be achieved through diligence by those who know the metaphysical truth, who have a deep desire for the reality and bliss of the Self, who have given up all rules, rituals and objects, and whose one continuous passion is devotion to the Self.

As the supreme purpose of a race-horse is to beat all other horses on the way to the goal, so the purpose of the human soul is to acquire freedom and illumination by awakening the seeds of divine wisdom in its own being. If the horse leaves the allotted track, what will happen? The spurs, the whip which inflicts great pain, shouts, scolding and subsequent want of affection are shown to the horse that does not run straight to the goal but indulges in a side-track. So the human soul which forgets the main purpose of life, and deviates from the straight and narrow path to spiritual illumination into the side-tracks of mundane and trivial pursuits—such as the pursuit of pleasure and power— is beset with immense difficulties, pain, suffering and all other kinds of hardship. When the heart has been purged by the application of discipline and virtue in daily life, when prejudices have been eliminated, pride and vanity expelled, and anger, avarice and attachment learnt to be futile; then the soul is ready for real spirituality, and not before.

sarvātmya-siddhaye bhikṣoḥ kṛta-śravaṇa-karmaṇaḥ
samādhiṃ vidadhāty eṣā śānto dānta iti śrutiḥ

> [342] 'To the monk who has completed the discipline of hearing, the Veda prescribes concentration (samādhi) as the means for "becoming the Self of all" in the words "restrained within" (śānta) and "restrained without" (dānta) (Bṛhadāraṇyaka Upanishad 4.4.23).

Doubtless in certain passages of the Acharya's writings the monastic life (samnyasa) is emphasized as an essential to Self-cognition and the attainment of spiritual illumination. But if we study his writings carefully, such monasticism is seen to imply not a special order but a point of view of the spiritual life. It is merely a most spiritual feeling towards the world which negates attachment to all unreal objects. It is not necessarily renouncing the world. The theory of the ashramas does not imply that monastic life is an essential. A man can be a spiritual renunciate while occupying a throne, as is clear from the instance of King Janaka.[1]

The first step is shravana, to hear the truth from a spiritual teacher. Will mere teaching or mere listening solve the riddle of life? No! There comes a time when the listening ends and something else begins. It is called reasoning (manana). Knowledge must be assimilated by reasoning. Whatever you listen to has no meaning unless in your calm moments you reason it out, with all the arguments for and against, making that knowledge your own knowledge.

Realization depends on the awakening through sustained meditation (nididhyasana) of a higher faculty of understanding. Our understanding operates on many levels. To a little child the toy is an object of amusement, to an engineer it is a machine which he wants to study, to a philosopher it is a symbol and he wants to know what it symbolizes. What is needed is to awaken in our intellect that faculty which apprehends Truth, and that faculty is above reason.

Yoga says that there is a special faculty of understanding in the human soul which has to be resuscitated so that the final Truth may be clear and may be realized. Reason proves the validity of a doctrine, but cannot make you realize the essence of that doctrine and take full advantage of that realization, unless your higher faculty of understanding is awakened through meditation. This is a factor which distinguishes the yogic teachings from those of the so-called 'rationalists'.

1 see *Bṛhadāraṇyaka Upanishad* 4.2.4 and *Gītā* 3.20. The 'ashramas' are the four stages of life traditionally followed in ancient times by orthodox Hindus: religious student, householder, forest-dweller and renunciate.

ārūḍha-śakter ahamo vināśaḥ
kartuṃ na śakyaḥ sahasāpi paṇḍitaiḥ
ye nirvikalpākhya-samādhi-niścalās
tān antarā 'nanta-bhavā hi vāsanāḥ

[343] 'Nor, in general, can the wise immediately halt the power of the ego once it is well entrenched. It is only those who are motionless in that form of concentration (samādhi) known as "void of all imagination" who can do so. For the subtle impressions derive from innumerable previous lives.

The mind of man, like a rose, has innumerable petals, and its depths have not yet been touched by Western psychology. When we have opened those secret petals of the rose of our mind, in which peace and tranquillity dwell, we call it 'samadhi'. People think that this word has something to do with shutting the nostrils alternately; but no, that only leads to nervous illness. Samadhi means that the mind contacts the region of peace and tranquillity within itself. This peace is creative. It is not like the peace and tranquillity of the drone who, having left the honeycomb, sleeps the whole day doing nothing. A few days more and the other bees kill him.

Never confound peace with negativity. Intense creativity is a characteristic of samadhi. Who has created the greatest poetry? Rishi Valmiki, a man of samadhi, the author of the *Ramayana*. Who has written the highest metaphysical classic? Shri Vyasa in the *Gita*. It is not running away from the world. It is running from the false world into the real world, and there, in the real world, creating forms of beauty and truth which will serve as the light of Jupiter when the moon of wisdom has withdrawn itself on a dark night. The man who says 'I am in samadhi', but does not create or appreciate anything, is a poser.

ahaṃ-buddhyaiva mohinyā yojayitvāvṛter balāt
vikṣepa-śaktiḥ puruṣaṃ vikṣepayati tad-guṇaiḥ

> [344] 'The power of projection (vikṣepa-śakti), having forcibly linked the soul with the delusive ego-notion, prompts it to act through the attributes of that very ego-notion.

Either the uncontrolled mind is distracted or it seeks complacency, which is not a spiritual state at all. That state in which our mind is distracted by the desire for pleasure is called vikshepa. The greatest distraction to the mind is caused by desires for power, pleasure and sex. This state of agitation is most detrimental to the growth of the mind and sends it hurtling downwards in the course of devolution. Then it loses the capacity to create beauty, harmony and peace, and that is the state of complacency, or laya.

vikṣepa-śakti-vijayo viṣamo vidhātuṃ
  niḥśeṣam āvaraṇa-śakti-nivṛtty-abhāve
dṛg-dṛśyayoḥ sphuṭa-payo-jalavad vibhāge
  naśyet tadā ''varaṇam ātmani ca svabhāvāt
niḥsaṃśayena bhavati pratibandha-śūnyo
  vikṣepaṇaṃ na hi tadā yadi cen mṛṣārthe

> [345] 'Unless the power of concealment (āvaraṇa-śakti) has been brought to a halt, it is difficult to acquire complete victory over the power of projection. But when the subject (i.e., metaphysical subject, the pure Self as universal witness) and object have been distinguished clearly like water and milk, then the concealing power dissolves of its own accord into the Self. When that has occurred, victory over the power of projection will certainly be complete and unhindered; for there will not be projection when objects are known to be unreal.

As the root of all sins is the feeling of duality, the concealing power (avarana) is sometimes called impurity (mala). The right hand never quarrels with the left hand or the eye or the neck; so the knower (jnani) who has seen the non-duality of all is at peace with all. The feeling of duality is ignorance (ajnana). The Veda declares: 'Verily all is Brahman (the Absolute)'.[1] It is only in delusion that the feeling of duality strikes us. 'O Gudakesha, I am the Self of all, abiding in all beings', says the Lord.[2]

The concealing power (avarana) does not allow the mind to come to the Yoga. It encourages scepticism and materialism, like that of Herbert Spencer, who said that Truth is unknown and unknowable. The power of projection (vikshepa) forms an obstacle to endurance in the practice of Yoga. It side-tracks the mind, showing the green gardens of a comfortable life and creating a thirst for alcohol, possession of wealth and sex-relationship. Mad pursuit of pleasure is the outcome of the projecting power. Its sure consequence is only suffering. It breeds fickleness, selfishness and sloth. It is hell.

What else is there to attain when avarana and vikshepa are overcome? Knowledge of Truth (jnana), a vision of the identity of the local self with the universal Self.

samyag-vivekaḥ sphuṭa-bodha-janyo
vibhajya dṛg-dṛśya-padārtha-tattvam
chinatti māyā-kṛta-moha-bandhaṃ
yasmād vimuktasya punar na saṃsṛtiḥ

> [346] 'Right discrimination arises from clear knowledge. It separates the subject from the object as two metaphysical principles (real and false respectively). It cuts the bonds of delusion set up by Māyā, so that the liberated one does not again undergo reincarnation in the world.

Discrimination means to be always vigilant, to know what is passing and what is eternal; to ignore the passing and to cling to the eternal with all the strength of your soul. Detachment means that you have the power to extricate yourself from any object, any experience

1 *Chāndogya Upanishad* 3.14.1

2 *Gītā* 10.20

in the world, however sweet, at a moment's notice. Unless a man has that power, his life is no good at all. Therefore discrimination and detachment are two most important words; they give you an empire over yourself, an empire worth having and which you have for ever. By the practice of these two, discrimination and detachment, the individual soul (jiva) realizes that the object and locus of avidya (ignorance) is its own consciousness, and it is purified by the expansion of being in knowledge, or God-consciousness. The locus of avidya is man's consciousness and the object of avidya is the individual (jivic) consciousness also. When you have overcome this avidya, you participate in the divine Consciousness, nothing less than God Himself.

parāvaraikatva-viveka-vahnir
dahaty avidyā-gahanaṃ hy aśeṣaṃ
kiṃ syāt punaḥ saṃsaraṇasya bījam
advaita-bhāvaṃ samupeyuṣo 'sya

[347] 'The fire of the discriminative knowledge of the identity of the soul with the Supreme demolishes the entire forest of metaphysical ignorance. When the soul has once acquired the non-dual state, how could it return to the life of reincarnation?

āvaraṇasya nivṛttir bhavati ca samyak-padārtha-darśanataḥ
mithyājñāna-vināśas tadvad vikṣepa-janita-duḥkha-nivṛttiḥ

[348] 'When the reality is truly known, the concealing power is brought to an end. From this follow the destruction of positive erroneous knowledge and the end of the pain produced by the power of projection.

As soon as the rope is recognized, the snake disappears; but the fear and agitation caused by the previously imagined presence of the snake in the room persist a little while longer.

46. The metaphysical substratum (adhiṣṭhāna)

etat tritayaṃ dṛṣṭaṃ samyag-rajju-svarūpa-vijñānāt
tasmād vastu sa-tattvaṃ jñātavyaṃ bandha-muktaye viduṣā

> [349] 'These three (i.e., destruction of concealment, of projection and of the fear and pain arising from projection) occur through right knowledge of the rope (which dispels the illusory snake). So a wise person should know the true nature of the real for the sake of liberation from bondage.

Avarana and vikshepa are negative; right knowledge (jnana) is positive. How does jnana come? By the grace of the Lord.

ayo 'gni-yogād iva sat-samanvayān
mātrādi-rūpeṇa vijṛmbhate dhīḥ
tat kāryam etad dvitayaṃ yato mṛṣā
dṛṣṭaṃ bhrama-svapna-manorathesu

> [350] 'The mind assumes the form of knower, knowledge and known through the constant presence (of the supporting and illumining force) of the real, as molten iron is able to assume various forms through the presence of fire. The fact that the duality it produces is illusory is seen from the cases of perceptual error, dream and day-dreaming.

In Advaita Vedanta, perception is held to be immediate consciousness, absolute cognition. It is a psychological process which is both subjective and objective, a determinate consciousness of an object and an indeterminate consciousness of the self knowing the object.

Three aspects of consciousness are recognized by the holy Acharyas of Advaita: (1) the transcendent though expressive Witness consciousness (sakshi cetana); (2) the logical subject consciousness (pramatri chetana) (3) the consciousness immanent in the psychological process (vritti cetana). Vritti is an idea which becomes definite as the mental consciousness functions according to a form or mould. It is the vritti which, going out through the sense orifices (indriya), assumes manifestation in the form of the object. An object is illumined by the Witness consciousness (sakshi chetana) and it is this Witness consciousness which reveals it.

tato vikārāḥ prakṛter aham-mukhā
dehāvasānā viṣayāś ca sarve
kṣaṇe 'nyathā bhāvitayā hy amīṣām
asattvam ātmā tu kadāpi nānyathā

[351] 'It follows from this that all modifications of Nature are false, both those that form the series from the ego to the body —that make up the individual—and those that form the objects he experiences. They are unreal because they change form every moment. But the Self never changes.

nityādvayākhaṇḍa-cid-eka-rūpo
buddhyādi-sākṣī sad-asad-vilakṣaṇaḥ
ahaṃ-pada-pratyaya-lakṣitārthaḥ
pratyak-sadānanda-ghanaḥ parātmā

[352] 'The supreme Self, indicated indirectly (but not correctly represented) by the notion promoted by the word 'I', is the one Consciousness, eternal, indivisible and non-dual. It is the witness of the mind and other factors in the human personality. Neither being nor non-being in the empirical sense, it is a homogeneous mass of bliss, the inmost reality.

The Spirit is the sun, ever luminous, never darkened, truth and bliss, infinite and imperishable. It is neither one nor two; there is no other existence beside the Spirit. When it is spoken of in relation to the personality of man, it is called Self (atman), the inmost reality. It is the basis of heaven and earth. The mind is like a cloud which is formed by the rays of the sun, the Self (atman). It has no reality of its own; where is any reality of the cloud other than the sun? The sun of the Spirit is reflected in the cloud of the mind as knowledge, activity and bliss. The world is like the cloud materialized externally. It, too, has no independent existence; it is from the sun, of the sun, a phase of the sun. The sun of Spirit conditioned by the cloud of the mind is the individuality in man.

itthaṃ vipaścit sad-asad vibhajya
niścitya tattvaṃ nija-bodha-dṛṣṭyā
jñātvā svam ātmānam akhaṇḍa-bodhaṃ
tebhyo vimuktaḥ svayam eva śāmyati

[353] 'In this way, a person of wisdom discriminates the real from the unreal and comes to know the reality through direct vision in his own consciousness. Having known his own Self as undifferentiated Consciousness, he is liberated from these unreal modifications and rests in the peace of his own true nature.

When the mind is pure and peaceful, the sun conditioned in it realizes its identity with the universal sun. This is the spiritual Truth and, when realized, it gives unbroken peace, blissfulness and a feeling of identity with the sun. Is there any practical value of this realization of identity? Yes. Before the individuality is finally dissolved, it is inspired under the rays of the illumination and it creates art, poetry, music and philosophy to lighten the material burden of mankind. It diffuses peace, light and bliss which are above emotion and which radiate from it like the rays from the sun.

The process of purification, elimination of vice and egoism, and the inner peace under which the identity is realized, is called Adhyatma Yoga.

47. Total concentration (samādhi)

ajñāna-hṛdaya-granther niḥśeṣa-vilayas tadā
samādhinā 'vikalpena yadā 'dvaitātma-darśanam

[354] 'The knot in the heart (Muṇḍaka Upanishad 2.2.8) formed by ignorance is only finally dissolved when there is vision of the non-dual Self through that form of concentration (samādhi) that is totally void of false imagination (nirvikalpa).

Etymologically, samadhi comes from 'sama', 'equal', and 'dhi', 'intellect', and means 'equality of intellect', the determinative quality by which you can see a running thread of unity in all diversity—you see the Lord in the saint and sinner alike. It means sustained meditation (nididhyasana) developed to the highest possible extent. Samadhi is the flowering out of the state of meditation and contemplation. In meditation your mind is peaceful only for the time being, but when you can continue it even when you are out of meditation, this is called samadhi. Follow the teaching of Shri Shankara on this and you are on the right lines. Don't be distracted by Patanjali and modern writers. In this condition, all ideas of one's being a contemplator and of the process of contemplation vanish, and the mind, witnessing its contemplation, is as still 'as a lamp sheltered from the wind' (*Gita* 6.19). Our object is to enrich the mind and to see the death of the mind consciously. This is samadhi. The mind is the only barrier between the soul and God, and when it is slain, the sacrifice is complete.

The wise, therefore, all the time keep before the mind either the holy name or a concept of God. If you worship anything as a symbol of the Lord with great intensity and devotion, the Lord will speak to you through this symbol. This is called 'pratika upasana' (worship through a symbol).[1]

1 See Swami Rama Tirtha's essay on 'Worship' included in *Scientist and Mahatma*, by H. P. Shastri, p.80 (published by Shanti Sadan).

tvam aham idam itīyaṃ kalpanā buddhi-doṣāt
prabhavati paramātmany advaye nirviśeṣe
pravilasati samādhāv asya sarvo vikalpo
vilayanam upagacched vastu-tattvāvadhṛtyā

[355] 'Through the defects of the mind, false notions like "you", "I" (as opposed to "you") and "this" are applied to the supreme Self, which is in reality without distinctions. But when concentration reigns, all these false imaginations are dissolved through a keen sense of reality as it is.

Samadhi is of two kinds: (a) samadhi with ideas (savikalpa)—the state of mind resembling a continuous stream of spiritual reflection; (b) samadhi without ideas (nirvikalpa)—withdrawal of it, the state of deep concentration in which there is a total and absolute absence of the triad of knower, knowledge and known, and the modification (vritti) of the mind assumes the form of the partless attributeless Brahman (the Absolute).

In the state of nirvikalpa samadhi there is a slight consciousness of duality, but it gives rise to no attachment and is not an obstacle. The triad of the knower, knowledge and the known does not appear in the form of duality. Just as a lump of salt dissolved in water remains in the water, yet you do not perceive it, so is the phenomenal universe (jagat) merged in Brahman (the Absolute) in the state of nirvikalpa samadhi. It has a slight, dim, unreal and phenomenal existence, but it is all Brahman (the Absolute).

śānto dāntaḥ param uparataḥ kṣānti-yuktaḥ samādhiṃ
kurvan nityaṃ kalayati yatiḥ svasya sarvātma-bhāvam
tenāvidyā-timira-janitān sādhu dagdhvā vikalpān
brahmākṛtyā nivasati sukhaṃ niṣkriyo nirvikalpaḥ

[356] 'The truly disciplined person continually concentrates his mind with inner and outer restraint, total desistance from self-interested action and patience in all circumstances. Thereby he

> attains to his true nature as the Self of all. Through this he burns up all false imagination born of the darkness of ignorance and lives happily in identity with the Absolute, actionless and without false imagination.

Dr Radhakrishnan quotes a beautiful simile in his translation of the *Gita*: 'As an acrobatic dancer twists and tortures her body in a million ways, but the object is to please the one for whom she is dancing, so the people of the world who have any wisdom, doing this or doing that, ever keep the mind concentrated on the Lord. The wise under no circumstances give up the contemplation of the lotus-feet of Mukunda'.[1] This is the real life of man. You need no psycho-analysis or treatment if you can do that, because the culmination of all life is to contemplate God with a pure heart, a heart from which all desires have been driven as poisonous beasts are driven out of the house, should they ever lodge themselves in it.

samāhitā ye pravilāpya bāhyaṃ
    śrotrādi cetaḥ svam ahaṃ cid-ātmani
ta eva muktā bhava-pāśa-bandhair
    nānye tu pārokṣya-kathābhidhāyinaḥ

> [357] 'Those who practise concentration and dissolve everything external, including the senses, the mind and the ego, into the Self as pure Consciousness—they alone are liberated from the bonds of worldly reincarnation, and not those who speak about what they only know abstractly.

When this state of concentration is matured and fixed, the mental modification (vritti) of knowledge (jnana) arises and nescience, as the mind, is burnt up.

Nobody has ever acquired God-vision by the mere study of books. The truth has to be expounded by the loving lips of a traditional teacher

1 'The Deliverer', a name of Vishnu.

who is a knower of Brahman (the Absolute). It must be listened to with faith and reverence, and in return the pupil must give his loving personal service (see *Gita* 4.34). The teachings are to be revered more than the teacher. The mind must be controlled and focused on the truth expounded. Mere hearing is not enough: what is heard has to be assimilated in inner silence. Mere intellectual appreciation of the truth will not bring the promised results.

upādhi-bhedāt svayam eva bhidyate
copādhy-apohe svayam eva kevalaḥ
tasmād upādher vilayāya vidvān
vaset sadā 'kalpa-samādhi-niṣṭhayā

[358] 'The Self undergoes (apparent) distinction through the distinctions of the apparent conditioning adjuncts, and when the adjuncts have been removed it stands transcendent. Therefore the person of wisdom should ever live in continuous concentration without false imagination in order to dissolve (every) conditioning adjunct.

sati sakto naro yāti sad-bhavaṃ hy eka-niṣṭhayā
kīṭako bhramaraṃ dhyāyan bhramaratvāya kalpate

[359] 'If a person is attached to the real, he "becomes" the real through one-pointed devotion. It is like the case of the insect which (according to popular tradition) turns into a bee through meditating on it (in paralytic terror).

kriyāntarāsaktim apāsya kīṭako
dhyāyan yathāliṃ hy ali-bhāvam ṛcchati
tathaiva yogī paramātma-tattvaṃ
dhyātvā samāyāti tad-eka-niṣṭhayā

[360] 'Just as the insect (according to popular belief) lays aside preoccupation with any other kind of activity and meditates

on the bee and thereby becomes the bee, so the yogi meditates on reality as the supreme Self and "enters into it" through one-pointed concentration on that.

atīva sūkṣmaṃ paramātma-tattvaṃ
  na sthūla-dṛṣṭyā pratipattum arhati
samādhinā 'tyanta-susūkṣma-vṛttyā
  jñātavyaṃ āryair ati-śuddha-buddhibhiḥ

[361] 'One cannot apprehend the extremely subtle reality as the supreme Self through coarse worldly vision. It can only be known by noble souls of very subtle intellect through an extremely subtle modification of the mind brought about by yogic concentration (samādhi).

When the subjective modification (vritti) is stable and issues from a pure desireless mind, it assumes the form of 'I am Brahman (the Absolute)'. This is the highest vritti.[1]

yathā suvarṇaṃ puṭa-pāka-śodhitaṃ
  tyaktvā malaṃ svātma-guṇaṃ samṛcchati
tathā manaḥ sattva-rajas-tamo-malaṃ
  dhyānena saṃtyajya sameti tattvam

[362] 'Just as gold when heated in a crucible loses its coat of impurities and attains its natural lustre, so the mind loses its impurities of sattva, rajas and tamas through meditation and attains its true natural state (as the Self).

nirantarābhyāsa-vaśāt tad itthaṃ
  pakvaṃ mano brahmaṇi līyate yadā
tadā samādhiḥ sa vikalpa-varjitaḥ
  svato 'dvayānanda-rasānubhāvakaḥ

1 Cp. verse 428 and comment, below.

[363] 'When the mind, thus matured by constant practice, dissolves in the Absolute, there ensues a natural concentration, void of all false imagination, which brings immediate experience of the savour of non-dual bliss.

samādhinā 'nena samasta-vāsanā-
granther vināśo 'khila-karma-nāśaḥ
antar bahiḥ sarvata eva sarvadā
svarūpa-visphūrtir ayatnataḥ syāt

[364] 'Through this concentration, there ensues the destruction of the whole knot of the subtle impressions and of all merit and demerit. Reality manifests effortlessly all the time, everywhere, on all sides, within and without.

śruteḥ śata-guṇaṃ vidyān mananaṃ mananād api
nididhyāsaṃ lakṣa-guṇam anantaṃ nirvikalpakam

[365] 'One should know that pondering over what one has heard from Vedic revelation is a hundred times better than the mere hearing. Sustained meditation on it is a hundred thousand times better than pondering. But the value of concentration without false imagination of any kind (e.g., without even the subject-object distinction implied by sustained meditation) is incalculable.

nirvikalpaka-samādhinā sphuṭaṃ
brahma-tattvam avagamyate dhruvam
nānyathā calatayā mano-gateḥ
pratyayāntara-vimiśritaṃ bhavet

[366] 'The Absolute as the real is known clearly through that form of concentration (samādhi) that is totally free from all false imagination (nirvikalpaka). It is not known in any other way, because elsewhere other ideas are intermixed on account of the mercurial nature of the mind.

When the ultimate Reality is understood under the supra-mental condition called samadhi, it is called the Self or Atman of man. It is described as imperishable, all-pervasive consciousness and bliss. It has no particular name and yet is known under thousands of names. The mind which tries to express the inexpressible speaks of It in symbols. The highest expression is Existence, Consciousness and Bliss (sat-chit-ananda).[1] It can also be described as Truth, Knowledge and Infinity (satyam-jnanam-anantam).[2] This is the nearest approach by speech and mind to an idea of the ultimate Reality.

The ultimate Reality is self-conditioned, though not absolutely, and the unillumined mind sees it in a mysterious form called Maya. The finite mind has to understand the infinite. The mind itself is a condition superimposed on Reality, and all that it *can* understand is Maya, a mystery. Reality is beyond it. Swami Vidyaranya says: 'The mind becomes no mind, all the latent impressions in it are blotted out and nothing is left of the mind or in the mind. Then the mystery is revealed. The Infinite in man, the Self (atman), sees the Infinite in nature, above the realm of time-space and causation, Maya'. As long as the ultimate Reality is not seen, it is Maya; when the ultimate Reality is known, It is Self (atman). As soon as a dream is known to be a dream, or unreal, it disappears and the state of waking follows. What was the dream? A mystery, a wonder, Maya.

The highest function of the mind of man is to know, to understand. In the West, since the time of Aristotle, man has been trying to unveil the Real, to understand Truth and live in the light of Truth. It is most reasonable to strive to rise above the sense of egoity. All ideas of race, family and caste superiority, all individual selfishness which seeks power over others, all desire for pleasure through hoarding and possessing is unnatural.

1 Cp. verse 291, above.

2 see *Taittirīya Upanishad* 2.1.1

ataḥ samādhatsva yatendriyaḥ sadā
nirantaraṃ śānta-manāḥ pratīci
vidhvaṃsaya dhvāntam anādy-avidyayā
kṛtaṃ sad-ekatva-vilokanena

[367] 'Therefore you should control your senses and ever concentrate on the inmost Self with a peaceful mind. Destroy the darkness, brought on by beginningless ignorance, by direct vision of your identity with (or, of the unity of) the real.

yogasya prathamaṃ dvāraṃ vāṅ-nirodho 'parigrahaḥ
nirāśā ca nirīhā ca nityam ekānta-śīlatā

[368] 'The first doorway into yoga consists of restraint of speech, non-accumulation of possessions, absence of anxious hopes for personal benefits, absence of efforts for personal gain and continuous living in solitude.

The solitude is not in space. It is a psychological condition. In space there is no real solitude. If there is no noise from mills or motor-cars in the forest, there is the noise of birds, insects and the wind also. Let it therefore be clearly understood that by 'solitude' is meant that state of consciousness in which there is no individual separative existence, which is free from beginning, middle or end, and which pervades the universe all the time.

ekānta-sthitir indriyoparamaṇe hetur damaś cetasaḥ
saṃrodhe karaṇaṃ śamena vilayaṃ yāyād ahaṃ-vāsanā
tenānanda-rasānubhūtir acalā brāhmī sadā yoginas
tasmāc citta-nirodha eva satataṃ kāryaḥ prayatnān muneḥ

[369] 'Living in solitude enables one to withdraw the sense-organs from activity. Control of the senses enables one to control the mind. The subtle impressions setting up an ego are dissolved through control of the mind. Hence the yogi ever

experiences the unchanging bliss of the Absolute. Therefore a sage should always practise with diligence restraint of the mind.

vācaṃ niyacchātmani taṃ niyaccha
buddhau dhiyaṃ yaccha ca buddhi-sākṣiṇi
taṃ cāpi pūrṇātmani nirvikalpe
vilāpya śāntiṃ paramāṃ bhajasva

[370] 'Restrain speech within the lower mind (i.e., do not use it, and meditate on it as inseparable from the lower mind and therefore nothing but the lower mind). Restrain the lower mind in the higher mind. Restrain the higher mind in the witness. And dissolve even the notion of "witness" in the infinite Self beyond all false imagination. Then enjoy supreme peace.

If you follow the discipline of meditation and devotion it will lead to (1) emergence of a higher faculty of knowledge, buddhi, (2) communion with the Absolute, the All-Highest and (3) absorption of the sense of individuality.

Who creates individuality? The mind. In deep sleep, when the mind has gone back to its cause, there is no sense of individuality: king and beggar are the same.

The state of dreamless sleep or torpor is not samadhi. Though there is no consciousness of the world (jagat) in such a state, there is no consciousness of Brahman (the Absolute) either—there is an absence of the consciousness 'I am Brahman'.

deha-prāṇendriya-mano-buddhy-ādibhir upādhibhiḥ
yair yair vṛtteḥ samāyogas tat-tad-bhāvo 'sya yoginaḥ

[371] 'The yogi attains identity with whatever conditioning adjunct his attention is connected, whether it be the body, the vital energy, the sense-organs, the lower mind, the higher mind or whatever.

tan-nivṛttyā muneḥ samyak-sarvoparamaṇaṃ sukhaṃ
saṃdṛśyate sad-ānanda-rasānubhava-viplavaḥ

[372] 'When the sage puts an end to all of them, then he has the joy of the cessation of all worldly experience, and is overflooded by his direct experience of the savour of the Absolute as reality and bliss.

Absorption results in illumination and then all doubts are resolved, all ties are broken and life's highest fulfilment is attained. There is nothing more to be known: 'I have known all that was to be known'. Read the utterances of Rama Tirtha, Nirbhayanandaji and Shri Dada. Do they speak with any reservations of it? There are no 'ifs' and 'buts': their statements are the naked truth. And to understand the truth you must be naked. Throw off the veils of individuality, both good and evil, then, lifting up the hands cry: 'I am Thine, Father, I am Thine', and you will hear from the heaven of your heart the answering cry: 'tat tvam asi!' 'That thou art!'

48. Detachment

antas tyāgo bahis tyāgo viraktasyaiva yujyate
tyajaty antar bahiḥ saṅgaṃ viraktas tu mumukṣayā

[373] 'Only he who is detached can give up the outer realm (of objects) and the inner realm (of thoughts and desires). But he who is detached is able to give up the inner as well as the outer realm through deep desire for liberation.

The starting point of the science of eternal freedom (moksha) is the firm and deep-rooted conviction of the reality of God and the unreality of the phenomenal world. The natural deduction of this spiritual principle is detachment (vairagya). Our aim in daily life should be to realize the hollowness of all ambitions and desires, the utter unreliability of the objects of the world and their failure to give us even a moment's pleasure unmixed with woe and anxiety. It is so, but in many cases it does not appear to be so.

Let us make it a vital fact that any material desire we have is useless and that our deepest yearning should be for God, the spiritual Truth, in our own being. You cannot go on thinking of a dinner of seven courses or a holiday in Portugal, and yet say that you are thinking of seeing God within you and obtaining spiritual perfection.

bahis tu viṣayaiḥ saṅgaṃ tathāntar aham-ādibhiḥ
virakta eva śaknoti tyaktuṃ brahmaṇi niṣṭhitaḥ

> [374] 'Only he who is detached and concentrated on the Absolute can give up attachment both for the external realm of objects and the inner realm of the ego, desires and so forth.

What really stands in the way of one's realization of spiritual perfection is the harbouring of any material desire. You will say 'May I not have a desire to win half a million dollars and open an orphanage with it?' If you are a disciple, your aim is simple, and it is nothing but the Lord Himself. And in Him is contained all that is best in this world or in the world to come.

vairāgya-bodhau puruṣasya pakṣi-vat
pakṣau vijānīhi vicakṣaṇa tvam
vimukti-saudhāgra-talādhirohaṇaṃ
tābhyām vinā nānyatareṇa sidhyati

> [375] 'O wise one, know that detachment and metaphysical understanding are the two wings of the soul whereby it soars upwards like a bird. It cannot alight on the pinnacle of liberation by the use of only one wing without the other.

When the soul becomes conscious of the world of reality (paramartha) it feels detached from this world of sorrow and incertitude and applies discipline, devotion and meditation in order to realize the world of God, the Kingdom of Heaven, as true disciples do.

atyanta-vairāgyavataḥ samādhiḥ
samāhitasyaiva dṛḍha-prabodhaḥ
prabuddha-tattvasya hi bandha-muktir
muktātmano nitya-sukhānubhūtiḥ

[376] 'Only he who has boundless detachment can have perfect concentration (samādhi). Only he who has perfect concentration can have firm metaphysical knowledge. He who is awake to the metaphysical truth has release from bondage. The soul that is released has experience of eternal joy.

vairāgyān na paraṃ sukhasya janakaṃ paśyāmi vaśyātmanas
tac cecchuddhatarātma-bodha-sahitaṃ svārājyasāmrājya-dhuk
etad dvāram ajasra-mukti-yuvater yasmāt tvam asmāt paraṃ
sarvatrāspṛhayā sad-ātmani sadā prajñāṃ kuru śreyase

[377] 'I do not know of anything better than detachment to produce joy for a person of self-control, and if that is supplemented by pure metaphysical knowledge of the Self, it produces the joy of sovereignty over the empire of the Self. This is an open door for the entry of that beautiful girl called "eternal liberation". Therefore, from now on you must always cultivate metaphysical knowledge of the Self as the real, without desire for anything anywhere else. Here lies your highest good!

Like a young pure-hearted girl who prepares for her wedding, detaching herself from the world of her relatives, home and friends, her town and its parks, in order to enter matrimony, so does a true yogi live in detachment and practise renunciation in order to enter the realm of Truth (atman).

āśāṃ chindhi viṣopameṣu viṣayeṣv eṣaiva mṛtyoḥ sṛtis
tyaktvā jāti-kulāśrameṣv abhimatiṃ muñcātidūrāt kriyāḥ
dehādāv asati tyajātma-dhiṣaṇāṃ prajñāṃ kuruṣvātmani
tvaṃ draṣṭāsy amalo 'si nirdvaya-paraṃ brahmāsi yad vastutaḥ

> [378] 'Give up desire for sense-objects (viṣaya) which (when sought for their own sake) are like poison (viṣa). Desire is the path to (forgetfulness of one's true nature and) death. Abandon pride in caste, family and your stage of life (e.g., monk). Keep far away from ritualistic activity. Break away from self-identification with the body and other unreal things. Cultivate metaphysical knowledge of the Self. You are the Witness. You are spotless. For in truth you are the Absolute, non-dual and transcendent.

Detachment (vairagya) means detachment from prejudices, biases, baneful habits and, more than anything else, unspiritual company. To be detached means to be able to see the One in the many. There is no need to become a slave to the detail in the individuals. If you are devoted to God, you can be a devoted friend, relative and companion, but if only devoted to yourself, you will be an exploiter in the garb of a philanthropist. These are the words of Meister Eckhart: 'The still, glorious, sublime Oneness, which finally satisfies all thirst for truth, the point where all lines meet and show their meaning, this is the end of life'.

49. The method of meditation

lakṣye brahmaṇi mānasaṃ dṛḍhataraṃ saṃsthāpya bāhyendriyaṃ
sva-sthāne viniveśya niścala-tanuś copekṣya deha-sthitim
brahmātmaikyam upetya tan-mayatayā cākhaṇḍa-vṛttyā 'niśaṃ
brahmānanda-rasaṃ pibātmani mudā śūnyaiḥ kim anyair bhramaiḥ

> [379] 'Fix the mind firmly on the Absolute, your goal. Confine the outgoing senses to their stations in the physical body. Leave your body motionless and pay no attention to its condition. Feel your identity with the Absolute. Absorbed in that, drink in joyously the bliss of the Absolute in your own Self continuously, without allowing the mind to undergo differentiation (lit. with an akhaṇḍa-vṛtti). What is the use of other erroneous and empty notions?

To prepare for meditation, you sit with a firm will to know the spiritual Truth: 'I am infinite Truth, I am Shiva (infinite bliss)'. You want to actualize the God in you as your Self. You start by letting your mind be absorbed in the idea, Truth itself: 'I am infinite bliss'. You feel it. You exclude contrary thoughts. You rise above the cognitive plane by asserting 'I am Shiva'. This is meditation.

'How do I know that I have meditated successfully?' Leave this pragmatic thought alone. You have come to the temple of Truth and you have loved the Lord of Truth. This is your offering to Him and it is for the universal good.

At the conclusion of the meditation, we should bless all, particularly any whom we think are our foes: 'Cover the world with the Lord' says the *Isha Upanishad*. Our spiritual interest is our highest self-interest. The highest expression of love is to meditate on the identity of the soul with God. A Sufi poet says: 'I have been led to the street of my Love. Now I have something to live for and to die for'.

anātma-cintanaṃ tyaktvā kaśmalaṃ duḥkha-kāraṇaṃ
cintayātmānam ānanda-rūpaṃ yan mukti-kāraṇam

> [380] 'Give up dwelling on the not-self, which is impure and a source of suffering. Dwell, rather, on your Self, which is of the nature of bliss, for this is the source of liberation.

The great realization of the Absolute Consciousness as the Self takes place, not in the mind through logic or reason, but in the awakening of the higher faculty called samadhi.

To awaken this faculty, you must be one-pointedly devoted to the Yoga and keep the discipline firmly. It means meditation with a firm mind and the utmost interest. The teacher communicates the truth in the form of a formula. To concentrate the mind on it, in silence and relaxation, is meditation. Shri Sadananda, the author of *Vedantasara*, describes it as the unceasing contemplation of Brahman (the Absolute) as taught by the teacher and established by reasoning and arguments. First shravana, listening, then manana, sustained reflection and thinking on what we have heard, to see that it is confirmed by reason and, when confirmed, then to submit it to a practical intuitive test through meditation so that we know its real significance and inner meaning. These combined together are called in the Upanishads 'tapas' (austerity).

eṣa svayaṃ-jyotir aśeṣa-sākṣī
vijñāna-kośe vilasaty ajasram
lakṣyaṃ vidhāyainam asad-vilakṣaṇam
akhaṇḍa-vṛttyā ''tmatayā 'nubhāvaya

> [381] 'The Self is self-luminous. It is the Witness, ever shining within the sheath of the higher mind. Make this your goal, different in nature from the unreal. Identify yourself with it through inhibiting all differentiation in the mind (lit. through an akhaṇḍa vṛtti).

On the path of knowledge, God is not worshipped as an object. There is no other reality than Self (atman). To realize the true nature of the Self is the consummation of worship. The Self is dearer than the body, the mind, the son, the wife or wealth. As such, the Self is the dearest thing in the world. The realization of Self by the self is not the knowledge of an object, nor is it the result of a process; it is the quest of reality in one's own Self.

That which is limited and passing and conditioned is not-self, and he who worships it will not have peace everlasting. What comes as the result of a process is impermanent. Brahman (the Absolute), or pure Consciousness (chit), is homogeneous identity. Liberation (mukti) is the realization of the identity of the subject with pure Consciousness.

The Absolute of Hegel, although free from contradiction, appears to the finite reason to be the highest synthesis of all theses and antitheses. The Vedanta realization of the Absolute is different from the realization of the Hegelian Absolute through love, as recommended by Dr McTaggart. It is above the subject-object consciousness.

etam acchinnayā vṛttyā pratyayāntara-śūnyayā
ullekhayan vijānīyāt sva-svarūpatayā sphuṭam

[382] 'Apprehending this Self with a mind raised beyond differentiation and void of any other idea, one should realize it clearly as one's own true nature.

atrātmatvaṃ dṛḍhīkurvann aham-ādiṣu santyajan
udāsīnatayā teṣu tiṣṭhed ghaṭa-paṭādivat

[383] 'One should strengthen one's conviction that one's Self lies here. One should remain surrounded by the ego and other factors of the individual personality without identifying oneself with them, treating them with indifference, as if they were external objects like a pot or a cloth.[1]

The lower mind loses the dross of egoism and pleasure-sense by the process of meditation. To devote an hour to meditation daily is just a preliminary to constant meditation in the spirit of renunciation.

Study the story of Bhrigu, the son of Varuna (*Taittiriya Upanishad* 3.1-6). He applied to his father for instruction in knowledge of Brahman (the Absolute). The father said: 'That from which all these things are born, that by which they live, and that to which they finally return, that is Brahman. Know It by tapas, for tapas is the means of knowing Brahman'. Bhrigu performed tapas— that is, he meditated and kept the discipline in faith. After several ups and downs in his conviction, Bhrigu concluded that bliss is Brahman. Now all his doubts were dissolved and his mind was fixed on Brahman.

The story of Indra (*Chandogya Upanishad* 8.7.1-12) is also worth studying. Indra lived with his Guru, Prajapati, for thirty-two years, performing tapas and serving the teacher. Then Indra knew that the Self is above the mind and its conditions, immutable and fearless.

1 Reading 'ghaṭa-paṭādi' with Muni Lāl and Bhāgavat.

Indra realized Brahman after many unsuccesful attempts. But as he persevered in tapas and service, he did realize the Self.

Various methods are described in the Upanishads. In the Shandilya-vidya (*Chandogya Upanishad* 3.14.1-4), Brahman is to be meditated on as pervading the whole universe: 'All this is Brahman'. In Bhuma-vidya (*Chandogya Upanishad* 7.23-24), Brahman is described as infinity and bliss. In Madhu-vidya, (*Brihadaranyaka Upanishad* 2.5.1-15) Brahman is to be meditated on as the honey of existence of the whole universe and the inner Self of man. In all the Upanishads, chanting and meditation on the name of God, OM, is extolled. The novice rises from the sound to the soundless Brahman in the course of this meditation. OM is both the means and the end of knowledge. 'Penetrate the OM with undistracted attention. OM is the cosmic force; it is bliss, it is the highest'. (*Mundaka Upanishad* 2.2.2-4)

50. Vision of the Self

viśuddham antaḥkaraṇaṃ svarūpe
nivesya sākṣiṇy avabodha-mātre
śanaiḥ śanair niścalatām upānayan
pūrṇaṃ svam evānuvilokayet tataḥ

[384] 'Apply your purified mind to the Witness, pure Consciousness, your own true nature. Gradually bring it to complete stillness. And then one should behold one's own Self as infinite.

dehendriya-prāṇa-mano-'ham-ādibhiḥ
svājñāna-kḷptair akhilair upādhibhiḥ
vimuktam ātmānam akhaṇḍa-rūpaṃ
pūrṇaṃ mahākāśam ivāvalokayet

[385] 'One should behold one's own Self infinite like the ether of space, undifferentiated, free from all apparent conditioning adjuncts arising through metaphysical ignorance such as body, senses, vital energy, mind, ego and so on.

An upadhi, or apparent conditioning adjunct, means a principle which in itself is unreal, but which creates the illusion of an appearance in the object which it conditions, and the appearance thus created by the upadhi is opposite in nature to that object in its unconditioned form. Maya, or illusion, is called the upadhi of the Lord (Ishvara); avidya, or nescience, is the upadhi of the individual soul (jiva). Maya, as an upadhi, is used by the Lord (Ishvara) to create, sustain and absorb the world by His independent will. He is not influenced by His upadhi; He is called Maya-pati, the Lord of Maya. Maya is refined, having a predominance of the constituent quality (guna) of sattva.

Avidya (nescience) is the upadhi of the individual soul, the jiva. Avidya is darker in its constitution than Maya and creates for the jiva the illusion of the reality of the world. The individual soul is a reflection of Ishwara in avidya, its upadhi; in reality it is Brahman (the Absolute). But while it is *apparently* conditioned by avidya, it forgets its nature as Truth, Consciousness and Bliss. Identifying itself with its upadhi in the form of the mind (antahkarana), the jiva considers itself as bound, subject to pleasure and pain, doing and reaping the fruits of action.

To illustrate this point: The ether (space) is pure, taintless, infinite, neither a cause nor an effect, and free from all attributes. But if it is enclosed, or conditioned, in a blue jar, it looks blue and seems to partake of the attributes of the jar. In this illustration, the ether stands for Brahman (the Absolute) and the jar for the upadhi.

The law of causation is in the upadhi and so are all the attributes and states of matter. The jiva takes these upadhis to be real. All evil is due to this fact. The characteristics of pure Consciousness are erroneously applied to them and *vice versa*. To undo this error and see the ever-free Brahman as one's Self (atman) is the purpose of Yoga.

ghaṭa-kalaśa-kuśūla-sūci-mukhyair
    gaganam upādhi-śatair vimuktam ekam
bhavati na vividhaṃ tathaiva śuddhaṃ
    param aham-ādi-vimuktam ekam eva

[386] 'The ether of space remains one and indivisible, even though apparently enclosed within hundreds of different apparent conditioning adjuncts (of different sizes) such as pot, jug, storehouse, eye of a needle. In the same way, the supreme Spirit is one only and is free from ego and all other apparent differentiations.

brahmādi-stamba-paryantā mṛṣāmātrā upādhayaḥ
tataḥ pūrṇaṃ svam ātmānaṃ paśyed ekātmanā sthitam

[387] 'All apparent conditioning adjuncts, from the creator-god Brahmā to the meanest clump of grass, are pure illusion. Therefore one should gain vision of one's own infinite Self, which is ever uniform.

There are two worlds. There is the world of being, which is real, untouched by time, unconditioned by causation, perfect in bliss and freedom, of which we can neither say that it is, or that it is not. The other world is the world of becoming, of time, space and causation, in which constant change is essential, which does not satisfy us for long, is full of incertitude and is subject to misfortune and death. As it is changing like a flowing river, it is called sansara. This is the world of Maya or appearance. It exists in the world of being, from which it comes, in which it abides and in which it is finally dissolved. It is not unreal like a dream or the son of a barren woman. It is a school in which we learn, if we are not abject dunces, the reality of the world of being. All that matters in the world is to be conscious, intuitively, of the existence of God, or our higher Self, and to work for its realization. It is by the practice of selfless benevolence and the service of man, without expecting any reward, that we qualify for God-consciousness.

yatra bhrāntyā kalpitaṃ yad viveke
tat tan-mātraṃ naiva tasmād vibhinnaṃ
bhrānter nāśe bhrānti-dṛṣṭāhi-tattvaṃ
rajjus tad-vad viśvam ātma-svarūpam

[388] 'Whatever is erroneously superimposed onto anything else is known to have been only that thing when the latter has been discriminated. Just as the truth of the snake is seen to have been the rope after the error has been removed, so is the truth of the universe found ultimately to be the Self.

svayaṃ brahmā svayaṃ viṣṇuḥ svayam indraḥ svayaṃ śivaḥ
svayaṃ viśvam idaṃ sarvaṃ svasmād anyan na kiñcana

[389] 'You are yourself Brahmā, you are Vishnu, you are Indra, you are Shiva, you are this whole universe. Nothing but yourself exists.

The Self (atman) is not the knower and, of course, not the known. Atman is the substratum and source of all the reality and intelligibility of the universe. It is an error to think that Shri Shankara's philosophy is subjective idealism. Deussen is wrong when he says that in the state of liberation, all plurality is annihilated and only the knower in us, Atman, remains as the unity. All the varied means of knowledge have Atman as the goal and, when Atman is comprehended, all are negated. Atman is the bedrock of certainty.

Plato's approach towards a monism of the Good is nearer to the Advaita of Shri Shankara than any other European theory. The argument of Descartes ('I think, therefore I am') regarding the existence of the self as an absolute certainty has little in common with Shri Shankara's position. To Shri Shankara, Self (atman) is the essence and basis of all epistemological enquiry, and not the performer of the mental operations resulting in true conception (pramatri), which is what Descartes understood by the self. Descartes says nothing definite about the nature of the self, whereas the Self of Shri Shankara is identified with bliss: 'Atman is Brahman (the Absolute)'. 'Brahman is Existence, Consciousness and Bliss (sat-chit-ananda)'.

Atman is not a theological conception; it is metaphysical, and its existence is self-revealed, above all proof.

antaḥ svayaṃ cāpi bahiḥ svayaṃ ca
svayaṃ purastāt svayam eva paścāt
svayaṃ hy avācyāṃ svayam apy udīcyāṃ
tathopariṣṭāt svayam apy adhastāt

[390] 'You are yourself all that is within, all that is without, all that is in front, all that is behind. You are what is to the south, you are what is to the north, you are what is above, you are what is below.

taraṅga-phena-bhrama-budbudādi
sarvaṃ svarūpeṇa jalaṃ yathā tathā
cid eva dehādy aham-antam etat
sarvaṃ cid-evaika-rasaṃ viśuddham

[391] 'Just as the waves, the foam, the eddies, the bubbles and so on are all in their true nature only water, so is all this from the body to the ego in its true nature only pure homogeneous Consciousness.

sad evedaṃ sarvaṃ jagad avagataṃ vāṅ-manasayoḥ
sato 'nyan nāsty eva prakṛti-parasīmni sthitavataḥ
pṛthak kiṃ mṛtsnāyāḥ kalaśa-ghaṭa-kumbhādy avagataṃ
vadaty eṣa bhrāntas tvam aham iti māyā-madirayā

[392] 'This whole world as we know it through speech and thought is only the one principle of reality, which exists transcending the bounds of Nature. Are the jug, the pot, the pitcher found to be anything different from the clay from which they are made? It is only he who has been deluded by the intoxication of Māyā who speaks of "you" and "I".

There are four categories of experience—Brahman (the Absolute), Maya (cosmic illusion), jiva (the individual soul) and jagat (the phenomenal world)—but this is not a doctrine of multiplicity. Jagat is an effect of Maya. Jiva is a projection of Brahman, Maya and jagat.

Being in relation to each other as cause and effect, they are analogous to clay and the jug, etc. The individual soul (jiva) is not a modification of Brahman (the Absolute), but is Brahman perceived through Maya. Maya is like a multi-coloured looking-glass and, when seen through it, Brahman appears as many. Now the four categories are reduced to two, Maya and Brahman. Macrocosmically, Maya is to the Absolute (brahman) what, microcosmically, mind is to the individual (jiva). One can imagine oneself to be many, but one does not become many.

Has the Absolute forgotten His nature? Is He deluded? No! It is the mind, animated by the presence of the Self (atman) in it, that dreams the dream of bondage and release. The mystery is inexplicable, but it is easily apprehended if we patiently listen.

kriyā-samabhihāreṇa yatra nānyad iti śrutiḥ
bravīti dvaita-rāhityaṃ mithyādhyāsa-nivṛttaye

[393] 'The Veda teaches the non-existence of duality in order to put an end to false superimposition by juxtaposing a number of verbs in the negative in the passage "When a person sees nothing else, hears nothing else, knows nothing else—that is the Infinite" (Chāndogya Upanishad 7.24.1)

There are many explanations of this mystery. Theories are only theories, as everybody knows. They are not facts, but instruments to explain a phenomenon.

Shankara Acharya and Sureshvara Acharya call this the theory of mutual superimposition. According to it, the conditioned form of Consciousness (chit), called the jiva, sometimes conceived as a reflection of Consciousness (chidabhasa), imposes its own nature—that is, Existence, Consciousness and Bliss—on Maya and imposes the nature of Maya—action, suffering, inertness and limitations—on itself.

This is an attempt to explain the mystery, but the truth is 'God alone is real and all else is unreal (transient)'. Yoga is the method, partly psychological and partly mystical, practised by the jiva to annul the mutual superimposition.

ākāśavan nirmala-nirvikalpa-
niḥsīma-niṣpandana-nirvikāram
antar-bahiḥ-śūnyam ananyam advayaṃ
svayaṃ paraṃ brahma kim asti bodhyam

[394] 'Could one say that the Absolute is knowable as an object? It is pure like the ether of space, void of all illusory imagination, limitless, motionless, formless, having nothing inside it and nothing outside it, having nothing other than itself over against it, non-dual, one's own Self and transcendent.

vaktavyaṃ kimu vidyate 'tra bahudhā brahmaiva jīvaḥ svayaṃ
brahmaitaj jagad ātataṃ nu sakalaṃ brahmādvitīyaṃ śruteḥ
brahmaivāham iti prabuddha-matayaḥ santyakta-bāhyāḥ sphuṭaṃ
brahmī-bhūya vasanti santata-cid-ānandātmanaiva dhruvam

[395] 'On this subject there is not much to say. The soul in its true nature is the Absolute. This whole expanded universe is (in reality only) the Absolute. The Veda says that the Absolute is the non-dual reality. The enlightened ones, who have clearly realized their true nature as the Absolute, undoubtedly reject whatever is external and live in the conviction "I am the Absolute and that alone", continuously identified with it as Consciousness and Bliss.

jahi mala-maya-kośe 'haṃ-dhiyotthāpitāśāṃ
prasabham anila-kalpe liṅga-dehe 'pi paścāt
nigama-gadita-kīrtiṃ nityam ānanda-mūrtim
svayam iti paricīya brahma-rūpeṇa tiṣṭha

[396] 'First give up desires arising from identifying your 'I' with this physical body, which consists of impurities. Then forcibly disidentify yourself from the subtle body, which consists of the air-element (i.e., consists principally of the vital energy). Recognize that your own true Self is that constant and eternal bliss that is taught and celebrated in the Veda. Stand fast in your true nature as the Absolute.

Duality is created by the mind because the mind is made up of nescience (avidya), ignorance (ajnana), illusion (maya). The mind must go; it must lose its individuality and finite character. Then the Truth is visible; then reality is known. The mind is meant to be surrendered to Truth, to Beauty, to Shiva (infinite bliss).

śavākāraṃ yāvad bhajati manujas tāvad aśuciḥ
parebhyaḥ syāt kleśo janana-maraṇa-vyādhi-nilayaḥ
yadā ''tmānaṃ śuddhaṃ kalayati śivākāram acalam
tadā tebhyo mukto bhavati hi tad āha śrutir api

[397] 'Man is impure so long as he identifies himself with the corpse-like body. He suffers at the hands of others. He is an abode of birth, death and illness. But when he attains to his pure Self, motionless, excellent (śiva) in every way, then he is released from these evils. That is also the verdict of the Veda.

51. The incongruity of the world of plurality

svātmany āropitāśeṣābhāsa-vastu-nirāsataḥ
svayam eva paraṃ brahma pūrṇam advayam akriyam

[398] 'When all the apparent realities that have been superimposed on the Self have been rejected, then what remains is one's true Self, the infinite, non-dual, actionless, transcendent Absolute.

samāhitāyāṃ sati citta-vṛttau
parātmani brahmaṇi nirvikalpe
na dṛśyate kaścid ayaṃ vikalpaḥ
prajalpa-mātraḥ pariśiṣyate tataḥ

[399] 'When the mind has been concentrated on the true Self, the Absolute that is devoid of all false imagination, then this falsely imagined world is not seen. From then on it remains recognized as the result of empty talk (as the clay of a clay-elephant is clay that is merely called an elephant).

Picture a house made of sugar; its rooms, doors, walls, floors, arches, windows and sills are all sugar and sugar only. Every bit of it is sugar and participates in the nature of sugar as a whole. This phenomenal existence (sansara) is a house made of Brahman (the Absolute); every bit of it is pure Consciousness (chit). Your mind is a part of the cosmic mind (Hiranyagarbha). Your body is a part of the cosmic body (Virat). The law of cause and effect is also, fundamentally, Brahman. The conscious part of you is the cosmic Consciousness (chit). It is a mystery! It looks a secret! But it must be discovered, otherwise you are like Newton's mice, running round and round on the wheel. The one loved by his Guru, who has withdrawn himself from all other interests and applied himself to its investigation, knows it. Maya and Brahman are names, but the reality is without a name.

asat-kalpo vikalpo 'yaṃ viśvam ity eka-vastuni
nirvikāre nirākāre nirviśeṣe bhidā kutaḥ

[400] 'The universe is no more than this trifling piece of imagination, for how could there be distinctions in the reality which is one and homogeneous, changeless, formless, undifferentiated. How could it undergo real distinctions?

draṣṭṛ-darśana-dṛśyādi-bhāva-śūnyaika-vastuni
nirvikāre nirākāre nirviśeṣe bhidā kutaḥ

[401] 'When reality is one and homogeneous, changeless, formless, undifferentiated and void of states such as seer, seeing and seen, how could it undergo real distinctions?

kalpārṇava ivātyanta-paripūrṇaika-vastuni
nirvikāre nirākāre nirviśeṣe bhidā kutaḥ

[402] 'When reality is one and homogeneous, changeless, formless, undifferentiated and infinite like the ocean that succeeds a world-period, how could it undergo real distinctions?

Imagine an infinite expanse of water and water only with nothing else. There are infinite ripples and waves lying in a state of latency in this water. What is the nature of the water as a whole? It can only be described in terms of perfection, which implies eternal immutability. Now imagine that some parts of the surface of the water are completely calm while other parts are ruffled. What has caused some parts to be ruffled? The power that has caused the ruffling on the surface was latent in the water itself. The agitation on the surface gives place to calmness again. The water, taken as a whole in its entire depth, is ever calm. Now substitute Brahman (the Absolute) for the water, Maya for the latent power that ruffles its surface, and sansara (phenomenal existence) for the agitation. All is one; there is no duality at all whatsoever.

tejasīva tamo yatra pralīnaṃ bhrānti-kāraṇam
advitīye pare tattve nirviśeṣe bhidā kutaḥ

[403] 'Where darkness, which is the cause of illusion, has been dissolved as if in light—how could there be distinctions in the supreme reality, which is non-dual and undifferentiated?

ekātmake pare tattve bheda-vārtā kathaṃ bhavet
suṣuptau sukha-mātrāyāṃ bhedaḥ kenāvalokitaḥ

[404] 'How could there be mention of distinctions in the supreme reality, which is one? Has anyone ever found any distinctions in dreamless sleep, a state of pure happiness?

na hy asti viśvaṃ para-tattva-bodhāt
sadātmani brahmaṇi nirvikalpe
kāla-traye nāpy ahir īkṣito guṇe
na hy ambu-bindur mṛga-tṛṣṇikāyām

[405] 'When there is direct knowledge of the supreme reality, it is seen that no universe of plurality exists in the real Self, the Absolute, devoid of all false imagination. No snake is ever truly seen in a rope, in past, present or future, nor is a drop of water ever truly seen in a mirage.

A few travellers from Peking have crossed the Great Wall of China from the town called Kalgan and are now in the mighty Gobi desert. For four hundred miles there are no springs, no rivers, no green grass: all is sand. When they are thirsty and fatigued, they see a river in which cool, refreshing water appears to be flowing, singing, towards the sea. A naive man, who thinks that the sense perceptions are real—who thinks that food, drink, soft beds and sweet voices are real—shouts with joy: 'Water! Water! How fortunate! Here is the river! I will run to it! Today the river is in flood!' And looking at his companions, he cries: 'Come on! Let us quench our thirst and bathe in the river!' There is a wise man among them who has experience of crossing the Gobi desert. He says: 'Don't exhaust yourself, young man, by this false enthusiasm. It is a mirage river, only an appearance. It has no reality'. But the other still insists: 'See, look, look! Only fifty yards away! How can you say it is not real?' The wise man says: 'Don't be silly, it is not a river, it is a mirage, have patience! Take out your bottle of water and drink that'. But the other says: 'I will throw away my bottle. I don't need it'.

The mirage river is sansara (the phenomenal realm). The spiritually ignorant man (ajnani) says: 'Let me conquer the world, possess wealth, have a couple of cars and a good cellar. I will enjoy life!' His friend, the enlightened man (jnani) says: 'Forget it! Do not exhaust your energy on them, it is all a mirage! They have never given lasting satisfaction to any. Cross this Gobi desert of sansara! Your real Self (atman) is the substratum on which this mirage river of sansara stands'.

Our home is Atman, God. Let us go home!

māyā-mātram idaṃ dvaitam advaitaṃ paramārthataḥ
iti brūte śrutiḥ sākṣāt suṣuptāv anubhūyate

[406] 'This realm of duality is a mere illusion, what is ultimately real is non-duality. So declares the Veda, and we experience the fact in dreamless sleep.

ananyatvam adhiṣṭhānād āropyasya nirīkṣitam
paṇḍitai rajju-sarpādau vikalpo bhrānti-jīvanaḥ

[407] 'The wise perceive that what is superimposed is non-different from what it is superimposed on. The false imagination in the case of the rope-snake and so on depends on the error (of the beholder and does not manifest without it).

Swami Rama Tirtha says: 'I had a dream. In the dream I was ploughing the land. Two strong bullocks were yoked to the plough. I was lashing them. I ploughed for two, three, four hours. The sun was hot and I was tired. Then I said: "Now let us go home, I have ploughed enough for today!" And when I started to go home, the dream ended. Where is the plough, the fatigue, the haste, the vision of a good crop? The dream has ended, all have gone!'

'And therefore', says Swami Rama Tirtha, 'let us go home to God. Return to Atman, the pure "I", and then this dream of fatigue, of perspiration, of false hopes, will come to an end'.

52. How to reflect on the Self

citta-mūlo vikalpo 'yam cittābhāve na kaścana
ataś cittaṃ samādhehi pratyag-rūpe parātmani

[408] 'This realm of false imagination depends on the mind. When there is no mind there is no false imagination. Therefore you should concentrate the mind on the supreme Self, the inmost principle.

The mind can enslave the soul of man, and it can also enrich, beautify and release the soul from the cumbersome bondages. To enjoy life we must dismiss from our mind all personal desires of pelf, power and comfort. Otherwise the mind remains impure, and whatever it creates causes grief and suffering, enslaving the soul to passions and prejudices. How hard is the task! Yes, but only in the beginning. The mind thus purified and lit with a little knowledge of the Spirit creates beauty if applied to outer objects. If devoted to inner contemplation it creates poetry, philosophy and other beautiful imageries. But if through Yoga practice it is deprived of all its activities, then, in the vacuity left by their elimination, is seen the Face of the Beloved, the Ruler of the universe, after which there follows a carefree life having a perpetual divine vision of peace (shanti) and bliss.

kim api satata-bodhaṃ kevalānanda-rūpaṃ
nirupamam ati-velaṃ nitya-muktaṃ nirīham
niravadhi gaganābhaṃ niṣkalaṃ nirvikalpaṃ
hṛdi kalayati vidvān brahma pūrṇaṃ samādhau

[409] 'The enlightened one perceives the infinite Absolute in his heart in a state of concentration—that mysterious Absolute, eternal Consciousness, of the nature of pure bliss, incomparable, timeless, ever liberated, actionless, endless, like the ether of space, partless, devoid of false imagination.

The visible universe is a fraction of the reality; it is just as much as is revealed to us by our empirical instruments of perception. The invisible, too, is only a limited aspect of the same reality. That which is grasped by the mind is the invisible. It is not the whole. Reality is that which is the root of both the visible and the invisible, and which yet transcends both.

The divine Jesus, God incarnate, who was an objective manifestation of reality, called it 'Our Father in heaven'. Mohammed, a God-man, styled it 'Allah'. The philosophy of Adhyatma Yoga calls it Atman, the real Self of man, or Brahman (the Absolute)—the Self of the universe. It is the object of the highest love; it is the home of delight.

This is reality, being free from change and limitations, conditions or attributes. It is the essence of God, man and the world. The yogis take delight in its contemplation. By saturating their minds in it, in a state of inner tranquillity created by the withdrawal of the mind from the objective and subjective spheres, they know directly: 'This Atman is Brahman (the Absolute)'.

prakṛti-vikṛti-śūnyaṃ bhāvanātīta-bhāvaṃ
sama-rasam asamānaṃ māna-sambandha-dūram
nigama-vacana-siddhaṃ nityam asmat-prasiddhaṃ
hṛdi kalayati vidvān brahma pūrṇaṃ samādhau

[410] 'The enlightened one perceives the infinite Absolute in his heart in a state of concentration—that Absolute which is void of Nature either in its potential or its developed form, which is beyond our conceptions, homogeneous, not comparable with anything we could imagine, totally unconnected with the means of empirical knowledge, known through the texts of the Veda, ever familiar to us as (the pure) "I".

ajaram amaram astābhāsa-vastu-svarūpaṃ
stimita-salila-rāśi-prakhyam ākhyā-vihīnam
śamita-guṇa-vikāraṃ śāśvataṃ śāntam ekaṃ
hṛdi kalayati vidvān brahma pūrṇaṃ samādhau

[411] 'The enlightened one perceives the infinite Absolute in his heart in a state of concentration—that Absolute which is not visited by old age or death, which is the real in its true nature, void of all illusory appearances[1], which, though without any name, is referred to as a perfectly still ocean, in which no play of the constituents (or "no modification of attributes") occurs, which is ever the eternal One, motionless and at peace.

samāhitāntaḥkaraṇaḥ svarūpe
vilokayātmānam akhaṇḍa-vaibhavam

1 Reading 'astābhāsa' with Muni Lāl and H.R. Bhāgavat.

vicchindhi bandhaṃ bhava-gandha-gandhitaṃ
yatnena puṃstvaṃ sa-phalīkuruṣva

[412] 'Concentrate your mind on your own true nature and behold the Self in its undifferentiated splendour. Cut away bondage, tainted by the odour of rebirth. Succeed in gaining the true goal of human existence by hard endeavour.

sarvopādhi-vinirmuktaṃ sac-cid-ānandam advayam
bhāvayātmānam ātma-sthaṃ na bhūyaḥ kalpase 'dhvane

[413] 'Concentrate on the Self in your mind—the Self which is free from all conditioning adjuncts and of the nature of non-dual Existence-Consciousness-Bliss. Then you will not have to continue on the round of birth and death.

The sensuous creations of the mind are evanescent. The inner creations have a higher value. But there is the highest value in surrendering the mind, reducing it to the position of an object of the Spirit. Men who have acquired this state will be just rulers, benevolent citizens, really spiritual artists, uplifting friends, edifying companions, exalting lovers and magnanimous in all relationships of life.

This state is called in the Bible 'the Kingdom of Heaven'. There there are no friends and no foes, no great and no small, but one Overlord of all.

53. Overlooking the realm of objects

chāyeva puṃsaḥ paridṛśyamānam
ābhāsa-rūpeṇa phalānubhūtyā
śarīram ārāc chava-van nirastaṃ
punar na sandhatta idaṃ mahātmā

[414] 'A great soul (mahātmā) perceives his body indeed in

experiencing the results of his deeds (of that fraction of his former deeds that prompted his present life, "prārabdha"), but he experiences it as a mere appearance, like a person's shadow. He rejects it from afar like a corpse, and never accepts it again.

The engagement of the enlightened man (jnani) in eating food in order to preserve his body, and so forth, is said to be caused by prarabdha karma. Karma is of three kinds: (1) sanchita karma—the accumulated karma created in former bodies, the fruition of which has not yet begun; (2) agami karma—future karma; (3) prarabdha karma—the part of one's karma created in the past which is the direct cause of the present body and its maintenance. Self-realization directly destroys the accumulated karma. The enlightened man (jnani) does not attribute action to the Self, as he knows it to be an illusion. He therefore has no further karma. The prarabdha karma which has caused the beginning of the body and which, in the case of the jnani, leads him to get alms and to teach disciples, has still to be fructified and experienced.

In some places (as later in *The Crest Jewel of Wisdom* and in *Direct Experience of Reality*), it is stated by Shri Shankara that in the case of a jnani, even prarabdha karma is destroyed.[1] The meaning is that the jnani is not aware of any karma, nor of its fruition. The Acharya has not, in fact, repudiated prarabdha. In the *Brahma Sutras* it is said that, in the case of the jnani: (1) the accumulated karma is destroyed by Self-realization; (2) there is no possibility of future action; (3) prarabdha has to be experienced in its fruition.

satata-vimala-bodhānanda-rūpaṃ sametya
tyaja jaḍa-mala-rūpopādhim etaṃ su-dūre
atha punar api naiṣa smaryatāṃ vānta-vastu
smaraṇa-viṣaya-bhūtaṃ kalpate kutsanāya

1 See verses 446 and 450 with comment, below.

> [415] 'Attain your own true nature as continuous Consciousness and Bliss, and leave this impure non-conscious conditioning adjunct (the physical body) far behind. Do not even call it to mind. Even the memory of what one has vomited out evokes a feeling of disgust.

We are what our karma has made us. It is in our hands either to become morally and spiritually excellent or to live as beasts, ignorant of truth and the need for benevolence, study of philosophy and devotion. Man builds karma through his mind, word and action. The only real happiness for man is found in creative ever-expanding love of God, and in selfless devotion to the good of his fellow men. Devotion to a spiritual ideal is the one and only way to peace and delight in this life. This is the karma of light which dispels the gloom and darkness of narrow self-love. It is the way out of the web of karma into the timeless and causeless region of knowledge of identity. The soul bound in the chain of causation will remain a prisoner for ever. 'The spirit of man comes from heaven', says Goethe. It must pass into the light of truth which is above causation.

sa-mūlam etat paridahya vahnau
  sad-ātmani brahmaṇi nirvikalpe
tataḥ svayaṃ nitya-viśuddha-bodhā-
  nandātmanā tiṣṭhati vid-variṣṭhaḥ

> [416] 'The highest kind of enlightened person burns up this world together with its cause in the fire of the real Self, the Absolute, void of false imagination. He then stands identified with his own true Self, pure and eternal Consciousness and Bliss.

Just as ether or space (akasha) is either conditioned or unconditioned, so the Self (atman) is either conditioned by illusion (maya) or is Brahman (the Absolute). Maya is mere appearance, slight (tuccha), not real though not wholly unreal. The effect of Maya, also called nescience (avidya or ajnana), is the illusion of the existence of difference or duality and its effects, desire and aversion (raga and dvesha).

The individual soul (jiva) can overcome nescience and enter the natural, ever-abiding samadhi of 'I am Brahman (the Absolute)'. By hearing, reflection and meditation on the Truth (shravana, manana and nididhyasana), and observance of the discipline of inner and outer control (yama and niyama), he annihilates his empirical ego which functions in duality, and thereafter lives according to his prarabdha karma.

prārabdha-sūtra-grathitaṃ śarīraṃ
prayātu vā tiṣṭhatu gor iva srak
na tat punaḥ paśyati tattva-vettā
''nandātmani brahmaṇi līna-vṛttiḥ

[417] 'He whose mind is dissolved in the Absolute of the nature of bliss, and who knows reality as it is, does not notice whether his body, woven from the threads of the merit and demerit that initiated his present life (prārabdha karma), comes or goes, even as a cow does not notice whether its neck is or is not decorated with a garland.

When the effect of prarabdha is exhausted, he enters the state of videha-mukti (release after death) and is united with the Absolute. There is no further birth or death for him.

akhaṇḍānandam ātmānaṃ vijñāya sva-svarūpataḥ
kim icchan kasya vā hetor dehaṃ puṣṇāti tattva-vit

[418] 'Having known the Self, unbroken bliss, to be one's own true nature, to what end or for whose sake would such a knower of reality cherish his body?

About the enlightened man (jnani), it is written in the *Vichara*

Sagara: 'As a dried fig leaf is propelled by the wind here and there, so does the jnani seem to appear in various states, led by his prarabdha karma. Sometimes he rides an elephant or a horse and goes to a garden; sometimes he walks alone, unnoticed. Sometimes he enjoys a meal of several dishes and sleeps on a soft bed; sometimes he fasts in a lonely cave. Sometimes he is worshipped by many; sometimes he is condemned as fallen in the two worlds. Those who worship him gain great benefit, while they who find fault with him earn the effect of sins. No order lays down how long his body shall last and it is subject to no law. He has no duty because his illusion of duality has gone. On the authority of the Veda he is known to be the light of the secondless Brahman (the Absolute). There is no pretence in him. He has no feeling of superiority and looks on no one as a sinner or fallen being'.

54. The rewards of Self-knowledge

saṃsiddhasya phalaṃ tv etaj jīvan-muktasya yoginaḥ
bahir antaḥ sad-ānanda-rasāsvādanam ātmani

[419] 'The reward of the yogi who has been successful in acquiring liberation in life is this, namely, that he enjoys the savour of reality and bliss in the Self, within and without.

vairāgyasya phalaṃ bodho bodhasyoparatiḥ phalam
svānandānubhavāc chāntir eṣaivoparateḥ phalam

[420] 'The reward for detachment is metaphysical knowledge. The reward for such knowledge is withdrawal from all self-interested action. The reward for withdrawal from all self-interested action is the peace arising from direct experience of the bliss of one's own true nature.

yady uttarottarābhāvaḥ pūrva-pūrvaṃ tu niṣphalam
nivṛttiḥ paramā tṛptir ānando 'nupamaḥ svataḥ

[421] 'As between detachment, metaphysical knowledge, withdrawal from self-interested action, and peace, each earlier member of the series is useless if not crowned by what follows. But cessation from all activity (i.e., peace) is the highest kind of realization (tṛpti). It is of its very nature incomparable joy.

dṛṣṭa-duḥkheṣv anudvego vidyāyāḥ prastutaṃ phalam
yat kṛtaṃ bhrānti-velāyāṃ nānā karma jugupsitam
paścān naro vivekena tat kathaṃ kartum arhati

[422] 'The reward for metaphysical knowledge is said to be indifference to perceived suffering. After achieving metaphysical discrimination, how could a person go on performing those disgraceful acts which he used to perform at the time he was under the sway of ignorance?

vidyā-phalaṃ syād asato nivṛttiḥ
pravṛttir ajñāna-phalaṃ tad īkṣitam
taj jñājñayor yan mṛga-tṛṣṇikādau
no ced vido dṛṣṭa-phalaṃ kim asmāt

[423] 'The reward for metaphysical knowledge is desistance from action for the sake of the unreal. The result of ignorance is seen to be action of just this kind. This is the same distinction that we see between the person who does and the person who does not know the truth in the case of a mirage and so on (i.e., the one who knows the truth does not go off in search of the non-existent water). If this were not so, what other tangible reward would a knower get for his metaphysical knowledge?

ajñāna-hṛdaya-granther vināśo yady aśeṣataḥ
anicchor viṣayaḥ kinnu pravṛtteḥ kāraṇaṃ svataḥ

[424] 'If there is total destruction of the knot of ignorance in

the heart, then how could an object be a natural cause of activity in a person who would not be desiring it?

vāsanānudayo bhogye vairāgyasya paro 'vadhiḥ
ahaṃ-bhāvodayābhāvo bodhasya paramo 'vadhiḥ
līna-vṛtter anutpattir maryādoparates tu sā

[425] 'The highest limit of detachment is the absence of all urges for desirable sense-objects. The highest limit of metaphysical knowledge is the absence of all individual ego-feeling. The highest limit of withdrawal from self-interested action (uparati) comes when the motions of the mind have been halted (lit. dissolved) and do not return.

55. The marks of one liberated in life

brahmākāratayā sadā sthitatayā nirmukta-bāhyārtha-dhīr
anyāvedita-bhogya-bhoga-kalano nidrālu-vad bāla-vat
svapnālokita-loka-vaj jagad idaṃ paśyan kvacil labdha-dhīr
āste kaścid ananta-puṇya-phala-bhug dhanyaḥ sa mānyo bhuvi

[426] 'He in this world is to be congratulated, he is to be revered, whose mind is permanently liberated from thoughts of external objects through having assumed the form of the Absolute (i.e., within the limits of human representation), who enjoys sense-objects like a child or one half sunk in sleep and only at the suggestion of others, who occasionally takes cognisance of this world, though it seems to him like a fantasy-world seen in a dream, and who rests in this way enjoying the rewards of innumerable good deeds in previous lives.

sthita-prajño yatir ayaṃ yaḥ sad-ānandam aśnute
brahmaṇy eva vilīnātmā nirvikāro viniṣkriyaḥ

> [427] 'That person of spiritual discipline is said to be "of steady knowledge" (sthita-prajña, Gītā 2.55) who attains to the principle of reality and bliss, whose mind is dissolved in the Absolute, who is actionless and undergoes no change.

The following verse from the concluding part of chapter two of the *Gita* is one of some twenty which describe the mental and spiritual condition of 'one established in wisdom', that is to say, one who has realized the Self (atman): 'When the yogi gives up all ambitions and desires existing in his mind and is fully satisfied with the Self (atman), then he is said to be one who is established in wisdom'.

The enlightened man (jnani) knows that as the mind and all its objects are Maya, there is neither contentment nor happiness in that region. Before the actual state of enlightenment (jnana) is realized, he trains his mind by meditating on the truth: 'Brahman (the Absolute) is real, all else is unreal'; and when jnana is obtained, he is confirmed in the truth. Before jnana arises, the yogi induces in himself the state of detachment (vairagya) and gives no attention to any of his desires and ambitions. This is the negative side of the attitude of the jnani. There is a positive side too, and it is to be wholly content in the knowledge of Self as Existence, Consciousness and Bliss. This state does not dawn suddenly like the appearance of a beautiful rainbow. It is the result of continuous practice and love of the Guru and God.

Suppose you dream that you are enjoying the pleasures of a palace as a king, and that suddenly you want to extend the sphere of your sovereignty. You struggle and are in a state of agitation. Then you realize the fact that it is a dream. What do you feel now? Either you smile at your condition of ignorance, or you become detached from it. Similarly, the yogi knows that all the ambitions abiding in the core of his mind are barren and have not the least shade of happiness in their fulfilment. Then 'he is fully satisfied with the Self (atman)'. It means that he is convinced without any doubt that he is Brahman (the

Absolute), Existence, Consciousness and Bliss (sat-chit-ananda), in which there is no want, no ambition and no imperfection.

brahmātmanoḥ śodhitayor eka-bhāvāvagāhinī
nirvikalpā ca cin-mātrā vṛttiḥ prajñeti kathyate
su-sthitā sā bhaved yasya sthita-prajñaḥ sa ucyate

[428] '"Knowledge" (prajñā) in this context is defined as an "idea" (vṛtti) which is in fact only pure Consciousness shorn of all false imagination. Such an "idea" (being in fact not a mental idea but pure Consciousness itself) is adequate to "Brahman" and "Ātman" in their pure form, where they are one. He who has well-entrenched knowledge in this sense is called "a man of steady knowledge".

In chapter four of the great classic *Advaita Siddhi*, that greatest of philosophers, Shri Madhusudana Saraswati, says: 'Self (atman) is not an object of knowledge, yet the ignorance regarding Atman is set aside by the mental modification (vritti) which is of the form of Atman (atmakara), undivided and indeterminate'.

The vritti here spoken of as 'of the form of Atman (ātmākāra)' is also called 'of the form of Brahman (brahmākāra)'. It means that the vritti, which is a composition of two elements, nescience (avidya) and Consciousness (chetana), assumes the form of Consciousness (chetana) although it cannot be called pure Consciousness. In this state, the nescience (avidya) element of the vritti is set aside and Consciousness (chetana) remains.

yasya sthitā bhavet prajñā yasyānando nirantaraḥ
prapañco vismṛta-prāyaḥ sa jīvan-mukta iṣyate

[429] 'He whose knowledge (of this kind) is well-entrenched, who enjoys continuous bliss and by whom the universe of plurality is almost forgotten—he is called "one liberated in life".

līna-dhīr api jāgarti yo jāgrad-dharma-varjitaḥ
bodho nirvāsano yasya sa jīvan-mukta iṣyate

[430] 'He who remains awake though his mind is dissolved in the Absolute, he who is (perfectly aware that he is in truth) without the attributes of the waking state, he who is possessed of enlightenment and void of all subtle urges—he is called "one liberated in life".

śānta-saṃsāra-kalanaḥ kalāvān api niṣkalaḥ
yaḥ sa-citto 'pi niścintaḥ sa jīvan-mukta iṣyate

[431] 'He whose dealings with the world are at an end, he who, though from the empirical standpoint possessed of a body and so on having limbs and parts, is (perfectly aware that he is) without limbs or parts, he who, though in one sense possessing a mind, is without any thoughts and worries (that usually characterize a mind)—he is said to be one liberated in life.

vartamāne 'pi dehe 'smiñ chāyā-vad-anuvartini
ahaṃtā-mamatā-'bhavo jīvan-muktasya lakṣaṇam

[432] 'The mark of one liberated in life is that he has no sense of "I" or "mine" in regard to the physical body, even though it is present and follows him about like a shadow.

atītānanusandhānaṃ bhaviṣyad avicāraṇam
audāsīnyam api prāpte jīvan-muktasya lakṣaṇam

[433] 'The mark of one liberated in life is that he does not remember the past with nostalgia, that he takes no special thought for the future and that he receives whatever comes at the present moment with indifference.

guṇa-doṣa-viśiṣṭe 'smin svabhāvena vilakṣaṇe
sarvatra sama-darśitvaṃ jīvan-muktasya lakṣaṇam

[434] 'The mark of one liberated in life is that he values everything everywhere exactly the same in this realm of Māyā, characterized by goods and bads and inherently different in nature from himself.

iṣṭāniṣṭārtha-samprāptau sama-darśitayā ''tmani
ubhayatrāvikāritvaṃ jīvan-muktasya lakṣaṇam

[435] 'The mark of one liberated in life is that, because he sees all as the same in the Self, it makes no special impression on him when he encounters either the pleasant or the unpleasant.

brahmānanda-rasāsvādāsakta-cittatayā yateḥ
antar bahir avijñānaṃ jīvan-muktasya lakṣaṇam

[436] 'The mark of one liberated in life is that he is a disciplined person whose mind is so absorbed in the taste of the bliss of the Absolute that he cannot distinguish within from without.

dehendriyādau kartavye mamāhaṃ-bhāva-varjitaḥ
audāsīnyena yas tiṣṭhet sa jīvan-mukta-lakṣaṇaḥ

[437] 'He has the mark of one liberated in life who attends to his duty with body and sense-organs in a spirit of detachment and without feelings of "I" and "mine".

Who acts in the human personality? It is Nature (prakriti) which acts. It is animated by the proximity of Consciousness, without which it is a nonentity. Let the wise man understand this truth and let him regulate his actions under the light of Consciousness, reflected through reason. In this process, the actions are not limited to the consideration of the individualizing factor. True action is undertaken by love and it refers, ultimately, to the transcendence of the conditioning personality. When this mode of conduct is judiciously adopted, the wise man knows that he is neither the actor nor the enjoyer. His Self reveals both the subject and the object. He sits at rest, in peace and harmony, and smiles at the state of ignorance under which he attributed action to the Self.

vijñāta ātmano yasya brahma-bhāvaḥ śruter balāt
bhava-bandha-vinirmuktaḥ sa jīvan-mukta-lakṣaṇaḥ

[438] 'He has the mark of one liberated in life who has realized through the power of the Veda that in his true nature he is the Absolute and has acquired freedom from bondage.

dehendriyeṣv ahaṃ-bhāva idaṃ-bhāvas tad-anyake
yasya no bhavataḥ kvāpi sa jīvan-mukta iṣyate

[439] 'He has the mark of one liberated in life who never has the feeling "I" in relation to his body and its organs (including the mind) or the feeling "this" in regard to other things.

na pratyag-brahmaṇor bhedaṃ kadāpi brahma-sargayoḥ
prajñayā yo vijānāti sa jīvan-mukta iṣyate

[440] 'He is said to be liberated in life who has such insight that he never thinks of his own inmost Self and the Absolute as different, or of the Absolute and the created world as different.

sādhubhiḥ pūjyamane 'smin pīḍyamāne 'pi dur-janaiḥ
sama-bhāvo bhaved yasya sa jīvan-mukta iṣyate

[441] 'He is said to be one liberated in life who feels the same whether his body is served with hospitality by the good people or tormented by bad ones.

yatra praviṣṭā viṣayāḥ pareritā
nadī-pravāhā iva vāri-rāśau
līyanti san-mātratayā na vikriyām
utpādayanty eṣa yatir vimuktaḥ

[442] 'That disciplined person is liberated into whom objects provided by others enter like rivers entering the ocean, and dissolve in him without introducing any change into his nature as pure Being.

vijñāta-brahma-tattvasya yathā pūrvaṃ na saṃsṛtiḥ
asti cen na sa vijñāta-brahma-bhāvo bahir-mukhaḥ

[443] 'He who has knowledge of the Absolute does not undergo reincarnation as before. And if he did undergo further reincarnation, then he would not have had metaphysical knowledge after all, and would have been an extroverted person.

prācīna-vāsanā-vegād asau saṃsaratīti cet
na sad-ekatva-vijñānān mandī-bhavati vāsanā

[444] 'If you were to say: "He will undergo further re-incarnation on account of the force of accumulated subtle impressions", this would be wrong. For knowledge of one's identity with the real undermines the power of the impressions.

Just as the waves rising and falling in the sea, and the water of rivers, finding lodgement ultimately in the sea, do not disturb the equilibrium of the sea, so that man is a mahatma whose soul is not disturbed by any impressions. This state is called in the *Gita* (2.48) samata, the light of inner tranquillity, equimindedness, undisturbability, by reason of the understanding that the impressions are illusory (mithya) and the reality which is the Self is not touched by them.

atyanta-kāmukasyāpi vṛttiḥ kuṇṭhati mātari
tathaiva brahmaṇi jñāte pūrṇānande manīṣiṇaḥ

[445] 'The desires even of the most lustful man are blunted in face of his mother. In just such a way, the desires of the sage who knows the Absolute are blunted all round in face of the bliss of infinity that he feels.

56. How the liberated one still appears to act

nididhyāsana-śīlasya bāhya-pratyaya īkṣyate
bravīti śrutir etasya prārabdhaṃ phala-darśanāt

[446] 'In the case of one who is habituated to sustained meditation, we notice that there is still awareness of external objects. The Veda speaks of this as "the portion of merit and demerit that served to initiate the present body" (prārabdha karma), and we see that this merit and demerit has to be worked out (despite the other remaining parts of his merit and demerit being "burnt up" by his metaphysical knowledge).

In these verses the traditional view of how the liberated man (jivan-mukta) continues to live in the world is explained on a relatively low basis for the good of aspirants in general.

The doctrine of prarabdha karma is here accepted as a working hypothesis, although in other great classics it is not mentioned. Swami Sacchidanandaji did not endorse it, nor does Shri Shankara in some of his other works. From the highest point of view, liberation is liberation and there are no stages in it such as liberation in life (jivan-mukti) and release after death (videha-mukti). When the illusory snake disappears and the rope, its substratum, is revealed, the snake does not disappear by stages. You cannot say that first the tail goes and then the teeth and the venomous hood. In the theory of ajata-vada,[1] which is accepted in

1 The 'no creation' doctrine: cp. Gauḍapāda in *Māṇḍūkya Upanishad Kārikā* 3.48: 'This is the highest truth: that nothing is ever born'. For this final view see verses 455-464 below and the *Śaṃkara Source Book*, vol.2 *Śaṃkara on the Creation*, p.185 ff. (published by Shanti Sadan).

the highest state of Vedanta, there is no such distinction as that between jivan-mukti and videha-mukti.

sukhādy-anubhavo yāvat tāvat prārabdham iṣyate
phalodayaḥ kriyā-pūrvo niṣkriyo na hi kutracit

[447] 'We accept that prārabdha karma must continue as long as there are experiences of pleasure and pain and so on. For results in the form of pleasure and pain spring only from action, and are never found without it.

aham brahmeti vijñānāt kalpa-koṭi-śatārjitam
sañcitaṃ vilayaṃ yāti prabodhāt svapna-karma-vat

[448] 'On the attainment of the concrete perception: "I am the Absolute", the merit and demerit accumulated in hundreds of millions of world-periods dissolves, like the merit and demerit (apparently) earned in a dream dissolving when one awakes.

yat kṛtaṃ svapna-velāyāṃ puṇyaṃ vā pāpam ulbaṇam
suptotthitasya kiṃ tat syāt svargāya narakāya vā

[449] 'Can the many meritorious and sinful actions committed at the time of dream by one who has now woken up continue to lead him either towards heaven or towards hell?

svam asaṅgam udāsīnaṃ parijñāya nabho yathā
na śliṣyate yatiḥ kiñcit kadācid bhāvi-karmabhiḥ

[450] 'That person of discipline who has realized that he is relationless (or unattached) and indifferent to all, like the ether of space, is never in any way affected by the results of the acts he may commit in the future.

To the one liberated in life (jivan-mukta) there is no associationship and no non-associationship (no asangata). When there is only one-without-a-second, free from all kinds of difference, what associationship or non-associationship can there be? The one Brahman (Absolute), ever the same, prevails. The sun is never obscured by clouds. There is nothing in the world that can obscure the effulgence of the sun. That sun is Brahman, ever the same, the real Self.

An important question arises: 'Is the enlightened man (jnani) subject to duality at all?' He is. If so, what is the difference between him and the unenlightened man (ajnani)? The difference is this: when the jnani teaches, he will have to use duality, as no teaching is possible in non-duality. When he takes his alms, he is in a state of duality. If you put before him quinine, he will not eat it. When it is summer, he will say: 'Is there any cold water available?' But this duality is in his mind (antahkarana) and he is Self (atman), perfectly dissociated from the antahkarana, and in Atman there is no cold and heat.

The unenlightened man (ajnani) is identified with the mind and he identifies Atman with the want: 'I want cold water'. But the jnani knows it is the mind that wants, and: 'Have I anything to do with the mind? Can the finite ever influence the infinite? I am infinite!' He enjoys all the tastes, yet he is not enjoying any, because he knows where the enjoyment takes place.

na nabho ghaṭa-yogena surā-gandhena lipyate
tathātmopādhi-yogena tad-dharmair naiva lipyate

[451] 'The ether of space apparently enclosed within a pot is not tainted by the odour of any spirits that may be kept in that pot. In the same way, the Self, even though apparently enclosed within conditioning adjuncts (to form an individual soul), is not tainted by any of the attributes of those apparent conditioning adjuncts.

jñānodayāt purārabdhaṃ karma jñānān na naśyati
adattvā sva-phalaṃ lakṣyam uddiśyotsṛṣṭa-bāṇavat

[452] 'The merit and demerit that has begun to fructify (to produce the present body) before the rise of metaphysical knowledge, is not destroyed by that knowledge before it yields its fruit. It is like an arrow loosed at a target.

vyāghra-buddhyā vinirmukto bāṇaḥ paścāt tu go-matau
na tiṣṭhati chinatty eva lakṣyaṃ vegena nirbharam

[453] 'An arrow that has been shot at what was supposed to be a tiger will not stop when the tiger is afterwards realized to have been a cow. It will pierce its target with violence and speed.

prārabdhaṃ balavattaraṃ khalu vidāṃ bhogena tasya kṣayaḥ
samyag-jñāna-hutāśanena vilayaḥ prāk-sañcitāgāminām
brahmātmaikyam avekṣya tanmayatayā ye sarvadā saṃsthitās
teṣāṃ tat tritayaṃ na hi kvacid api brahmaiva te nirguṇam

[454] 'The merit and demerit that initiated the present life in the case of enlightened people must be very powerful. It can only be exhausted through being experienced. But other accumulated merit and demerit from previous lives is dissolved in the fire of right metaphysical knowledge, along with the merit and demerit that would have been engendered by acts performed after enlightenment. But those who have perceived their own identity with the Absolute and who are perpetually intent on that—for them, none of the three kinds of merit and demerit exists anywhere. They are the Absolute alone, and that is without empirical attributes.

upādhi-tādātmya-vihīna-kevala-
brahmātmanaivātmani tiṣṭhato muneḥ
prārabdha-sad-bhāva-kathā na yuktā
svapnārtha-sambandha-katheva jāgrataḥ

[455] 'For the sage who is established in his true Self as identical with the transcendent Absolute, free from any feeling of identity with conditioning adjuncts, this talk of the existence of the merit and demerit that initiated the present life does not seem right. It is like talk of the things seen in a dream to one who is awake.

na hi prabuddhaḥ pratibhāsa-dehe
dehopayoginy api ca prapañce
karoty ahantāṃ mamatām idantām
kintu svayaṃ tiṣṭhati jāgareṇa

[456] 'For one who has awoken from a dream does not feel "I", "mine" or "this" with regard to the patently unreal dream-body or the dream-world that seemed to support it. Being awake, he stands independently.

na tasya mithyārtha-samarthanecchā
na saṅgrahas taj-jagato 'pi dṛṣṭaḥ
tatrānuvṛttir yadi cen mṛṣārthe
na nidrayā mukta itīṣyate dhruvam

[457] 'He does not wish to defend the reality of the dream-world, since it is illusory; he is not seen to adopt it as his own either. If he were seriously to pursue the illusory objects of that world, one would have to conclude that he had not really awoken from his sleep.

tadvat pare brahmaṇi vartamānaḥ
sad-ātmanā tiṣṭhati nānyad īkṣate
smṛtir yathā svapna-vilokitārthe
tathā vidaḥ prāśana-mocanādau

[458] 'The same is the case with the one established in the Absolute: he stands identified with the real and sees nothing else. The eating, defecation and so on on the part of the enlightened one proceed like the memory of things seen in a dream.

karmaṇā nirmito dehaḥ prārabdhaṃ tasya kalpyatām
nānāder ātmano yuktaṃ naivātmā karma-nirmitaḥ

[459] 'The body has come into being as a result of action. The merit and demerit that initiated the present life must be thought of as pertaining to it. It is not right to attribute them to the beginningless Self. The Self is not the result of action.

ajo nitya iti brūte śrutir eṣā tv amogha-vāk
tad ātmanā tiṣṭhato 'sya kutaḥ prārabdha-kalpanā

[460] 'The Veda is infallible and speaks of the Self as unborn and eternal. So how could one truly attribute "the merit and demerit initiating the present birth" to one (i.e., an enlightened person) who remains identified with the Self?

prārabdhaṃ sidhyati tadā yadā dehātmanā sthitiḥ
dehātma-bhāvo naiveṣṭaḥ prārabdhaṃ tyajyatām ataḥ

[461] '"The merit and demerit initiating the present birth" is a concept that can subsist only so long as there is identification with the physical body. You do not accept that the body is the Self. So you should drop this notion of the merit and demerit that initiated the present body.

śarīrasyāpi prārabdha-kalpanā bhrāntir eva hi
adhyastasya kutaḥ sattvam asattvasya kuto janiḥ
ajātasya kuto nāśaḥ prārabdham asataḥ kutaḥ

[462] 'Even attributing the merit and demerit that initiated the present life to the body is an error. How can the superimposed be real? How can the unreal be born? How can what has never been born die? How can one attribute "the merit and demerit that initiated the present life" to something which has no reality whatever?

jñānenājñāna-kāryasya sa-mūlasya layo yadi
tiṣṭhaty ayaṃ kathaṃ deha iti śaṅkāvato jaḍān
samādhātuṃ bāhya-dṛṣṭyā prārabdhaṃ vadati śrutiḥ

[463] 'The Veda speaks of "the merit and demerit that initiated the present life" to satisfy from an external point of view those dull-witted objectors who ask: "If knowledge has dissolved the effects of ignorance together with their cause, how can the body continue to exist?"

na tu dehādi satyatva-bodhanāya vipaścitām
yataḥ śruter abhiprāyaḥ paramārthaika-gocaraḥ

[464] 'The Veda does not intend to teach the reality of the body to intelligent people. For the sole aim of the Veda is to teach (directly or indirectly according to the capacity of the student) the final reality.

57. Rejection of plurality

paripūrṇam anādy-antam aprameyam avikriyam
ekam evādvayaṃ brahma neha nānāsti kiñcana

[465] 'Only the Absolute exists, superabundant, beginningless, immeasurable (or unknowable), not subject to change, one without a second. Here there is no diversity whatsoever.[1]

sad-ghanaṃ cid-ghanaṃ nityam ānanda-ghanam akriyam
ekam evādvayaṃ brahma neha nānāsti kiñcana

[466] 'Being as an undifferentiated mass, Consciousness as an undifferentiated mass, eternal, actionless, Bliss as an

1 *Bṛhadāraṇyaka Upanishad* 4.4.19, etc.

undifferentiated mass—the Absolute is one without a second. Here there is no diversity whatsoever.

pratyag-eka-rasaṃ pūrṇam anantaṃ sarvato-mukham
ekam evādvayaṃ brahma neha nānāsti kiñcana

[467] 'Having the one savour of interiority, infinite, endless, all-pervading—the Absolute is one without a second. Here there is no diversity whatsoever.

aheyam anupādeyam anādheyam anāśrayam
ekam evādvayam brahma neha nānāsti kiñcana

[468] 'Not subject either to rejection or acceptance, having nothing else for its support or resting place—the Absolute is one without a second. Here there is no diversity whatsoever.

nirguṇaṃ niṣkalaṃ sūkṣmaṃ nirvikalpaṃ nirañjanam
ekam evādvayaṃ brahma neha nānāsti kiñcana

[469] 'Without attributes, without parts, subtle, free from false imagination, taintless—the Absolute is one without a second. Here there is no diversity whatsoever.

anirūpya-svarūpaṃ yan mano-vācām agocaram
ekam evādvayaṃ brahma neha nānāsti kiñcana

[470] 'Its nature is indescribable. It is beyond the range of mind and speech. The Absolute is one without a second. Here there is no diversity whatsoever.

sat samṛddhaṃ svataḥ-siddhaṃ śuddhaṃ buddham anīdṛśam
ekam evādvayaṃ brahma neha nānāsti kiñcana

[471] 'It is real, magnificent, independently self-established, pure, conscious, without an equal. The Absolute is one without a second. Here there is no diversity whatsoever.

58. Teaching for direct experience of the Self

nirasta-rāgā nirapāsta-bhogāḥ
śāntāḥ su-dāntā yatayo mahāntaḥ
vijñāya tattvaṃ param etad ante
prāptāḥ parāṃ nirvṛtim ātma-yogāt

[472] 'It is the great souls of disciplined life who come to know the supreme metaphysical principle and finally achieve the highest happiness through realizing the Self, but only when they are equipped with inner and outer control in high measure and have dropped all attachment and personal individual enjoyment.

bhavān apīdaṃ para-tattvam ātmanaḥ
svarūpam ānanda-ghanaṃ vicārya
vidhūya mohaṃ sva-manaḥ-prakalpitaṃ
muktaḥ kṛtārtho bhavatu prabuddhaḥ

[473] 'So you, also, should reflect over this highest nature of your own Self as a mass of bliss. Shake off this delusion imagined by your mind. Wake up to enlightenment, acquire liberation, fulfil your true destiny.

samādhinā sādhu viniścalātmanā
paśyātma-tattvaṃ sphuṭa-bodha-cakṣuṣā
niḥsaṃśayaṃ samyag-avekṣitaś cec
chrutaḥ padārtho na punar vikalpyate

[474] 'Behold your own Self with the clear eye of enlightenment with well-maintained motionless concentration. When something that is first only heard about is later correctly and indubitably seen, then there are no further misconceptions about it.

Concentration (samadhi), in the highest sense, is the state following enlightenment (jnana). The enlightened man (jnani) is still in samadhi when he finds himself fighting a battle for righteousness promoted by his prarabdha karma and the prarabdha karma of the world. When he rules, like Shri Krishna in Dwaraka, all is samadhi.

svasyāvidyā-bandha-sambandha-mokṣāt
satya-jñānānanda-rūpātma-labdhau
śāstraṃ yuktir deśikoktiḥ pramāṇaṃ
cāntaḥ-siddhā svānubhūtiḥ pramāṇam

[475] 'In realizing the true nature of your own Self as Existence-Consciousness-Bliss through liberation from the bondage of ignorance about your own true state, the authoritative knowledge comes from the Veda, from reasoning, from the words of the teacher and from your own personal experience perceived within.

bandho mokṣaś ca tṛptiś ca cintā-''rogya-kṣudādayaḥ
svenaiva vedyā yaj jñānaṃ pareṣām ānumānikam

[476] 'Bondage, liberation, satisfaction, anxiety, recovery from illness, hunger and so on are directly known only to oneself and for others are a subject of mere inference.

taṭa-sthitā bodhayanti guravaḥ śrutayo yathā
prajñayaiva tared vidvān īśvarānugṛhītayā

[477] 'Teachers and Vedic texts can only instruct one from outside. The enlightened one has to cross over transmigratory life through his own personal spiritual experience (prajñā), aided by the grace of the Lord.

Liberation in life (jivan-mukti) is not acquired but realized. When it is realized, what is the attitude of the enlightened man (jnani) towards the world? 'Where has the world disappeared to? Who has taken it away? It was seen just now by me; now it is not. What a great wonder!' (see verse 484).

Enlightenment (jnana) is not subject to achievement. The Veda says that neither by ritual, nor charity, nor prayer, nor devotion is the Self (atman) to be realized. Then what is the purpose of Yoga, or good living, or discipline? The answer is given in the words of Arjuna in the *Gita* when he says, after having experienced the grand vision of the Lord described in chapter eleven: 'O Janardana (Krishna), my ignorance has gone. I have acquired the memory of the holy state. All this is the result of Thy grace'.

In many instances in the *Gita* the Lord says: 'I give this state of spiritual consciousness to My devotees'. In the *Katha Upanishad* also it is said: 'He whom the Self chooses, by him the Self can be gained'.

Is the grace of God arbitrary, or does it fall on everybody indiscriminately like the snow in winter? No, the devotee has to earn the grace. As in the course of biological evolution, the survival of a species is not arbitrary but depends on the adaptability of the organism, so the grace of the Lord is attracted when the individual (jiva), through discipline and the practice of righteousness (dharma), meditation and devotion, has created a vacuum in his soul by expelling the love of all that is not-self. Nature abhors a vacuum and, as in the physical world, this vacuum in the soul is filled by the light of 'All is Brahman (the Absolute)'.

The grace of the Lord comes when we please Him. By carrying out His commandments (dharma), by living a life of detachment and devotion, we render our mind fit to receive His grace.

svānubhūtyā svayaṃ jñātvā svam ātmānam akhaṇḍitam
saṃsiddhaḥ sa-sukhaṃ tiṣṭhen nirvikalpātmanā ''tmani

[478] 'Having known his own true undifferentiated Self in direct experience, he should rest happily and without false imagination in that Self, having attained perfection.

vedānta-siddhānta-niruktir eṣā
brahmaiva jīvaḥ sakalaṃ jagac ca
akhaṇḍa-rūpa-sthitir eva mokṣo
brahmādvitīye śrutayaḥ pramāṇam

> [479] 'The right explanation of the final upanishadic teaching is that both the soul and the whole world are in truth (not what they appear to be but) only the Absolute. Liberation is permanent establishment in this undifferentiated principle. The Vedas are the authority declaring that the Absolute is one without a second'.

In the third chapter of the *Taittiriya Upanishad* there is a progressive revelation of the ultimate nature of reality to an enquiring mind, in the discussion between the father Varuna and his son Bhrigu. Varuna tells his son that the Absolute, called in the Vedanta philosophy Brahman, is something infinite which includes everything else and sustains the whole universe: 'That from whence these things are born, That by which when born they live, That into which they enter at their death: try to know That, That is Brahman'. The father describes to his son in outline the general features of reality, and advises him to discover the content of it by supra-intellectual reflection and meditation.

The son identifies the reality in turn with matter, vitality and mind, and rejects them. Materialism does not satisfy him because it fails to explain the whole of experience. The idea that vitalism is the absolute truth he also finds unsatisfactory. Mind also is not Brahman; the intellect is not satisfied with the adequacy of mind, for it does not exhaust the nature of reality. Intellect operates in the realm of duality. It splits the world into two factors, Self and not-self, a state in which struggle and endeavour must continue forever. There is no peace possible in this state. To know the unchanging, infinite reality in one's own being—and it cannot be known elsewhere—man must transcend the limitations which veil infinity in him.

Bhrigu, in the end, is taught: Bliss (ananda) is Brahman; It is the heart of things; both the Self and the not-self are included in Brahman, the Absolute. Then he sees, in the tranquillity of his soul, bliss as the Absolute. He is freed from fear and doubts. The divine vision described in chapter eleven of the *Gita* is seen by Bhrigu, mirrored in the calm of his soul. This intuitive experience is the crown of human life, the summit of evolution.

59. The pupil's enlightenment

iti guru-vacanāc chruti-pramāṇāt
param avagamya sa-tattvam ātma-yuktyā
praśamita-karaṇaḥ samāhitātmā
kvacid acalākṛtir ātma-niṣṭhito 'bhūt

[480] Having known the supreme in its true nature from the above teaching of the Guru and the authority of the Upanishads, together with his own reasoning, and with his senses stilled and mind concentrated, at a rare moment in time a certain person became established in the Self, motionless in form.

kañcit kālaṃ samādhāya pare brahmaṇi mānasam
vyutthāya paramānandād idaṃ vacanam abravīt

[481] For a time he concentrated his mind on the Absolute in its highest form. Then he broke away from this supreme bliss and spoke as follows:

buddhir vinaṣṭā galitā pravṛttir
brahmātmanor ekatayādhigatyā
idaṃ na jāne 'py anidaṃ na jāne
kiṃ vā kiyad vā sukham asty apāram

[482] 'My mind has disappeared and my self-interested activity has dropped away through direct knowledge of the identity of my own true Self with the Absolute. I am aware neither of a "this" nor a "not-this". I know neither the nature nor the extent of my limitless joy.

vācā vaktum aśakyam eva manasā
mantuṃ na vā śakyate
svānandāmṛta-pūra-pūrita-para
brahmāmbudher vaibhavam
ambho-rāśi-viśīrṇa-vārṣika-śilā-
bhāvaṃ bhajan me mano
yasyāṃśāṃśa-lave vilīnam adhunā
''nandātmanā nirvṛtam

[483] 'Speech cannot express and mind cannot encompass the glory of the ocean of the Absolute filled with the nectar of the bliss of one's own Self. My mind is like a hailstone melted in that ocean. Dissolved into a drop of a fraction of a fraction of that ocean, it is now satisfied with the essence of bliss.

kva gataṃ kena vā nītaṃ kutra līnam idaṃ jagat
adhunaiva mayā dṛṣṭaṃ nāsti kiṃ mahad adbhutam

[484] 'Where has this world gone? Who has taken it away? Where has it dissolved? Just now I could see it. Now it has gone. What a strange miracle![1]

kiṃ heyaṃ kim upādeyaṃ kim anyat kiṃ vilakṣaṇam
akhaṇḍānanda-pīyūṣa-pūrṇe brahma-mahārṇave

[485] 'In the ocean of the Absolute filled with the nectar of unbroken bliss, what is there to reject? What is there to accept? What exists other than one's own Self? What is there that is in any way different from oneself?

na kiñcid atra paśyāmi na śṛṇomi na vedmy aham
svātmanaiva sad-ānanda-rūpeṇāsmi vilakṣaṇaḥ

1 Cp. verse 477 with comment, above.

[486] 'I see nothing here, hear nothing, know nothing. Having assumed my true nature as reality and bliss, I have become completely different from what I appeared to be before.

namo namas te gurave mahātmane
vimukta-saṅgāya sad-uttamāya
nityādvayānanda-rasa-svarūpiṇe
bhūmne sadā 'pāra-dayāmbu-dhāmne

[487] 'Reverence, reverence to you, O great soul (mahātmā), O my teacher! You are liberated from attachment. You occupy the highest place amongst the good. You are the essence of eternal non-dual bliss in its true form. You are infinity. You are ever a shoreless ocean of compassion.

yat kaṭākṣa-śaśi-sāndra-candrikā-
pāta-dhūta-bhava-tāpa-ja-śramaḥ
prāpta-vān aham akhaṇḍa-vaibhavā-
''nandam ātma-padam akṣayaṃ kṣaṇāt

[488] 'My scorched sufferings in repeated worldly existences have been (cooled and) washed away by the watery beams of a glance from your moon-like eye. In a trice they have wafted me to the glory of the unbroken and inexhaustible bliss of the Self.

dhanyo 'haṃ kṛta-kṛtyo 'haṃ vimukto 'haṃ bhava-grahāt
nityānanda-svarūpo 'ham pūrṇo 'ham tad-anugrahāt

[489] 'Blessed am I. I have done all that has to be done. I am liberated from the curse of repeated worldly lives. I am eternal bliss in its true form. I am infinite and perfect—all through his (the teacher's) grace.

asaṅgo 'ham anaṅgo 'ham aliṅgo 'ham abhaṅguraḥ
praśānto 'ham ananto 'haṃ amalo 'haṃ cirantanaḥ

[490] 'I am relationless. I have no body. I have no characteristic whereby I could be identified. (Or: I have no physical body or subtle body.) I am indestructible. I am in profound peace. I have no bounds. I am pure.[1] I have existed from primordial time.

akartāham abhoktāham avikāro 'ham akriyaḥ
śuddha-bodha-svarūpo 'haṃ kevalo 'haṃ sadā-śivaḥ

[491] 'I am not a performer of action. I do not enjoy individual experience. I have nothing to do with change or action. I am pure Consciousness in its true nature, I am transcendent, the eternal good (sadā-śiva).

draṣṭuḥ śrotur vaktuḥ kartur bhoktur vibhinna evāham
nitya-nirantara-niṣkriya-niḥsīmāsaṅga-pūrṇa-bodhātmā

[492] 'I am other than the seer, the hearer, the speaker, the performer of action or the enjoyer of individual experience. My nature is infinite Consciousness, eternal, unbroken, actionless, limitless, relationless and perfect.

nāham idaṃ nāham ado 'py ubhayor
avabhāsakaṃ paraṃ śuddham
bāhyābhyantara-śūnyaṃ pūrṇaṃ
brahmādvitīyam evāham

[493] 'I am neither "this" nor "that" but that supreme pure principle which illumines both (i.e., which illumines all things relative). There is nothing outside me and nothing inside (interior to) me. I am the infinite Absolute, one without a second.

1 Reading 'amalo' with Mādhavānanda and Bhāgavat.

nirupamam anādi-tattvaṃ tvam
aham idam ada iti kalpanā-dūram
nityānandaika-rasaṃ satyaṃ
brahmādvitīyam evāham

[494] 'I am the Absolute, one only without a second, the beginningless principle to which nothing else can be compared, far removed from all vain imaginations such as "you", "I", "this", "that", real and ever of the one homogeneous savour of bliss.

nārāyaṇo 'ham narakāntako 'ham
purāntako 'haṃ puruṣo 'ham īśaḥ
akhaṇḍa-bodho 'haṃ aśeṣa-sākṣī
nirīśvaro 'ham nirahaṃ ca nirmamaḥ

[495] 'I am Nārāyaṇa, I am the slayer of the demon Naraka (that is, again, "I am Vishnu"), I am the slayer of the demon Tripura (i.e., "I am also Shiva"), I am the Spirit, I am the Lord, I am undifferentiated Consciousness, I am the witness of all, I have no overlord, I have no (individual) sense of "I" and "mine".

sarveṣu bhūteṣv aham eva saṃsthito
jñānātmanā 'ntar-bahir-āśrayaḥ san
bhoktā ca bhogyaṃ svayam eva sarvaṃ
yadyat pṛthag-dṛṣṭam idantayā purā

[496] 'I alone am the reality present in all creatures, I exist everywhere, the support of all, within and without, as Consciousness. I am the sole reality in all that was previously seen as separate and as "such and such". In this sense I am the experiencer and the object of his experience.

mayy akhaṇḍa-sukhāmbhodhau bahudhā viśva-vīcayaḥ
utpadyante vilīyante māyā-māruta-vibhramāt

[497] 'It is in me as the undifferentiated ocean of joy that the false appearance of waves of various kinds of sense-objects arise and subside through the play of the wind of Māyā.

sthūlādi-bhāvā mayi kalpitā bhramād
āropitā nu sphuraṇena lokaiḥ
kāle yathā kalpaka-vatsarāyan-
artvādayo niṣkala-nirvikalpe

[498] 'It is in me that physical (perceptible) and subtle (imperceptible) beings are imagined through error. But people merely superimpose them as empty phenomena. It is as when people imagine, in time, which is partless and undifferentiated, divisions such as world-periods, years, half-years, seasons and so on.

āropitaṃ nāśraya-dūṣakaṃ bhavet
kadāpi mūḍhair mati-doṣa-dūṣitaiḥ
nārdrīkaroty ūṣara-bhūmi-bhāgaṃ
marīcikā-vāri-mahāpravāhaḥ

[499] 'Things superimposed by people who are deluded by the defects in their minds have no deleterious effect on that onto which they are erroneously superimposed. A great flood of water seen in a mirage in no way dampens the ground in the desert where it is seen.

ākāśa-val lepa-vidūra-go 'ham
āditya-vad bhāsya-vilakṣaṇo 'ham
ahārya-van nitya-viniścalo 'ham
ambhodhi-vat pāra-vivarjito 'ham

[500] 'Like the ether of space, I am far removed from all stain. I am not capable of being illumined by anything else, like the sun. I am motionless like a mountain. I am shoreless like a (vast) ocean.

na me dehena sambandho megheneva vihāyasaḥ
ataḥ kuto me tad-dharmā jāgrat-svapna-suṣuptayaḥ

[501] 'I am no more connected with or affected by the body than the ether of the sky is connected with or affected by a cloud. So how can I be affected by its states—waking, dream and dreamless sleep?

upādhir āyāti sa eva gacchati
sa eva karmāṇi karoti bhuṅkte
sa eva jīryan mriyate sadā 'haṃ
kulādri-van niścala eva saṃsthitaḥ

[502] 'It is (not myself but) my apparent conditioning adjunct (the physical body and also the subtle body associated with senses, mind, etc.) that comes and goes. It is that which grows old and dies, while I remain fixed and immovable like a great mountain range.

na me pravṛttir na ca me nivṛttiḥ
sadaika-rūpasya niraṃśakasya
ekātmako yo nibiḍo nirantaro
vyomeva pūrṇaḥ sa kathaṃ nu ceṣṭate

[503] 'Partless and ever the same, I neither engage in action nor desist from it. How could that act which is infinite like the ether of the sky, homogeneous, close-packed and void of interstices?

puṇyāni pāpāni nirindriyasya
niścetaso nirvikṛter nirākṛteḥ

kuto mamākhaṇḍa-sukhānubhūter
brūte hy ananvāgatam ity api śrutiḥ

[504] 'I am undifferentiated Consciousness and Bliss, changeless, formless, not possessed of sense-organs or mind. How could I perform meritorious or sinful acts? The Veda also declares that I am not accompanied by merit or demerit.[1]

chāyayā spṛṣṭam uṣṇaṃ vā śītaṃ vā suṣṭhu duṣṭhu vā
na spṛśaty eva yat kiñcit puruṣaṃ tad-vilakṣaṇam

[505] 'The heat and the cold, the good and the bad, that touch a man's shadow do not affect the man himself at all, who is different from the shadow.

na sākṣiṇaṃ sākṣya-dharmāḥ saṃspṛśanti vilakṣaṇam
avikāram udāsīnaṃ gṛha-dharmāḥ pradīpavat

[506] 'In the same way, the attributes of the objects of the vision of a witness do not affect the witness, which is different from them, not subject to change and indifferent. The witness is untouched and unaffected by what it illumines, like a lamp illumining the contents of a house.

raver yathā karmaṇi sākṣi-bhāvo
vahner yathā vāyasi dāhakatvam
rajjor yathāropita-vastu-saṅgas
tathaiva kūṭastha-cid-ātmano me

[507] 'As the rock-firm Self and Consciousness, my relation to objects is like the indifferent witness-relationship of the sun to an act (which it illumines indifferently whether it is good or bad), like the relationship of "burner" on the part of fire in red-

1 *Bṛhadāraṇyaka Upanishad* 4.3.22

hot iron (where the fire rests motionless and any activity belongs to the iron)[1] and like the relationship of a rope to that which is superimposed upon it (which is only an appearance, is subject to cancellation, and does not in the last resort exist).

kartāpi vā kārayitāpi nāhaṃ
bhoktāpi vā bhojayitāpi nāham
draṣṭāpi vā darśayitāpi nāhaṃ
so 'haṃ svayaṃ-jyotir anīdṛg-ātmā

[508] 'I am neither a performer of action nor one who promotes action in others; I am neither an individual experiencer nor one who promotes individual experience in others. I neither perceive nor promote perception in others. "I am He" (so 'ham)—the self-luminous Self without a parallel.

calaty upādhau pratibimba-laulyam
aupādhikaṃ mūḍha-dhiyo nayanti
sva-bimba-bhūtaṃ ravi-vad-viniṣkriyam
kartāsmi bhoktāsmi hato 'smi heti

[509] 'In the case of a medium in which an object is reflected, confused people attribute the movement of the medium to the stationary object reflected in it, as in the case of the sun (reflected in waves). In the same way, the metaphysically ignorant one attributes to his (motionless) Self the movements of the mind in which it is reflected, and feels, 'I am the actor and the enjoyer. Alas, I am done for!'

jale vāpi sthale vāpi luṭhatv eṣa jaḍātmakaḥ
nāhaṃ vilipye tad-dharmair ghaṭa-dharmair nabho yathā

1 Reading 'ayasi dāhakatvam' for 'dāha-niyāmakatvam' with Muni Lāl.

[510] 'This non-conscious body may be writhing about on the ground or struggling to stay alive in water, but I am no more tainted by its attributes than the ether of space is tainted by the attributes of a pot in which it appears to be enclosed.

kartṛtva-bhoktṛtva-khalatva-mattatā-
jaḍatva-baddhatva-vimuktatādayaḥ
buddher vikalpā na tu santi vastutaḥ
svasmin pare brahmaṇi kevale 'dvaye

[511] 'Being a performer of action, being an individual experiencer, mischievousness, intoxication, being non-conscious, being in bondage, being liberated and so on, are all imaginations of the mind which have no real existence in my true Self, the Absolute, the supreme, the transcendent, one without a second.

santu vikārāḥ prakṛter daśadhā śatadhā sahasradhā vāpi
kiṃ me 'saṅga-cites tair na ghanaḥ kvacid ambaraṃ spṛśati

[512] 'Nature may undergo modifications ten-fold, a hundred-fold or a thousand-fold. What does it matter to me, who am relationless Consciousness? The ether of space in the sky can never be touched by a thick band of clouds.

avyaktādi-sthūla-paryantam etad
viśvaṃ yatrābhāsa-mātraṃ pratītam
vyoma-prakhyaṃ sūkṣmam ādy-anta-hīnaṃ
brahmādvaitaṃ yat tad evāham asmi

[513] 'I am that Absolute, one without a second, subtle and without beginning or end, similar to the ether of space in the sky, in which the whole universe from the Unmanifest principle to the gross physical body is seen as a mere illusory appearance.

sarvādhāraṃ sarva-vastu-prakāśaṃ
sarvākāraṃ sarvagaṃ sarva-śūnyam
nityaṃ śuddhaṃ niścalaṃ nirvikalpaṃ
brahmādvaitaṃ yat tad evāham asmi

[514] 'I am that Absolute, one without a second, which is the support of all, the illuminator of all, which assumes all forms, pervades all and yet is void of all, which is eternal, pure, motionless and void of false imagination.

yat pratyastāśeṣa-māyā-viśeṣaṃ
pratyag-rūpaṃ pratyayāgamyamānam
satya-jñānānantam ānanda-rūpaṃ
brahmādvaitaṃ yat tad evāham asmi

[515] 'I am that Absolute, one without a second, bereft of all the distinctions of Māyā, of the nature of interiority and not to be encompassed by a mental idea, of the nature of Bliss, "Reality, Knowledge, Infinity" (Taittirīya Upanishad 2.1).

niṣkriyo 'smy avikāro 'smi niṣkalo 'smi nirākṛtiḥ
nirvikalpo 'smi nityo 'smi nirālambo 'smi nirdvayaḥ

[516] 'I am actionless, not subject to modification, partless, formless, bereft of false imagination, eternal, without a support, without a second.

sarvātmako 'haṃ sarvo 'haṃ sarvātīto 'ham advayaḥ
kevalākhaṇḍa-bodho 'ham ānando 'haṃ nirantaraḥ

[517] 'I am the Self of all, I am all, yet am I beyond all, one without a second, transcendent, undifferentiated Consciousness. I am unriven Bliss.

svārājya-sāmrājya-vibhūtir eṣā
bhavat-kṛpā-śrī-mahima-prasādāt
prāptā mayā śrī-gurave mahātmane
namo namas te 'stu punar namo 'stu

[518] 'O my teacher! Reverence, reverence, and again reverence unto you, O great soul! By your compassion, glory, divine power and grace, I have attained the glorious state of spiritual sovereignty and empire.

mahā-svapne māyā-kṛta-jani-jarā-mṛtyu-gahane
bhramantaṃ kliśyantaṃ bahulatara-tāpair anudinam
ahaṅkāra-vyāghra-vyathitam imam atyanta-kṛpayā
prabodhya prasvāpāt param avitavān mām asi guro

[519] 'O my teacher! You are my supreme benefactor who have awoken me by your boundless compassion from my great sleep. I was wandering and suffering in the forest of repeated birth, decrepitude and death created by Māyā, afflicted with many troubles every day, and molested by the tiger of individual ego-feeling.

namas tasmai sad-ekasmai kasmaicin mahase namaḥ
yad etad-viśva-rūpeṇa rājate guru-rāja te

[520] 'O King among Gurus! Reverence, reverence, to that one great unfathomable glory of yours, which manifests in splendour as this universe'.

60. Conclusion of the teaching on enlightenment

iti natam avalokya śiṣya-varyaṃ
samadhigatātma-sukhaṃ prabuddha-tattvam
pramudita-hṛdayaḥ sa deśikendraḥ
punar idam āha vacaḥ paraṃ mahātmā

[521] Glancing down at that excellent pupil bowing before him, who had realized the joy of the Self and was awake to reality, the lordly Guru, that great soul, began to utter glorious words again as follows, feeling delight in his heart.

brahma-pratyaya-santatir jagad ato
brahmaiva sat sarvataḥ
paśyādhyātma-dṛśā praśānta-manasā
sarvāsv avasthāsv api
rūpād anyad avekṣituṃ kim abhitaś
cakṣuṣmatāṃ vidyate
tad-vad brahma-vidaḥ sataḥ kim aparaṃ
buddher vihāraspadam

[522] 'The world is but a continuous series of perceptions (i.e., of misrepresentations) of the Absolute and therefore is the Absolute and nothing else. From every standpoint, it is the real. Contemplate with the eye of spiritual insight and with a heart in profound peace in all states of experience. What is it but colour that can be seen all round by those possessed of eyes? Similarly, in the case of him who knows the Absolute, what other refuge can there be for the mind apart from That?

A vast region of Consciousness lies uncharted and unexplored by the mind. Some mental concepts have emerged from Consciousness, but infinite concepts are implicit in it. Western philosophy, from Aristotle to Croce, has made no efforts towards widening our conception of what is potential in Consciousness; it has been labelled 'unknown' and 'unknowable'. The philosophy of Yoga claims to know this 'unknowable', not by dialectics, but by love and free-will.

The autonomy of Consciousness lies beyond the mind. When the tranquillized mind melts in contemplation, or effects meditation, to establish a link between the relative and the Absolute, there emerges the feeling of the true meaning of 'I am'.

kas tāṃ parānanda-rasānubhūtim
utsṛjya śūnyeṣu rameta vidvān
candre mahā-hlādini dīpyamāne
citrendum ālokayituṃ ka icchet

[523] 'What person of sense would give up this experience of supreme bliss and wander in the empty desert of sense-objects? Who would wish to look at a picture of the moon when the moon itself was showering coolness all around?

asat-padārthānubhave na kiñcin
na hy asti tṛptir na ca duḥkha-hāniḥ
tad advayānanda-rasānubhūtyā
tṛptaḥ sukhaṃ tiṣṭha sad-ātma-niṣṭhayā

[524] 'There is no advantage in the experience of unreal objects. For it leads neither to contentment nor to diminution of suffering. Therefore remain happy, enjoying satisfaction through the direct experience of the taste of non-dual bliss, in devotion to the real Self.

svam eva sarvathā paśyan manyamānaḥ svam advayam
svānandam anubhuñjānaḥ kālaṃ naya mahāmate

[525] 'O noble-minded one! Seeing your Self everywhere, think yourself to be the non-dual Self. Pass your time in enjoyment of your own bliss.

akhaṇḍa-bodhātmani nirvikalpe
vikalpanaṃ vyomni puraḥ-prakalpanam
tad advayānandamayātmanā sadā
śāntiṃ parām etya bhajasva maunam

[526] 'Any imagination of a finite appearance manifesting in the Self, which is undifferentiated Consciousness and without false imagination, is like an aerial city imagined in the empty sky. Therefore, having attained the supreme peace, practise silence, identified with your Self, which is non-dual bliss.

tūṣṇīm avasthā paramopaśāntir
buddher asat kalpa-vikalpa-hetoḥ
brahmātmanā brahmavido mahātmano
yatrādvayānanda-sukhaṃ nirantaram

[527] 'The mind is the cause of false imagination, and its silence is the supreme peace. Here that great soul who knows the Absolute enjoys the bliss of non-duality, himself being the Absolute.[1]

The mind is not pure Consciousness but, like a cloud in the sky, or space, it is born of Consciousness, rests in Consciousness and is finally dissolved in it. We try to understand the mystery of being and becoming. The cloud, being a product of space and being finite, will not be able to grasp the infinite space. So does reality, or infinite Consciousness, elude the grasp of the mind. The mind is a help to an understanding of certain phases of life in the empirical realm (sansara), but in its existential form it obscures Consciousness. The real metaphysical effort should therefore be to negate the mind and thus establish the autonomy of Consciousness in which there is real freedom.

1 Reading 'brahmātmanā' and not 'brahmātmano', following Muni Lāl and Bhāgavat, cp. *Muṇḍaka Upanishad* 3.2.9

It is difficult to meet successfully the dialectics of determinism, and as long as there are divided elements and a law which governs their union and separation and *vice versa*, the deterministic conception is unavoidable. Freedom is the flooding of the mind, and the laws governing it, with the inrush of the Absolute. This process is called meditation in identity consciousness.

The analytical process of psychology cannot determine the basic factor of Consciousness. In the realm of empirical science and philosophy we hear so much of the improvement of the mind and expansion of mental consciousness, but the real way to freedom is to establish the autonomy of Consciousness.

To negate the mind, no strenuous psychic efforts are needed. It is by rising above the tyranny of the mind, by which it imposes limitation on Consciousness by creating a net of desire and aversion and other pairs of opposites, that we realize freedom. Our aim is to acquire freedom by regarding the mind and its products as space looks upon the clouds within it. The philosopher must cease to worry, the scientist to hurry. It is in the silence of pure Consciousness, the Absolute, that our spirit finds its rest and peace.

This is the real message of the philosophy of Shri Shankara.

nāsti nirvāsanān maunāt paraṃ sukha-kṛd uttamam
vijñātātma-svarūpasya svānanda-rasa-pāyinaḥ

[528] 'For one who has known the true nature of his own Self and is tasting the savour of his own bliss, there is no greater joy than silence void even of subtle urges.

In this state of spiritual peace (shanti), when all desire and aversion have ceased, the mind becomes transparent and reflects the Self as Existence, Consciousness and Bliss. This is termed the 'no-mind' state.

gacchaṃs-tiṣṭhann-upaviśañ-chayāno vānyathāpi vā
yathecchayā vased vidvān ātmārāmaḥ sadā muniḥ

[529] 'The enlightened sage who delights in the Self should ever live in relaxation, whether walking about, standing still, sitting down or otherwise occupied.

There are two keys to a life of real utility and joy. The first is nervous relaxation and the second is conscious living. I have been repeating this word 'relaxation' during the past fifty years. Whenever you do something which is not right, you are not relaxed. When you relax, you will be able to forgive and forget the wrongs which have been done to you. I always forget the wrongs anybody does to me, and very soon forget the good I have done to anybody. These two principles have helped me in my life and have enabled me to bear my poverty and illness. In the state of relaxation, no pleasure-desire, no anger, no hate, no egoism will ever torment you. Therefore I hope you will practise it in your home and abroad, and in order to practise it, use only as many words as are necessary. We waste far too much of our energy by using words which are not necessary. If one word can express our meaning, why use two?

Even the highest yogis, like Shri Shuka, Shri Vyasa and Shri Shankara, teach the holy scriptures and perform the legitimate and necessary functions of the body, such as begging for alms. Shri Shankara worshipped the Lord Shiva for a few hours daily in a temple to set an example in devotion to his pupils and others.

It is therefore clear that Yoga does not condemn the activities of the mind, but teaches a change in their nature and gives a spiritual purpose to them. Let us remember the fundamental truth that the Self is not the mind, and that there is no activity in the Self. The Self is the witness. But the witness is not the whole of the individuality (jivahood): it is the essence of it. To realize the Witness of the mind, the mind is not to be killed but taught to function in the right way, in detachment and in devotion to the Lord by way of service to His creatures.

The worst state of the mind is fatigue, when it loses all discrimination and is restless. Its activities when in this state are not spiritually purposive and not productive of any good results. A relaxed mind can produce the best of service by way of study of the spiritual classics and contributing to the good of one's fellow-men, and it is a mind in rest and peace, stilled and balanced, that can practise devotion and meditation.

na deśa-kālāsana-dig-yamādi-
lakṣyādy-apekṣā pratibaddha-vṛtteh
saṃsiddha-tattvasya mahātmano 'sti
svavedane kā niyamādy apekṣā

[530] 'The great soul who has controlled his mind and realized the truth does not depend on subordinate aims to do with place of meditation, posture for meditation, direction facing which one sits for meditation or disciplinary codes of conduct (yama, etc.). When one has knowledge of the true nature of one's own Self, what need does one have for rules?

ghaṭo 'yam iti vijñātuṃ niyamaḥ ko nv apekṣyate
vinā pramāṇa-suṣṭhutvaṃ yasmin sati padārtha-dhīḥ

[531] 'What rule could one need in order to know "This is a pot", apart from having those means of knowledge in good order (healthy eyes, light, pot in proximity, etc.) which are requisite for knowledge of such an object?

ayam ātmā nitya-siddhaḥ pramāṇe sati bhāsate
na deśaṃ nāpi vā kālaṃ na śuddhiṃ vāpy apekṣate

[532] 'This Self, which is always self-established as present, manifests when the means of knowledge (Vedic texts, teacher, discipline, etc.) have done their work. For this it does not depend on a particular place, a particular time or a particular degree of purity.

devadatto 'ham ity etad vijñānaṃ nirapekṣakam
tad-vad brahmavido 'py asya brahmāham iti vedanam

[533] 'The knowledge "I am Devadatta" does not depend on anything external. The same is true of the knowledge "I am the Absolute" on the part of a knower of the Absolute.

bhānuneva jagat sarvaṃ bhāsate yasya tejasā
anātmakam asat tucchaṃ kiṃ nu tasyāvabhāsakam

[534] 'What could illumine that whose light itself illumines the whole world like the sun—the world that is not-self, non-being, intrinsically paltry and insignificant?

Light is that principle which reveals something, that is, which brings something hidden into light, which makes the unknown known. To a layman, the sun is the light and the senses are revealers of the unknown; the unknown electrons are made known through scientific instruments—and that is the end of light. Let us expose this error.

This morning I was lying in my bed like a lazy fellow. My eyes were closed, my ears were stopped by the pillows, my nose was defunct, my sense of touch was also inoperative. I thought of the golden days when the earth was young and Tubal came hammering iron into swords. I thought of the stars shining together in the firmament, singing a chorus, the notes of which were wafted into gardens on the wings of the breeze. I imagined myself clad in raiments of light piping my flute in praise of the Master Light of the world. This thought soon vanished and I found myself a beggar, holding the bowl of my senses, soliciting beauty which was really deformity. Now consider, noble reader, what is that light which revealed to me those two visions of the past and present?

I then looked out of my window and I saw the sun slowly emerging above the horizon. In a few moments it had risen to the length of two yards, its effulgence increased. Under what light did I see these changes in the sun? The light of a candle suffers an eclipse in the light of the sun. Under whose light did the light and rise of the sun suffer an eclipse? What light issuing from my mind and my eyes covered the face of the sun and located it in its topographical situation? Surely that light must be infinitely stronger than the light of the sun. There is darkness when the sun has set and the stars have gone. Under what light do I see that darkness, and see that the darkness is not so thick now as it was two days ago? What is that light? It is the light of Self (atman). As Goethe says: ''Tis I who raised the sun from out the sea; The moon began her changeful course with me'.

veda-śāstra-purāṇāni bhūtāni sakalāny api
yenārthavanti taṃ kiṃ nu vijñātāraṃ prakāśayet

[535] 'What could illumine that knower, in whose light alone the Vedas, traditions and Purāṇas and all beings have meaning?

eṣa svayaṃjyotir ananta-śaktir
ātmā 'prameyaḥ sakalānubhūtiḥ
yam eva vijñāya vimukta-bandho
jayaty ayaṃ brahma-vid uttamottamaḥ

[536] 'This Self is self-luminous, possessed of unlimited power, not itself open to being known as an object of a means of knowledge, and is immediate experience wherever the latter is found. When he has known it, a knower of the Absolute reigns supreme; he is liberated from bondage and is the best among the best of men.

It is often asked whether consciousness is subject to evolution or mutation of any kind. The question is based on the statements of those philosophers who erroneously attribute expansion to the region of pure Consciousness. The Sufi teachers speak of stations of consciousness, and the sage Vasishtha speaks of landmarks of the rise of consciousness in the heart of the yogi; but the final teaching is that Consciousness is like the sun, which remains perpetually at its meridian.

That part of Consciousness which is conditioned by the human mind is subject to expansion as the layers of the mind are removed, just as the lids of a box in which a crest-jewel is kept are opened up. When a child is born, his consciousness, expressing itself as the sense of touch, is very limited; but very soon, as a certain lid over the mind is lifted, it expresses itself through all five senses. When perception is complete, conception begins to evolve.

Western philosophers think that the dawn of rational consciousness is the summit of consciousness, but the conception is elementary. There are many layers above the rational consciousness which have to be lifted up one after another before consciousness in its pristine purity as Existence, Consciousness and Bliss (sat-chit-ananda) reveals itself to that complex of the psychic and the conscious planes called the individual soul (jiva). When the door of the time-spatial consciousness is crossed, the jiva obtains admission into the divine Consciousness.

na khidyate no viṣayaiḥ pramodate
na sajjate nāpi virajyate ca
svasmin sadā krīḍati nandati svayaṃ
nirantarānanda-rasena tṛptaḥ

[537] 'He is neither resentful nor joyful on account of the presence of objects. He is neither attached to them nor detached from them. He ever sports and feels ecstasy alone in his own Self, enjoying intense satisfaction from the continual savour of bliss.

kṣudhāṃ deha-vyathāṃ tyaktvā bālaḥ krīḍati vastuni
tathaiva vidvān ramate nirmamo nirahaṃ sukhī

[538] 'Just as a child plays with a toy and forgets hunger and physical jars and jolts, so the enlightened one sports happily in the Self, forgetting "I" and "mine".

cintā-śūnyam adainya-bhaikṣam aśanaṃ pānaṃ sarid-vāriṣu
svātantryeṇa niraṅkuśā sthitir abhīr nidrā śmaśāne vane
vastraṃ kṣālana-śoṣanādi-rahitaṃ dig vāstu śayyā mahī
saṅcāro nigamānta-vīthiṣu vidāṃ krīḍā pare brahmaṇi

> [539] 'The enlightened ones sport in the Absolute, the supreme. Their food is whatever alms come by chance, and is not linked with anxiety or appeals for pity; they drink the water of rivers; their condition is one of indomitable independence; they know no fear; they sleep indifferently in a charnel house or in the forest; their robe is space, which does not need to be washed and dried; their dwelling-place and bed is the earth and they wander in the paths chalked out by the Upanishads.

The one great reason which makes the mystics fearless of death and indifferent to the vicissitudes of material life is that they become conscious of greater and greater vistas of consciousness, which are revealed to them by the grace of the Lord after their death. To a mystic, death is neither a negation of consciousness nor a suspension of it; it is a continuation of it in more and more intensified forms.

vimānam ālambya śarīram etad
  bhunakty aśeṣān viṣayān upasthitān
parecchayā bālavad ātma-vettā
  yo 'vyakta-liṅgo 'nanuṣakta-bāhyaḥ

> [540] 'The knower of the Self sits in the chariot of the body and enjoys, like a child, whatever objects are brought before him at the will of others. No one knows his true state. He is not attached to the external.

It is said in the *Katha Upanishad*: 'The wise say that the Self is the rider, the body is the chariot and the intellect (buddhi) the charioteer. The mind (manas) is the reins, the senses are the horses and their objects are the roads...The man whose charioteer is wise, who applies the reins of the mind well, attains the goal of life, the transcendental state of Vishnu'.[1]

1 *Kaṭha Upanishad* 1.3.3 ff.

In order to drive the chariot to its goal, reason (buddhi) should instruct the mind (manas) which way to drive. (We are not talking of what men usually call reason—rationalism, Marxism or dialectical materialism—which is not reason but merely a form of desire or emotion). Buddhi is the spiritual part of man's mind.

How does he get knowledge of how the body is to be guided? First from the accumulated experience of the holy and wise saints of the past—the saints of all religions. When the buddhi is sufficiently stilled by meditation, devotion and the practice of fraternity, then it receives direct instructions from the eternal repository of Truth or God. Then he attains the goal, 'the transcendental state of Vishnu'.

According to Shri Shankara, Vishnu means Vasudeva, 'He in Whom the world abides and Who abides in the world'. Spiritual teachings have their own goal according to the path chosen, but the supreme goal, in one word, is the state of Vishnu (Vishnu-loka) as described in the *Vishnu Purana*. This realm is higher than the stars. It is located in the region of all light. Those who dwell there are free from old age, they have pure desires and need no material support.

dig-ambaro vāpi ca sāmbaro vā
tvag-ambaro vāpi cid-ambara-sthaḥ
unmatta-vad vāpi ca bāla-vad vā
piśāca-vad vāpi caraty avanyām

[541] 'He walks the earth clothed in pure Consciousness, whether he appears to be naked or robed or clothed in bark. He walks like a lunatic or like a child or an imp.

kāmānnī kāma-rūpī saṃś caraty eka-caro muniḥ
svātmanaiva sadā tuṣṭaḥ svayaṃ sarvātmanā sthitaḥ

[542] 'The sage wanders about alone, eating if and when he fancies, assuming whatever form he fancies, but ever fully content through identification with his own true Self and established as being himself the Self of all.

The *Brihadaranyaka Upanishad* says: 'When, embraced by Brahman (the Absolute), man knows nothing that is within (cause) and nothing that is without (effect), when the father does not exist, nor the mother, nor the world, nor gods, nor the thief, nor the murderer; he overcomes all the sorrows of life forever and is one eternal, luminous Spirit'.[1] Then man sees infinity in all finite things. To a man who has realized this Consciousness, each and every object is a mirror reflecting his own light in perpetual glory. Jesus spoke against sin but not against the sinner. He came to save the sinner and offered Himself for the sinner. In His eyes there was no sinner, nor sin intrinsically, but only one God.

kvacin mūḍho vidvān kvacid api mahā-rāja-vibhavaḥ
kvacid bhrāntaḥ saumyaḥ kvacid ajagarācāra-kalitaḥ
kvacit pātrībhūtaḥ kvacid avamataḥ kvāpy aviditaś
carаty evaṃ prājñaḥ satata-paramānanda-sukhitaḥ

[543] 'The enlightened person wanders the earth in this way, continuously enjoying the highest bliss. Sometimes he seems like a lunatic, sometimes he has the majesty of an emperor, sometimes he seems like a happy vagabond, sometimes he is prompted to remain motionless like a python, sometimes he is treated with honour, sometimes with contempt, and sometimes he is not noticed at all.

nirdhano 'pi sadā tuṣṭo 'py asahāyo mahā-balaḥ
nitya-tṛpto 'py abhuñjāno 'py asamaḥ sama-darśanaḥ

[544] 'Though he is externally indigent, he is internally deeply content; though he appears to be without allies, he has immense strength (and, by a pun, "has an army [of friends]"); he is ever satisfied, though refraining from worldly enjoyments; though no one is his equal, he sees equality everywhere.

1 *Bṛhadāraṇyaka Upanishad* 4.3.21-22

api kurvann akurvāṇaś cābhoktā phala-bhogy api
śarīry apy aśarīry eṣa paricchinno 'pi sarvagaḥ

[545] 'Such a person is actionless though apparently acting, is a non-experiencer though apparently experiencing the results of his (prārabdha) merit and demerit, is not embodied though apparently embodied, is omnipresent though apparently limited.

In his own experience, the enlightened man (jnani) is like the sun which moves all but is itself unmoved. Let us rule out all consideration of an individual condition when we examine the state of the jnani. Does he sneeze when he catches a cold? Does he enjoy a drink of cold water in hot weather? Is he provoked when insulted? These are all individual experiences and he is above them. Is he a highly virtuous man? Is he beyond both virtue and vice? It is an experience which cannot be described.

Perhaps it is safe to postulate the following: (1) He is the universal Self. He is like an individual wave which, when conscious of its individuality, was subject to error, jealousy and uncertainty, but now realizes that it is water. All its feelings of limitation are at an end. (2) He has no further birth. (3) The karmas do not touch him at all.[1] (4) His real Self, enjoying identity with the Lord omniscient and omnipotent, rests in sovereignty, though his body may be begging alms in the street. Shri Nischala Dasa once remarked: 'He is neither great nor small. He is the sea which supports the pearl oysters and also the worthless shells'.

It is certain that his body delivers from sins those who serve it. His words have magic; his thoughts become a torch to those who have faith.

aśarīraṃ sadā santam imaṃ brahma-vidaṃ kvacit
priyāpriye na spṛśatas tathaiva ca śubhāśubhe

1 See comment on verse 414, above.

> [546] 'Never does the pleasant nor the unpleasant nor the good nor the bad have any effect on the knower of the Absolute, who is in truth ever bodiless.

According to Nirbhayanandaji Swami, his body and its functions are maintained by the karma of his disciples, but the fact is: 'In begging, in looking after the body, neither do I desire, nor do I act. The deluded ones imagine these conditions in me. I am not responsible for their fancies'. (*Panchadashi* 14.45)

sthūlādi-sambandha-vato 'bhimāninaḥ
sukhaṃ ca duḥkhaṃ ca śubhāśubhe ca
vidhvasta-bandhasya sadātmano muneḥ
kutaḥ śubhaṃ vāpy aśubhaṃ phalaṃ vā

> [547] 'Happiness and suffering, good and bad, apply to him who identifies himself with a physical body and a subtle body. But how can good or bad experiences accrue to the sage who has overcome bondage (also "has destroyed all connections") and is united with the real?

Enlightenment (jnana) means the realization by the enlightened man of the actionlessness of the Self (atman), of the existence of all minds in him. Saints and sinners are all conditions imposed on him. Neither does he cry nor laugh, but through contact with him, many souls (jivas) cross over the sea of ignorance.

tamasā grasta-vad bhānād agrasto 'pi ravir janaiḥ
grasta ity ucyate bhrāntyā hy ajñātvā vastu-lakṣaṇam

> [548] 'In the case of an eclipse, people who do not know the truth of the matter say in error that the sun has been swallowed by darkness, when it has not actually been swallowed but only appears to have been.

tadvad dehādi-bandhebhyo vimuktaṃ brahma-vittamam
paśyanti dehi-van mūḍhāḥ śarīrābhāsa-darśanāt

[549] 'In the same way, people still in error behold the great knower of the Absolute as if he were embodied, although he is free from all connection with the body and so on, because they see the appearance of a body.

ahir nirlvayanīvāyaṃ mukta-dehas tu tiṣṭhati
itas tataś cālyamāno yat kiñcit prāṇa-vāyunā

[550] 'And this enlightened person stands liberated from the body like a snake freed from its slough; he is tossed about hither and thither as prompted by the wind of his vital energy.[1]

srotasā nīyate dāru yathā nimnonnata-sthalam
daivena nīyate deho yathā kālopabhuktiṣu

[551] 'The body of such a person is led by (prārabdha) karma downwards and upwards to different experiences at the appointed time, like a piece of wood carried along in a stream.

A ship made of wood, the parts of which are held together by iron nails and screws, has come into proximity with a magnetic rock. All the nails and screws have been drawn and have gone to the rock. What remains? Only the planks which are floating outside. By realization of the identity of the individual (jiva) and Brahman (the Absolute)—of the local and the universal—all the ties which keep the body in the region of birth and death (sansara) are drawn, like the iron nails and screws of the ship, and just a little residue of karma remains floating by, which has no real meaning, no real sense and no real existence.

1 The reading follows Muni Lāl, Bhāgavat and Mādhavānanda's footnote.

prārabdha-karma-parikalpita-vāsanābhiḥ
samsāri-vac carati bhuktiṣu mukta-dehaḥ
siddhaḥ svayaṃ vasati sākṣivad atra tūṣṇīṃ
cakrasya mūlam iva kalpa-vikalpa-śūnyaḥ

[552] 'The one who is liberated from the body moves about amidst varying experiences just like one still subject to re-incarnation and prompted by urges imagined through "prārabdha karma". But in this situation the perfect one himself remains a mere silent witness, like the motionless pivot of a wheel, without either espousing or rejecting any personal end.

naivendriyāṇi viṣayeṣu niyuṅkta eṣa
naivāpayuṅkta upadarśana-lakṣaṇa-sthaḥ
naiva kriyā-phalam apīṣad avekṣate sa
svānanda-sāndra-rasa-pāna-sumatta-cittaḥ

[553] 'The enlightened one is intoxicated with the joy of drinking the bliss of his own Self. He does not engage his senses in the enjoyment of sense-objects nor withdraw them from it. He stands indifferent. He has no regard whatever for any personal reward from his actions.

lakṣyālakṣya-gatiṃ tyaktvā yas tiṣṭhet kevalātmanā
śiva eva svayaṃ sākṣād ayaṃ brahma-vid uttamaḥ

[554] 'That great knower of the Absolute, who does not care whether his earthly state is sound or unsound, who remains at one with the transcendent principle of reality, is verily Shiva Himself.

jīvann eva sadā muktaḥ kṛtārtho brahma-vittamaḥ
upādhi-nāśād brahmaiva san brahmāpyeti nirdvayam

[555] 'The great knower of the Absolute is liberated and has

realized all possible ends even while yet alive. Through the disappearance of his conditioning adjuncts, he dissolves in the non-dual Absolute, being verily the Absolute itself (Bṛhad-āraṇyaka Upanishad 4.4.6-7).

The final faculty of the mind is the supra-mental faculty. The mind has to be made a stepping-stone to the consciousness of infinity. It is to be purified, stilled and enriched, and all the factors which disturb the mind have to be reduced to nothing. When the mind has acquired that state of serenity, then, by meditation, by practice of the higher discipline, it is to be absorbed in the infinite Consciousness. This is called nididhyasana. The spiritual Consciousness beyond the mind, which is realized through the individual (jiva) making the mind a stepping-stone, is called samadhi or direct experience (aparoksha).

What happens to such a man? The words of the *Brihadaranyaka Upanishad* are: 'When the desires which cling to the human heart are abandoned, then the mortal man becomes immortal and attains bliss here below. His body is cast away like the slough of a snake, but the disembodied spirit becomes infinite and immortal, becomes all-light'. Do not think that the body becomes immortal. But he becomes consciously immortal, not after death but 'here below'.

śailūṣo veṣa-sad-bhāvābhāvayoś ca yathā pumān
tathaiva brahma-vic chreṣṭhaḥ sadā brahmaiva nāparaḥ

[556] 'Just as an actor remains a man whether he is wearing his actor's costume or not, so the great knower of the Absolute ever remains the Absolute alone and nothing else (whatever he may appear to be to others).

The world of names and forms has been described by Shri Shankara as inexplicable (mithya). The reason is as follows: Brahman is the Absolute Reality (sat); the world is neither absolutely real (sat) nor is it unreal (asat), that is, something absolutely different from Brahman—it is therefore inexplicable.

In the Acharya's commentary on the *Chandogya Upanishad*, he says that prior to its production and manifestation, the world was real (sat) as Brahman; but when the world came out of Brahman (i.e., when it actually appeared) it began to be looked upon as something absolutely different from Brahman. Taken in the latter sense, as the aggregate of names and forms, the world is unreal; but from the higher standpoint, it is inseparably connected with Brahman. Hence we can see that the world is neither real nor absolutely unreal—in other words, it is inexplicable (mithya).

Even from the practical point of view, we must look upon the world from the higher standpoint, namely that it stands inseparably connected with its cause, Brahman, the underlying reality. It is through the world that the underlying reality is being expressed and realized. Shri Shankara's view of unreality is that he does not deny the existence of the world as such; he only wants us to treat it as something non-different from Brahman. In the Acharya's view, the world is not something self-existent or independent of Brahman.

In his commentary on the *Vedanta Sutras*, he does not absolutely identify Brahman, the causal reality, with its effects. The world is not to be taken as identical with Brahman or as real; the real nature of the Cause is transcendental in the system of Shri Shankara. The world is simply to be taken as the means through which the underlying nature of Brahman is being expressed and realized.

Shri Shankara remarks: 'As a player, taking successive characters upon himself, enacts on the stage the parts of each of these characters in succession but yet retains his own distinct character; so the underlying Causal Unity, retaining Its own distinct identity, realizes Itself successively in each of these changes produced'.

yatra kvāpi viśīrṇaṃ sat parṇam iva taror vapuḥ patanāt
brahmī-bhūtasya yateḥ prāg eva hi tac cid-agninā dagdham

[557] 'Let the body of the disciplined one who has realized the Absolute fall down dead anywhere at the moment of final decay, like a leaf falling from a tree. (There is no need of a funeral

pyre since) it has already been burnt away by the fire of pure Consciousness.

sadātmani brahmaṇi tiṣṭhato muneḥ
pūrṇādvayānanda-mayātmanā sadā
na deśa-kālādy-ucita-pratīkṣā
tvaṅ-māṃsa-viṭ-piṇḍa-visarjanāya

[558] 'The sage who rests in the Absolute, united with the real, ever of the nature of perfect non-dual bliss, does not care about an appropriate time or place to get rid of his body, composed of flesh, excrement and skin.

dehasya mokṣo no mokṣo na daṇḍasya kamaṇḍaloḥ
avidyā-hṛdaya-granthi-mokṣo mokṣo yatas tataḥ

[559] 'For liberation is not liberation from the body any more than it is liberation from the staff and the water-pot. Liberation from the knot in the heart formed by ignorance is the only true liberation.

kulyāyām atha nadyāṃ vā śiva-kṣetre 'pi catvare
parṇaṃ patati cet tena taroḥ kiṃ nu śubhāśubham

[560] 'How does it affect the tree for good or for ill whether a leaf from it falls into a ditch or a river or onto holy ground consecrated to Shiva?[1]

patrasya puṣpasya phalasya nāśa-vad
dehendriya-prāṇa-dhiyāṃ vināśaḥ
naivātmanaḥ svasya sadātmakasyā-
''nandākṛter vṛkṣa-vad asti caiṣaḥ

1 Cp. verse 418 with comment, above.

[561] 'It is the body, senses, vital energy and mind (in the case of the enlightened one) that are subject to destruction, not the Self, the real, of the nature of bliss, just as it is the leaves, flowers and fruit that are subject to destruction but not the tree itself.

The Self (atman) is said to be undecaying or imperishable. It means that the bliss which accompanies Self-realization does not diminish under any circumstances, unlike the vision of the founder of Neo-Platonism, Plotinus, which gave him glimpses of truth and then left him. The freedom from grief and limitations, which realization of Self (atman) gives, abides forever under all circumstances.

prajñāna-ghana ity ātma-lakṣaṇaṃ satya-sūcakam
anūdyaupādhikasyaiva kathayanti vināśanam

[562] 'The Veda speaks of the Self as "a mass of Consciousness" (Bṛhadāraṇyaka Upanishad 4.5.13) to indicate its true nature, and speaks of "dissolution" there only with regard to the soul limited by conditioning adjuncts as it would appear to the student.

avināśī vā are 'yam ātmeti śrutir ātmanaḥ
prabravīty avināśitvaṃ vinaśyatsu vikāriṣu

[563] 'But it says "Verily, this Self is indestructible" (Bṛhadāraṇyaka Upanishad 4.5.14) to show that the Self stands indestructible amidst the things that change and pass away.

pāṣāṇa-vṛkṣa-tṛṇa-dhānya-kaṭāmbarādyā
dagdhā bhavanti hi mṛd eva yathā tathaiva
dehendriyāsu-mana-ādi-samasta-dṛśyaṃ
jñānāgni-dagdham upayāti parātma-bhāvam

[564] 'Just as when stones, trees, grass, crops, carpets, robes and so on (all conceived as ultimately products of earth) are burnt away, they dissolve into the element "earth", so does all the

objective realm beginning with body, senses and mind assume the nature of the supreme Self when burnt up by the fire of knowledge.

vilakṣaṇaṃ yathā dhvāntaṃ līyate bhānu-tejasi
tathaiva sakalaṃ dṛśyaṃ brahmaṇi pravilīyate

[565] 'Just as darkness, being different from the light of the sun, dissolves in it, so all the objective realm dissolves in the Absolute (in the case of the enlightened person).

ghaṭe naṣṭe yathā vyoma vyomaiva bhavati sphuṭam
tathaivopādhi-vilaye brahmaiva brahma-vit svayam

[566] 'Just as the ether of space apparently enclosed within a pot is clearly nothing but space on the destruction of the pot, so is the knower of the Absolute nothing but the Absolute on the destruction of conditioning adjuncts (at the death of the body).

kṣīraṃ kṣīre yathā kṣiptaṃ tailaṃ taile jalaṃ jale
saṃyuktam ekatāṃ yāti tathātmany ātma-vin muniḥ

[567] 'The sage who knows the Self stands identical with the Self (on the death of the body) just as milk poured into milk is milk, oil poured into oil is oil, water poured into water is water.

evaṃ videha-kaivalyaṃ san-mātratvam akhaṇḍitam
brahma-bhāvaṃ prapadyaiṣa yatir nāvartate punaḥ

[568] 'When such a disciplined soul attains (at death) the nature of the Absolute as pure undifferentiated Being, total transcendence without (even the appearance of) a body, he does not again return for reincarnation.

sadātmaikatva-vijñāna-dagdhāvidyādi-varṣmaṇaḥ
amuṣya brahma-bhūtatvād brahmaṇaḥ kuta udbhavaḥ

[569] 'Since he has become the Absolute and has burnt up the whole complex of limitations stemming from ignorance through knowledge of his identity with the real—well, how could the Absolute be reborn?[1]

māyā-kḷptau bandha-mokṣau na staḥ svātmani vastutaḥ
yathā rajjau niṣkriyāyāṃ sarpābhāsa-vinirgamau

[570] 'Both bondage and liberation are illusory appearances produced by Māyā. They do not really exist in the Self, any more than the illusory snake really enters or leaves the unchanging rope.

āvṛteḥ sad-asattvābhyāṃ vaktavye bandha-mokṣaṇe
nāvṛtir brahmaṇaḥ kācid anyābhāvād anāvṛtam
yady asty advaita-hāniḥ syād dvaitaṃ no sahate śrutiḥ

[571] 'Bondage and liberation are defined as presence and absence of concealment (āvṛti) of the Self. It is (in truth ever) unconcealed, because nothing else exists to conceal it. If there were anything else, that would contradict non-duality. The Veda does not tolerate duality.

bandhaṃ ca mokṣaṃ ca mṛsaiva mūḍhā
buddher guṇaṃ vastuni kalpayanti
dṛg-āvrtiṃ megha-kṛtāṃ yathā ravau
yato 'dvayāsaṅga-cid-ekam akṣaram

[572] 'Bondage and liberation are attributes of the mind; it is only in error that the deluded suppose that they apply to the real. To attribute these to the Self is like attributing the obstruction to

1 Mādhavānanda identifies 'ignorance' with the causal body here, and says that what are burnt up are the three bodies, causal, subtle and physical. This may be the correct interpretation.

> our eyes produced by clouds to the sun (i.e., like supposing that because we could not see the sun, it was not shining). For the real is the one principle of Consciousness, without a second, relationless, indestructible.

The Self is the light under which the world, external and internal, shines. The mind throws the picture of the world on the canvas of time-space under the light of Self. The Self is Absolute, and yet when you consider it in relation to the world of cause and effect, it is omnipotent and omniscient. When it is mixed up with the mind and deluded by the promises of the senses, and runs after the objects of pleasure and power, it is limited and unconscious of its limitless power of bliss and awareness.

astīti pratyayo yaś ca yaś ca nāstīti vastuni
buddher eva guṇāv etau na tu nityasya vastunaḥ

> [573] 'The ideas "it exists" and "it does not exist" in relation to the real are but attributes of the mind. They do not belong to the eternal reality itself.

The mind is the link between the physical and spiritual worlds; it is the lamp which reflects the light of the Self and imparts the properties of knowledge to the senses. To realize its infinite potentialities, the Self must make the mind its instrument of Self-realization and not a cage in which to imprison itself. The mind is like a cage fitted with mirrors and the Self is imprisoned in it like a bird. The impermanent is not real; it is imaginary. The bird in the cage sees its own Self reflected in the mirrors of the cage. Under a delusion it imagines that the reflection is real and runs after it. The result is fatigue and unrest.

Swami Rama Tirtha, in one of his Urdu verses, says: 'O beauties of the world, your grace, your charm, is a mere reflection of my black locks (maya). It is the shadow-worshippers who run after you under delusion'.

atas tau māyayā kḷptau bandha-mokṣau na cātmani
niṣkale niṣkriye śānte niravadye nirañjane
advitīye pare tattve vyomavat kalpanā kutaḥ

[574] 'And so bondage and liberation are notions set up by Māyā and do not exist in the Self. How could such false imaginations apply to the supreme transcendent principle, which is like the ether of space, partless, actionless, totally at rest, faultless, taintless, one without a second.

To enjoy the bliss of the Self, the mind must be made tranquil and rid of the thirst for pleasure and power. Then, by meditation on the great sentences of the Upanishads, such as 'I am Brahman (the Absolute)', let the mind be absorbed in the Self. This is the highest good. This is the only way to real peace. This is realization of Truth.

na nirodho na cotpattir na baddho na ca sādakaḥ
na mumukṣur na vai mukta ity eṣā paramārthatā

[575] 'There is nothing produced and nothing suppressed, there is no one in bondage and no spiritual seeker, there is no seeker of liberation and no liberation. This is the final truth.[1]

sakala-nigama-cūḍā-svānta-siddhānta-rūpaṃ
param idam ati guhyaṃ darśitaṃ te mayādya
apagata-kali-doṣaṃ kāma-nirmukta-buddhiṃ
sva-suta-vad asakṛt tvām bhāvayitvā mumukṣum

[576] 'Because I knew that you were deeply desirous of liberation, void of the characteristic taints of Kali Yuga[2], with

1 Quotation of *Amṛtabindu Upanishad* 10. Compare Gauḍapāda's *Kārikā* 2.32 on the *Māṇḍūkya Upanishad*.

2 Kali Yuga: the last and worst of the four *yugas* or ages, the present age, characterized by unrighteous conduct.

a mind free from desires for pleasure, I am repeatedly teaching you today this supreme secret, the final teaching and heart and crown of all the Veda, as if to a son'.

61. Farewell to the pupil

iti śrutvā guror vākyaṃ praśrayeṇa kṛtānatiḥ
sa tena samanujñāto yayau nirmukta-bandhanaḥ

[577] After hearing these words of the Guru, the pupil bowed to him humbly and, with his permission, left the Guru's presence, liberated from bondage.

gurur evaṃ sadānanda-sindhau nirmagna-mānasaḥ
pāvayan vasudhāṃ sarvāṃ vicacāra nirantaram

[578] As for the teacher, he incessantly wandered the whole earth, purifying it, with his mind drowned in the ocean of the bliss of the real.

62. Purpose of the work

ity ācāryasya śiṣyasya saṃvādenātma-lakṣaṇam
nirūpitaṃ mumukṣūṇāṃ sukha-bodhopapattaye

[579] Here in this present work we have indicated the true nature of the Self in the form of a dialogue between a teacher and a pupil for the ease of comprehension of those truly desirous of liberation.

hitam imam upadeśam ādriyantāṃ
vihita-nirasta-samasta-citta-doṣāḥ
bhava-sukha-viratāḥ praśānta-cittāḥ
śruti-rasikā yatayo mumukṣavo ye

[580] Those disciplined people, who are steeped in the Veda and deeply desirous of liberation, indifferent to the pleasures of the world and profoundly peaceful in their minds, who have eliminated all harmful mental faults—may they pay attention to this helpful teaching.

63. Eulogy of the work

saṃsārādhvani tāpa-bhānu-kiraṇa-
prodbhūta-dāha-vyathā-
khinnānāṃ jala-kāṅkṣayā maru-bhuvi
śrāntyā paribhrāmyatām
atyāsanna-sudhāmbudhiṃ sukha-karaṃ
brahmādvayaṃ darśayanty
eṣā śaṅkara-bhāratī vijayate
nirvāṇa-sandāyinī

[581] To those who, on the path of reincarnation, are weary and wandering painfully in the desert in search of water, troubled by the scorching rays of the sun of worldly suffering, this eloquent work of Shankara points out the extremely close ocean of the nectar of the non-dual Absolute that brings joy. Supreme in its field, it will confer nirvāṇa on the earnest student!

If any of you have travelled along the coast of Brittany, you may know of a local legend that there was once a splendid palace there inhabited by kings and queens which, in the course of time, was engulfed by the sea; and there are still those who say that their parents have heard music and seen the spires of this palace.

Man's outer personality is like the sea, and in that sea is submerged a palace with spires which is sometimes glimpsed in dreams or brought to memory by sweet music or the glory of a sunset. That palace is the spiritual nature of man's soul hidden in his personality. Religion and Yoga are the methods whereby the mind can dive deep into the personality and possess this hidden palace of freedom and bliss.

When we started this classic, we began a study of the means of discovering this palace in our being. In our philosophy, and also in life, discrimination (viveka) is a most important word. A man without discrimination is not entitled to be called a man. If it rains, you look for an umbrella. This is discrimination. Then why not apply this principle to life itself?

The soul is a king who has ministers and subjects. Among the subjects are rogues and robbers, and there are also beautiful singing birds and lovely gardens in the kingdom. The first minister is discrimination, and another is constructive thinking. The rogues are desires, ambitions, anger, greed and the habit of giving our heart to anything other than God.

It is proper that a king should rule his own kingdom and not let it be ruled by thieves and robbers. Therefore, make your Spirit the real king of your mind and senses, and create the love of the Lord within you by self-study. Others cannot help you. Find out for yourself. Study the *Gita* with the commentary of Shankara Acharya. Let us live in a way that is helpful to others as well as ourselves.

Right discrimination (viveka) means to pursue that which brings us nearer to the consummation of the goal of our life: freedom and everlasting happiness. God means man to be happy, but man is determined to be unhappy. God has provided man with every means to happiness, but man uses them to become a slave and miserable. Holy Shankara, following those in the great spiritual tradition, says that happiness and freedom, dearest to the heart of man, can be found in the personality of man himself.

OM

Translator's Note on the Text

As a spiritual vade-mecum of the Yoga of Self-Knowledge, the *Viveka-Chudamani* might be compared with *The Imitation of Christ* of Thomas À Kempis in the Christian tradition, but its author and date are much less certain. On grounds of style and terminology, it is thought today to have been composed by some outstanding Advaitic author who lived some centuries after the great Shankara of the commentaries. The last verse, which attributes the work to 'Shankara', can hardly have been composed by Shankara himself, as it was not his practice elsewhere to name himself at the conclusion of a work. Amongst the considerable number of terms used in the work that are not found in Shankara's commentaries, we might refer to the 'powers of concealment and projection' attributed to Ignorance (verses 110 to 117), the latter conceived as a kind of entity wielding them, a conception found in Shankara's contemporary Mandana Mishra, but not found in his own commentaries.

In Shankara's one independent work of known authenticity, the *Upadesha Sahasri*, the terminology does not stray beyond that found in the commentaries. The tone is fully as lofty as that of the *Viveka-Chudamani*, but cooler: references to the 'bliss' of the Absolute, which occur in nearly a fifth of the verses of the *Viveka-Chudamani*, are sparse. The pupil who is introduced is realistically conceived. The teacher forces him to examine his assertions and correct them in the light of further reflection, whereas in the *Viveka-Chudamani* the questions of the pupil are accepted immediately with congratulation and used as a mere literary device for the presentation of teaching. The proliferation of different metres in which the *Viveka-Chudamani* is composed is uncharacteristic of Shankara and his contemporaries, recalling rather Sarvajnatma Muni or the logician Udayana, who belonged to a later age. The date and authorship of the *Viveka-Chudamani* are in fact not known, but the style and flavour of the work often recall the *Yoga Vasishtha*. Verse 431 is manifestly a quotation of verse 3.9.12 of that work. The *Yoga Vasishtha* is known from its references to kings of Kashmir to have been composed towards the end of the tenth century.

INDEX TO TOPICS

Numbers refer to verses or the commentary on them.
***Bold** figures indicate the more important references.*
'Passim' denotes topics referred to throughout the text.

SHANTI SADAN

Centre of Adhyatma Yoga

Founded by Hari Prasad Shastri in 1933

Lectures and courses at Shanti Sadan
are held each
Wednesday and Friday at 8.00 pm
during the term, and also
at other venues in Central London.

For details of the current term's activities,
contact Shanti Sadan, 29 Chepstow Villas,
London W11 3DR, UK.
Tel. +44 (0)171 727 7846
Fax. +44 0)171 792 9817